Ecclesiology
and
Postmodernity

Questions for the Church in Our Time

Gerard Mannion

A Michael Glazier Book

LITURGICAL PRESS
Collegeville, Minnesota

www.litpress.org

A Michael Glazier Book published by Liturgical Press

Cover design by David Manahan, O.S.B. Photo courtesy of iStockphoto.com, © Christina Richards.

1   2   3   4   5   6   7   8   9

Library of Congress Cataloging-in-Publication Data

Mannion, Gerard, 1970–
    Ecclesiology and postmodernity : questions for the church in our time
/ Gerard Mannion.
        p.   cm.
    Includes index.
    ISBN-13: 978-0-8146-5223-7
    ISBN-10: 0-8146-5223-9
    1. Church.   2.Catholic Church—Doctrines.   3. Postmodernism—
Religious aspects—Christianity.   I. Title.

BX1746.M338 2007
262'.02—dc22   2006023218

With deep gratitude:

For Two Wonderful Sisters, Maria and Julie,

and for their marvelous families.

Never a dull moment in their company!

and

In Memoriam: Patrick Joseph Mannion

(1923–2006)

and Bridie Josephine Mannion

(1916–2006)

Two Selfless Servants of the Church All Their Years

Contents

Charity is the key to everything. It sets all to rights. There is nothing which charity cannot achieve and renew. Charity "beareth all things, believeth all things, hopeth all things, endureth all things" (1 Cor 13:7). Who is there among us who does not realize this? *And since we realize it, is not this the time to put it into practice?*

—Pope Paul VI, *Ecclesiam Suam* §56

Speak Truth to Power

—18th Century Quaker Book of Sayings

Preface

A New Paradigm for the Catholic Church?

> The very fact that there is such an enormous number of particular questions facing the church today in theory and practice involves a danger of not being able to see the wood for the trees, that the interested parties and experts in a single question will be blind to the church's task as a whole, in which alone the particular task can be properly mastered.
>
> Karl Rahner[1]

This volume seeks to explore the situation in which the Catholic Church finds itself and consider the strategies it might employ to live out its mission in faithfulness to the gospel today. There has been an enormous amount of debate within theological circles concerning the notion of postmodernity and postmodern thought, which has even led to the emergence of postmodern theology as a subdiscipline in its own right. This particular work is concerned more with the current age than the actual plethora of postmodern theories in detail. That is to say, my primary focus is on the impact on church life of the fundamental changes in human social existence and culture that have taken place in the present historical period.[2] The church's *response* to those challenges is central. This book contends that the Catholic Church has been left somewhat in limbo since Vatican II and still awaits an energizing ecclesiological vision for the future.

1. Karl Rahner, *The Shape of the Church to Come,* translated and introduced by Edward Quinn (London: SPCK, 1974), "Epilogue," 135.
2. I briefly explore the impact of more specifically postmodern *theories* on ecclesiology itself in my chapter, "Postmodern Ecclesiologies," in Gerard Mannion and Lewis Mudge, eds., *The Routledge Companion to the Christian Church* (London: Routledge, 2007).

I am also aware that some might object that the nature of engagement and discussion here could be perceived to be polemical. They would see this as an irony, given that the volume seeks to promote ecclesial charity and dialogue. I hope that a considered engagement with the text will ultimately refute any such charges.

Any essay on topics such as those that concern this volume cannot avoid engaging with schools of ecclesiological thought and of ecclesial practice that are, themselves, often polemical, which may frequently lack charity, and which do not admit genuine dialogue. In order to identify and discuss such "problematic" ecclesiological approaches, one must obviously employ *descriptive* language which is of a critical nature. But, given the hermeneutical concerns of the volume as a whole, here please allow me to emphasize that there is a great difference between polemic and critical engagement. The trend toward intolerance of language that challenges those ecclesiological voices that claim to be representing the "true" tradition, and of those who are in particular positions of authority is, in itself, a worrying development for the church in postmodern times and runs counter to the spirit of open dialogue that prevailed at Vatican II.

However, what does appear ironic is that some who feel uncomfortable about critical engagement with certain quarters of the church today, particularly those who decry such critique as being polemical, are often the very same people who can also be excessively polemical and judgmental of those positions they disagree with themselves.

So I am fully aware that to enter into the discussion of the matters covered in this volume is an undertaking that should not be entered into lightly. It can be a painful process. Why this approach, then? It may help to explain that, in chapters 6 and 7 of this volume, we encounter the thought of scholars who believe that the difficult task of fostering dialogue within and without the church today cannot be served by any weak or woolly version of pluralism or any overt relativistic denial of genuine differences. Instead, conflict will often be inevitable and difficult disagreements will come to the fore. Any harmony that might emerge in the church of these times will necessarily involve holding in creative and conflictual tension differing elements, standpoints, and ways of ecclesial being in the church today. Such has always been the case. Thus, in many ways, this book, while a few might still perceive some of its argument as being merely polemical, falls into that genre of difficult conversation: it engages in painful critique in order to help move debates onward toward the healing medicine of greater ecclesial dialogue. Thus, especially in chapters 3 and 4, we consider some particular and representative examples of potential stumbling blocks in the way of dialogue and ecclesial flourishing in the world today. Then, from chapter 5 onward, we turn to consider more constructive discussions toward the latter ends.

We begin, then, by seeking to identify a number of challenges. There are, of course, many *specific* issues and problems the church must confront. But this volume is not primarily about the intricacies of all-too-familiar issues such as women's ministry and women priests, sexual ethics, contraception, homosexuality, clerical sexual abuse,[3] financial impropriety, and so on. The chapters mention specific challenges, but primarily as they enable us to clarify broader ecclesiological issues that must be confronted.

Instead, this volume addresses the broader ecclesiological, structural, and administrative problems at the root of those specific instances of disagreement and concern—in other words, the perceived "fault lines" within and throughout the church of our times. Many such specific issues raise further moral issues and belong to the domain of moral theology and ethical discourse. However, as we shall see, there is a still broader moral debate to be engaged, concerning the moral vision, practice, and, indeed, aspiration toward holiness of the church itself (understood in both its local and universal manifestations).

By no means does this book claim to be, nor is it intended to be, a comprehensive study of every debate and every major work about the church in postmodern times. The literature is so vast that a single volume could not do it justice and would not have room for the constructive suggestions that will receive most of our attention in this book.

On the whole, in contrast to some recent ecclesiological thinking, I here take as my task to explore, develop, and promote the ways in which ecclesiology can benefit from various particular aspects of a comparative methodology. The emergence of "comparative ecclesiology" offers the most hope-filled method and approach for the present era. Indeed, this volume itself is but a modest attempt at shaping a work in that field of comparative ecclesiology, and one that might be termed an example of "critical" or hermeneutical comparative ecclesiology.

---

3. I have recently addressed this specific issue vis-à-vis the wider ecclesiological issues in "'A Haze of Fiction'—Legitimation, Accountability and Truthfulness," in Francis Oakley and Bruce Russet, eds., *Governance, Accountability and the Future of the Church* (New York: Continuum, 2003) 161–77.

The book offers some constructive suggestions about ways in which the church might bring greater harmony between its self-understanding—its ecclesiological vision—and the day-to-day reality of life in the church (ecclesial practice). To this end the volume commends the development of an ecclesiology inspired by virtue ethics, so that any disjuncture between ecclesiological theory and practice is increasingly healed. It is hoped that the church may become ever more truly a sacramental sign and mediation of the triune God who is love: so that the church might demonstrate all the more vividly in its relations both *ad intra* and *ad extra* that *Deus caritas est.*

Some further notes for clarification:

There are, of course, perceived normative sources for Christians with regard to the church such as Scripture, the Creeds, the marks or notes of the church and various confessional and catechetical statements on the part of various different communions. This essay is not intended to be a study of such. Much that is agreed as normative will be taken as read. Some areas where disagreements arise will be discussed, particularly, in a few instances, where further additional criteria perceived as normative have proved divisive. But the volume works toward an attempt to discern what might be normative for healthy dialogue and enhanced communion within the church, as well as for relations between the church and the world *ad extra* in the contemporary era. It is thus partly for the sake of discursive convenience, although also because a great deal of agreement can be discerned on the subject matter, that I denote this era by reference to the term "postmodernity." Certain trends, features, and challenges of that era are also treated insofar as there exists much agreement on these issues also. Where differences emerge, as we shall see, is in relation to the *response* to the same.

Along similar lines, note, also, that I do not here indulge in any *detailed* study and critique of *Lumen gentium*, not primarily because so much excellent and more comprehensive literature on this topic already exists, but because I believe this to be a less contentious and more widely accepted document of Vatican II than others. That the council, and in particular this document, sought to offer some (including normative) criteria for being church is beyond question. But the intentions behind such, the rightful interpretation of the same, and the various claimants to be true heirs of the "legacy" of *Lumen gentium* and Vatican II are different matters altogether. That is to say, differing approaches to ecclesiology in recent times have nonetheless shared a high estimation of this document which was itself, of course, the product of a long and protracted series of debates and disagreements among fathers and peritii of differing ecclesiological outlook during the council itself.

Throughout this work, I take ecclesiology to mean not simply the *doctrine* of the church, but also the self-understanding of any given ecclesial community and of the church as a whole, along with study of the same. It also embraces the study of the story and ongoing development of church, the conversations and disagreements within and without the church, and must also include the *aspirations* of church, in local and universal contexts alike. Ecclesiology also embraces practical elements (or applied if one prefers), for ecclesial practices can influence any given self-understanding of the church, as well as vice-versa. Of course, it will always involve engagement with Scripture and ongoing Christian tradition(s). Historical consciousness and hermeneutical principles will always be of central importance to any ecclesiological undertaking. For the sake of brevity, ecclesiology is thus here taken to mean that science of *envisioning* the church, in a variety of ways. Ecclesiology is thus a sub-discipline of theology, not simply the teaching of a particular community on a specific subject.

As I have said elsewhere, ecclesiology is, above all else, an *aspirational* undertaking. I should here from the outset say a little about the direction in which the ecclesial aspirations informing this study proceed. Throughout, the essay seeks to suggest what sort of community, what sort of ecclesial vision and practice, that the contemporary church might aspire toward. The church should seek to be truly and fully sacramental, pointing toward and emulating the divine community of Trinity. It should aspire toward being a community where theory (or indeed, perhaps better termed, aspirations), teaching, and practice are in greater harmony, a community that works to build the kingdom of love, justice, and righteousness. It should live in and through the Spirit and allow the Eucharist, the breaking of bread, to be both the source and sign of the communion that reflects the divine community of love.

Alas, space has also not permitted a detailed discussion of various "emerging ecclesiologies," especially the promise of trinitarian ecclesiologies in various guises throughout the world. Nor has this essay been able to dwell at length on new understandings and patterns of ministry, the place of the laity, or of detailed discussions or precisely *how* the church might be more in the world if not of the world etc. These are discussions for another day and in another place.

Finally, note also that, throughout, the term "Catholic Church" is employed, except where obvious, to refer to the *Roman Catholic* communion. This volume follows the conventions employed in US publishing, as opposed to those of European, and particularly UK, publishing. Of course, the term "Catholic Church" can also be employed to include Christians and communities beyond the confines of the Roman Catholic communion. Thus an ecumenical note is sounded here to avoid misunderstanding.

Except where stated, for the sake of consistency I have quoted the "official" translation of church teaching documents, as included in the public Vatican archives, made available at www.vatican.va. I am aware that these translations have their numerous faults and imperfections but have reluctantly opted to use them for the sake of accessibility and consistency. Of course, the original Latin texts are available via the same archives.

Gerard Mannion
Feast of St David, 2006

Acknowledgments

There are so many who deserve my deepest gratitude, and so, once again, I offer my apologies for any omissions. Special thanks are due to those who read chapters or parts thereof at various stages of their formation and whose suggestions and advice helped make this volume immeasurably better than it would have been, including Richard Gaillardetz, Philomena Cullen, Nicholas Lash, and members of the Association of Teachers of Moral Theology, particularly Jacqui Stewart. Naturally, the remaining imperfections are my responsibility alone. Many thanks are due also to those who listened to various papers that found their way in some form or other into this volume, including all who attended the conference on "Ministry, Authority, Leadership—What is the Future for the Laity?" at the University of Lampeter, Wales, in June 2002, especially Paul Gadie who organized the conference and invited me to speak. My deep gratitude, also, to those who organized and hosted "Pluralism from the Perspective of Hindus and Christians: an Ecumenical Symposium," at the Orthodox Seminary, Kottayam, India, in July 2005. For support in making it possible for me to participate in the latter I am enormously grateful to the British Academy. My appreciation is also due to all present at the inaugural lecture of the Church in Our Times Series of the Hope Theological Society of Liverpool Hope University in January 2006. Thank you, also, to St Deiniol's Library, Hawarden, Wales, for hosting my "retreats" on the final push to the volume's completion.

My deep gratitude, also, to Mary Stommes, Colleen Stiller, and all the team at Liturgical Press for believing in this project and to Professor Kenneth Newport for his enormous encouragement and support in seeing it through to completion. Deep gratitude also is due to Bradford Hinze, Gregory Baum, and Paul D. Murray. To all at Liverpool Hope

University for its daring to believe in a vision against the grain of our postmodern times: let us hope collectively that this new ecumenical university really does flourish as a "virtuous community" itself. And above all else to my father, Michael Mannion, who has tirelessly committed himself to the church of past and present times, and no doubt will continue to do so in future times. His faith, hope, and love, his unswerving support, encouragement, and dedication, have all been a constant inspiration to me in all these efforts to discern what hope there is for the church in the future.

The overall thesis of this volume appeared in embryonic form in "Ecclesiology and Postmodernity—A New Paradigm for the Church?" *New Blackfriars* 85 (May 2004) 304–28. I have also utilized some ideas and expanded on the material from my "A Virtuous Community: The Self-Identity, Vision and Future of the Diocesan Church," in Noel Timms, ed., *Diocesan Dispositions and Parish Voices* (Chelmsford: Matthew James, 2001) 79–130. I am most grateful to the editors and publishers of these publications for permission to use these earlier writings here.

Citations of Vatican Documentation

Second Vatican Council, *Gaudium et Spes* (*Pastoral Constitution on the Church in the Modern World*), http://www.vatican.va/archive/hist_councils/ii_vatican_council/documents/vat-ii_cons_19651207_gaudium-et-spes_en.html, 1965.

Pope Paul VI, Encyclical, *On the Church, Ecclesiam Suam,* http://www.vatican.va/holy_father/paul_vi/encyclicals/documents/hf_p-vi_enc_06081964_ecclesiam_en.html, 1964.

Pope Paul VI, Apostolic Exhortation on Evangelization in the Modern World, http://www.vatican.va/holy_father/paul_vi/apost_exhortations/documents/hf_p-vi_exh_19751208_evangelii-nuntiandi_en.html, 1975.

Pope Paul VI, *Evangelii Nuntiandi,* 1974, Congregation for the Doctrine of the Faith, *Communionis notio,* (*Letter To The Bishops Of The Catholic Church On Some Aspects Of The Church Understood As Communion*), 1992.

Congregation for the Doctrine of the Faith, *Dominus Iesus* (*On The Unicity And Salvific Universality Of Jesus Christ And The Church*), http://www.vatican.va/roman_curia/congregations/cfaith/documents/rc_con_cfaith_doc_20000806_dominus-iesus_en.html, 2000.

Permissions

Excerpts from Vatican documents, including *Gaudium et Spes, Ecclesiam Suam, Communionis notio,* and *Dominus Iesus,* from Libreria Editrice Vaticana. Reprinted with permission.

Excerpt from Philip J. Murnion, "Beyond Competing Ecclesiologies," private paper for ecclesiological elucidation, *Queen's Foundation Working Party on Authority and Governance in the Roman Catholic Church,* July 1999. Reprinted with permission, courtesy of the National Pastoral Life Center (with deep gratitude to Liz Sullivan, editor of *Church* magazine, for her assistance here also).

Excerpt from Gregory Baum, "Commentary," in *De Ecclesia: The Constitution on the Church of Vatican Council II* (London: Darton Longman and Todd, 1965). Reprinted with permission.

Excerpt from Eugene D'Souza, "Intellectual Humility," in Yves Congar, Hans Küng, and Daniel O'Hanlon, eds., *Council Speeches of Vatican II* (London and New York: Sheed and Ward, 1964) 142. Reprinted with permission of Hans Küng.

Excerpts from Hermann J. Pottmeyer "Dialogue as a Model for Communication in the Church," in Patrick Granfield, ed., *The Church and Communication* (Kansas City, MO: Sheed and Ward, 1994). Reprinted with permission.

Excerpts from John Beal, "'It Shall Not Be So Among You!' Crisis in the Church, Crisis in Canon Law," in Francis Oakley and Bruce Russet, eds., *Governance, Accountability and the Future of the Church* (New York: Continuum, 2003). Reprinted with permission.

PART I

A NEW PARADIGM FOR THE CATHOLIC CHURCH?

Chapter One

Church in Our Time:
Introducing the Themes and Concerns

[T]he church has always had the duty of scrutinizing the signs of the times and of interpreting them in the light of the gospel. Thus, in language intelligible to each generation, she can respond to the perennial questions which men ask about this present life and the life to come, and about the relationship of the one to the other. We must therefore recognize and understand the world in which we live, its explanations, its longings, and its often dramatic characteristics.[1]

We believe that it is a duty of the church at the present time to strive toward a clearer and deeper awareness of itself and its mission in the world, and of the treasury of truth of which it is heir and custodian. Thus before embarking on the study of any particular problem and before considering what attitude to adopt vis-à-vis the world, the church must here and now reflect on its own nature, the better to appreciate the divine plan which it is the church's task to implement.[2]

The Catholic Church stands, it seems, at the beginning of one of the most difficult phases of its history. For it too is implicated in the new and imponderable *problems of our future*. Since it professes to be "universal" it manifests more elemental cultural, geopolitical and social opposition than are to be found elsewhere. It also questions Christian existence, questions how the world can be fashioned in a Christian way. But, more radically than other faith-communities, it can put into play the dynamic energies of new possibilities and impulses within it. The Catholic Church sets an example; consequently the path it takes will be of wide interest.[3]

1. *Gaudium et Spes,* §4.
2. *Ecclesiam Suam,* §18.
3. Hermann Häring, "The Rights and Limits of Dissent," in Hans Küng and Jürgen Moltmann, eds., *The Right to Dissent. Concilium* 158 (1982) 95.

Introduction:
The Dilemmas of Historical and Ecclesiological Paradigms

Scholars and researchers from a variety of academic disciplines inform us that we live in an era known as "postmodernity." Hence it is necessary to begin by saying a little about what I understand postmodernity to mean. This chapter will attempt to settle upon a "working thesis" in "naming the present," but also note the various dilemmas that present themselves to the construction and articulation of historical and ecclesiological paradigms alike. The term "postmodernity," as I have stated elsewhere,

> . . . describes the current historical epoch and, on certain interpretations, stretches as far back as the latter half of the nineteenth century. For some, Nietzsche was both its prophet and its chief intellectual midwife. It is marked by the increasing disillusionment with all overarching explanatory hypotheses for the world in general and human beings and societies in particular. Thus "grand narratives" such as religion, political ideologies and even science itself are no longer seen to have "all the answers" to humanity's questions. The postmodern era is thus marked by a shift from belief in certainties and truth claims to more localised and piecemeal factors. The individual is seen as creating his or her own meaning to a certain extent, rather than receiving it from without.[4]

And the term is far from exhausted by such definitions, as the remainder of this chapter will seek to show. It was Jean-François Lyotard who famously defined the term "postmodern" as meaning "incredulity to meta-narratives," but the various understandings of this term and the associated terms "postmoderni*ty*" and "postmodern*isms*" that have emerged since take his own highly influential work beyond even the far-reaching and very loose boundaries envisioned by Lyotard himself.[5]

---

4. Gerard Mannion, "A Virtuous Community—The Self-identity, Vision and Future of the Diocesan Church, in Noel Timms, ed., *Diocesan Dispositions and Parish Voices in the Roman Catholic Church* (Chelmsford: Matthew James, 2001) 125. Cf. Roger Haight, who sees the word as a loose term that enables the description of a "culture." Under its umbrella are gathered a diverse set of experiences, including "a historical consciousness that is deeper and more radical than that of modernity; an appreciation of pluralism that is suspicious of all absolute or universal claims; a consciousness of the social construction of the self that has completely undermined the transcendental ego of modernity and, ironically, encouraged a grasping individualism; a sense of the size, age, complexity, and mystery of reality that modern science never even suspected." *Christian Community in History.* (New York: Continuum, 2004) vol. 1, Historical Ecclesiology, 57.

5. Jean-François Lyotard, *The Postmodern Condition—A Report on Knowledge,* tr. Régis Durand (Manchester: Manchester University Press, 1984) xxiv; cf. also xxv. On both pages, as throughout the work in general, he considerably expands on

Thus fundamental changes in human social existence and culture can become so widespread and influential that they take on the significance of being viewed as changes that perhaps dictate and/or capture the character (dare one say something of the "essence," in a non-philosophical sense of that term?) of a historical epoch and hence become known as "paradigmatic" changes. Such developments, of course, affect the religions prominent in the respective eras, and this volume explores the impact of the present era on one particularly large branch of one particular world religion.[6] One prominent commentator on the interplay between religion and postmodernity, Peter Hodgson, has indicated how ". . . we can also speak of a paradigm with reference to a culture or to an intellectual activity such as theology, meaning thereby a confluence of factors or elements that determine the predominant shape or pattern of the culture or theology in question. Major shifts in the cultural paradigm have generally elicited corresponding shifts in the theological paradigm."[7]

---

this definition. Lyotard himself offers further clarification in an appendix to his *The Postmodern Condition*, "Answering the Question: What is Postmodern?" 71–82, trans. Régis Durand, and see also his *The Postmodern Explained* (Minneapolis: University of Minnesota Press, 1992). Note, however, that Lyotard is not suggesting that the cultural, technological, economic, scientific, and intellectual currents of modernity suddenly disappear; they rather fragment and continue in various other forms. As Lieven Boeve states, commenting on Lyotard's work, "With the collapse of these master narratives, however, it becomes clear that they had been attempts to direct and guide the processes of modernization. Modernization, however, enjoys its own dynamic, one that continues to unfold, detached from the master narratives. In this sense, 'postmodernity' might also be characterized as 'radicalized modernity': the era in which functional differentiation, or viewed more broadly, the pluralization of the world, can no longer be kept together under one single perspective." Boeve, *Interrupting Tradition* (Leuven: Peeters, 2004) 51. Hence, in this respect, Christianity no longer forms a dominant part of a modern master narrative—but, more positively, it is no longer in any sense obliged to feel the need to follow the modernist form of logic. Here see also Graham Ward, *The Blackwell Companion to Postmodern Theology* (Oxford: Blackwell, 2001) xivff.

6. This is said prior to and aside from any assessment of the particular claims of that branch to religious or, more accurately, soteriological preeminence over other major religions. For an interesting but accessible discussion of the notion of postmodernity and its relation to Christianity in general see Daniel J. Adams, "Towards a Theological Understanding of Postmodernism," *Cross Currents* 47/4 (Winter 1997–98). For a more critical discussion of the possibility of religion's continued relevance in the postmodern era see Zygmunt Bauman, "Postmodern Religion," in a further collection of valuable essays on the various aspects of religion in relation to the current age, Paul Heelas, ed., *Religion, Modernity and Postmodernity* (Oxford: Blackwell, 1998).

7. Peter C. Hodgson, *Winds of the Spirit* (London: SCM, 1994) 53–54. Cf. also his *Revisioning the Church: Ecclesial Freedom in the New Paradigm* (Philadelphia: Fortress Press, 1988) 11–12 and elsewhere (preceded by an earlier article in *Theology Today* that articulates many of the core arguments of this work).

However, while fundamental changes, shifts, and developments in culture naturally have produced corresponding changes, shifts, and developments in theology, the relationship should never ultimately be interpreted as unidirectional. The reverse process is often the case. For example, consider the theological and philosophical debates that, at least in part, paved the way for the upheavals of the period of the Reformation(s) and therefore also led to profound social and cultural changes. Yet such theological and philosophical changes were themselves a result of the cultural developments in the Renaissance period and the advent and spread of Renaissance humanism. So culture and theology obviously do influence one another, despite the protests of some who would seek to keep them strictly apart (and yet contradict their own assertions by their tone, manner of discourse, and choice of intellectual and cultural "tools" and achievements employed). Of course, whether this is for good or for ill should be judged separately for particular periods and particular developments, taking the balance of historical evidence.

Hodgson's own work in this area allows us to illustrate how others have sought to understand the present era and have variously engaged in exploring the *ecclesiological* implications of "postmodernity." In a broad sweep Hodgson divides history into *three* distinct and "great" paradigms: the *classic* (from the Patristic to the Reformation era, characterized, he believes, by a "theological consensus" from "Augustine through Calvin"); the *modern* (from the seventeenth to the *late* twentieth century, what he calls the "Enlightenment age"), and the "postmodern era."[8] Yet Hodgson's attempt to sketch these eras illustrates how difficult it is to reach agreement about the dividing lines between the various paradigms or even about what is most distinctive in those particular paradigms. For example, it could be argued that the Reformation(s) era came about partly as a result of theological *pluralism* as opposed to consensus. Furthermore, Hodgson's positing of Calvin's theology as part of that consensus is only intelligible or even acceptable from within a (Protestant) reformed Christian framework. So also, some would place the beginning of the modern era at least a century earlier and, indeed, suggest that it ended a little over a century *before* Hodgson would have it. Finally, whether the "modern period" was most distinctive because of the development of the intellectual ferment known as the "Enlighten-

---

8. Ibid., 54. See also his *Revisioning the Church,* 12.

ment," as Hodgson suggests, is, again, open to debate.[9] A David Tracy would interpret these respective "epochs" somewhat differently, as we shall soon see. And amid the many alternative attempts to describe where *Christianity* stands vis-à-vis the various cultural "epochs" through which it has lived, Johann Baptist Metz (following Karl Rahner, his onetime teacher and later collaborator), prefers to describe the specific history of the church and Christian theology by reference to a very different threefold scheme: "The epoch of Jewish Christianity, relatively short in terms of years but fundamental for the identity of the church and of theology; then the very long epoch within a single culture, even if one with many different strands, in other words the epoch of Hellenism and European culture and civilization up to our own days; and finally the epoch of a culturally polycentric genuinely universal church whose first hints and beginnings showed themselves at Vatican II."[10]

Of course, as Metz would acknowledge, this latter period of ecclesial and theological reality is one that is far from universally acknowledged or universally perceived as desirable. Indeed, much of this book will seek to offer a positive assessment of such a development over and against those who feel the church and theological communities should resist all such cultural developments.

Despite these caveats, Hodgson is attentive to the fact that there are dangers in bracketing history within such strictures, for he writes that "Of course, the discernment of paradigms and of shifts between them is a matter of perspective."[11] So here I will acknowledge the potential pitfalls of such historical analysis and suggest that, if we admit the importance of realizing that *perspective* plays a large part in the discourse of any era, we may be permitted to proceed in speaking of the "postmodern era" with reference to the church. In all, we bear in mind the

9. A particularly critical account—often unjustly so—of Hodgson's work is given by Nicholas M. Healy, *Church, World and the Christian Life: Practical-Prophetic Ecclesiology* (Cambridge: Cambridge University Press, 2000) 44–45, 82–87, 92–93.

10. Johann-Baptist Metz, "Theology in the Modern Age, and Before its End," in Claude Geffré, Gustavo Gutiérrez, and Virgil Elizondo, eds., *Different Theologies, Common Responsibility: Babel or Pentecost? Concilium* 171 (Edinburgh: T & T Clark, 1984) 16.

11. Peter C. Hodgson, *Winds of the Spirit* (London: SCM, 1994) 54. However, he then somewhat commits the same "offense" while trying to illustrate its danger (!) when he continues: "From *our* perspective, the important distinctions between the patristic, the medieval, and the Reformation periods of the church lessen in significance since these are now all seen as variations on the classic paradigm, which was prescientific and precritical. From the perspective of later centuries, our proposed distinction between the modern and postmodern paradigms will likely pale by comparison with even far-reaching changes."

warnings of John O'Malley that different forms of *historical consciousness* lead to notably differing assessments especially of the church and the need for (and form of) its reform and renewal.[12]

On Presenting a "Name"

Although I have already introduced the term "postmodernity," for clarity let me here also acknowledge David Tracy's assertion that "We live in an age that *cannot* name itself."[13] We recognize that no such universal agreement exists with regard to the "name" of the present time. And yet, as already indicated, if one is to talk about the church's challenges and prospects in the present age, it is first necessary to say a little more about the various attempts at naming and discerning our present age, epoch, or era. As Tracy has illustrated, such attempts can be profitably divided into various "camps," although here I again stress that one must proceed, initially at least, by employing the "ideal type" device as opposed to seeking to offer decisive and comprehensive accounts of the various differing perspectives.

With that ever-present further caveat in mind, however one chooses to describe the present "age," whether as modernity, late-modernity, post-modernity, or even post-post-modernity, and in whichever manner one assesses the developments in cultural, intellectual, historical, political, societal, and, of course, religious dimensions of reality over the previous century and a half, we nonetheless are speaking *about* roughly the same thing, though what we make of all this may differ considerably. Thus to some extent I concur with Paul Lakeland when he writes that "[Postmodernity] is in the air we breathe, and the semantic implications of 'postmodernity' mislead us if we think the word itself contains mean-

---

12. John O'Malley, "Reform, Historical Consciousness and Vatican II's *Aggiornamento*," *TS* 32 (1971) 573–601.

13. David Tracy, "On Naming the Present," in Claude Geffré and Jean-Pierre Jossua, eds., *The Debate on Modernity. Concilium* 1992/6 (London: SCM, 1992), italics supplied. This essay was later reproduced in Tracy's book of the same name, *On Naming the Present: Reflections on God, Hermeneutics and the Church* (Maryknoll, NY: Orbis, 1994) ch. 1. For a survey of his developing thoughts on this debate see also his *Blessed Rage for Order: The New Pluralism in Theology* (New York: Crossroad, 1975), *The Analogical Imagination: Christian Theology and the Culture of Pluralism* (New York: Crossroad, 1981), and *Dialogue with the Other: the Inter-Religious Dialogue* (Leuven: Peeters, 1990). See also Werner G. Jeanrond and Jennifer L. Rike, eds., *Radical Pluralism and Truth. David Tracy and the Hermeneutics of Religion* (New York: Crossroad, 1991), and Gareth Jones, "Tracy: Halting the Postmodernist Slide," chapter 5 of his *Critical Theology* (Cambridge: Polity, 1993) 113–34.

ing. It is a way of saying 'our time, not some other.'"[14] From an Anglican perspective, Graham Ward has suggested that "Postmodernity promises neither clarification nor the disappearance of perplexity," but that does not mean we should not seek (paraphrasing Thomas Carlyle's *Signs of the Times*) to "take stock of where we stand" and investigate the "profundity" of the relationship between "our thinking and our cultural/historical context."[15] In particular, Ward's own work is concerned with explicating "the ways in which theological speaking and doing are implicated in contemporary culture, both as its products and its producers."[16]

But more can be said, and here Tracy's descriptive analysis of the situation vis-à-vis so-called "Western culture" is helpful:

> For *modernity* the present is more of the same—the same evolutionary history of the triumph and taken-for-granted superiority of Western scientific, technological, pluralistic and democratic Enlightenment. For *anti-modernity*, the present is a "time of troubles"—a time when all traditions are being destroyed by the inexorable force of that same modernity. For the anti-moderns ours is a time to retreat to a past that never was and a tradition whose presumed purity belies the very meaning of tradition as concrete and ambiguous history. For *post-modernity*, modernity and tradition alike are now exposed as self-deceiving exercises attempting to ground what cannot be grounded: a secure foundation for all knowledge and life. For the post-moderns at their best, the hope of the present is in the reality of otherness and difference—the otherness alive in the marginalized groups of modernity and tradition alike—the mystics, the dissenters, the avant-garde artists, the mad, the hysterical. The conscience

14. *Postmodernity: Christian Identity in a Fragmented Age* (Minneapolis: Fortress Press, 1997) 1.

15. *The Blackwell Companion to Postmodern Theology*, xii.

16. Ibid. For Ward this era brings *two* forms of cultural transformation. The first is "within the logics of a certain movement" that "might radicalize elements already apparent within an historical epoch" and "may develop what is already there in the tradition," while the second type of transformation "is a radical break with the cultural logic of the past or present." Here some form of rupture takes place and encounter with "The Other" leads to the "fracture" of "the symbolic systems that constitute any given cultural milieu. Some cultural analysts suggest that postmodernity performs such a radical break with respect to the thinking and practices of modernity" (ibid., xiii). Note, however, that Ward himself challenges much of the second type of analysis. Still, he concurs, along with several of the scholars whose analysis we have already discussed, that "the cultural situation we find ourselves in both develops certain themes evident in modernity (like the social arena as composed of barely repressed struggles and competitions regulated through contract), but also breaks with categories that maintained the hegemony of modernity (its naturalisms, positivism, essentialisms, dualisms, and humanisms, for example)" (ibid.).

of post-modernity, often implicit rather than explicit, lives more in those groups than in the elite intellectual classes constituting their ranks.[17]

And what of the consequences of such developments? Does this mean that we can reach little agreement in relation to naming and character-izing this age? Not necessarily. More recently Lieven Boeve has shown that the likes of Metz and Tracy were nonetheless right in their portrayal of the end of that "era" characterized by the centrality of Christianity to certain cultures and civilizations: "Whatever the proposed remedy, the *diagnosis* leads one to the unavoidable conclusion that an *ever-in-creasing gulf exists between contemporary culture and the Christian faith.* The days of 'traditional,' cultural Christianity are numbered."[18]

Of course, even Tracy's lengthy quotation does not exhaust the possible interpretations of our age. We must at least mention certain further options that investigate the challenges of postmodern*ism* as opposed to simply looking at the interpretation of the current age—postmodern*ity*.[19] As Boeve suggests, we can note key differences when distinguishing between (post)-modernization/(post)-modernity and (post)-modernism (along with pluralization/plurality in relation to plural*ism*). "The initial terms should be understood as descriptive while the terms ending in 'ism' stand for particular ways of interacting with the described situation whereby elements of the description are brought to the fore as normative."[20]

Some such further options take on board these critiques of the present age and seek to construct or live by the values of an already present "new enlightenment."[21] Hugo Meynell has recently offered one interpretation of this kind.[22] He believes that sufficient time has elapsed

17. Tracy, "On Naming the Present," 66–67.

18. Lieven Boeve, *Interrupting Tradition* (Leuven: Peeters, 2004) 6.

19. Graham Ward offers a discussion of the merits of distinguishing between the two in *The Blackwell Companion to Postmodern Theology,* xxii–xxv, including his statement that "Postmodernism enables us to distinguish certain elements in our contemporary world which are other than postmodern and yet, all too often, can be lumped together as characteristics of postmodernity" (ibid., xxi).

20. Boeve, *Interrupting Tradition,* 52.

21. And/or, as with certain proponents of critical theory, they perceive modernity as an *unfinished* project, one that took several wrong turnings along the way.

22. See Hugo A. Meynell, *Postmodernism and the New Enlightenment* (Washington, D.C.: Catholic University of America Press, 2000). On Meynell's take on postmodernity see Gerard Mannion, "Being True: Williams and Meynell on Reason and Virtue," *The Heythrop Journal,* forthcoming. On such themes see also Bernard Lonergan's influential "The Second Enlightenment" in Bernard Lonergan, *A Third Collection,* ed. Frederick E. Crowe (London: Geoffrey Chapman, 1985) 63–64. Of course, Tracy himself develops an approach that seeks to take on board the positive elements of modernity and integrate

now to judge the major achievements and faults of the (reductivistic) postmodern "movement" and some of its key theorists. Meynell understands postmodern*ism* as follows: "Postmodernism may usefully be looked at as a set of related beliefs and attitudes that oppose the 'modernism' that derives from the Old Enlightenment. Basically, a restricted and debilitating view of the norms of rationality has provoked a reaction in which such norms are (at least explicitly) rejected altogether."[23] However, the "New Enlightenment" is typified by an attempt to reassert a commitment to the existence of authentic foundations for "our knowledge of what is true and good."[24] Such an approach might be understood as one variety of what is termed "constructivistic postmodernism," to counter "reductivistic" and "eliminative" versions.[25]

Along similar lines, others have also sought to offer a more constructive response to postmodernity, suggesting that while overarching "grand narratives" may no longer hold the universal validity they once did (*if* ever they did so, in any case), that is no reason why we cannot operate with and hold as valid such explanatory hypotheses as "major narratives," certainly less "grand" in character but nonetheless still relevant for certain communities and their seeking after truth.[26] Lieven

---

them with aspects of Catholic tradition and postmodern thought. As well as the article and text named above, see especially his "The Uneasy Alliance Reconceived: Catholic Theological Method, Modernity, and Postmodernity," *TS* 50/3 (1989).

23. Meynell, *Postmodernism and the New Enlightenment*, 40. Further, very different perspectives come in the form of such theories as those of Francis Fukuyama, who has suggested that we have now entered into a period in which we may speak of the "end of history." Cf. his *The End of History and the Last Man* (New York: Free Press, 1992) and his later *The Great Disruption* (London: Profile, 1999). For an interesting theological commentary on Fukuyama's theories, and of the relation between theology and history in general, cf. Nicholas Lash, "Remembering Our Future," *The Month* (January 2001) 4–14.

24. Meynell, *Postmodernism and the New Enlightenment*, 29.

25. Further studies of particular relevance here include Paul Lakeland, *Postmodernity: Christian Identity in a Fragmented Age*, and Nicholas M. Healy, *Church, World, and the Christian Life*. As will become evident, the line of argument in this present volume is more sympathetic, in general, to Lakeland's position than to elements of how Healy critiqued other approaches in *that particular work*. However, Healy has since clarified and developed his position considerably.

26. For an example of such an attempt from an evangelical perspective see Richard Middleton and Brian Walsh, *Truth is Stranger than It Used to Be. Biblical Faith in a Postmodern Age* (London: InterVarsity, 1995). Although he believed in 1992 that history is still locked in the conflicts caused by the forces of modernity, Gregory Baum also helps illustrate that there have been and continue to be constructive alternatives in the various responses to modernity and what is now termed postmodernity. See his "Modernity: A Sociological Perspective," in Geffré and Jossua, eds., *The Debate on Modernity* (1992) 4–9. His own conclusion then was that "We are still . . . in the

Boeve, whose work we shall encounter at various stages throughout the latter parts of this volume, prefers to speak in terms of offering an "open narrative" as opposed to attempting to encircle and retreat within a "closed narrative" in the face of postmodernity's challenges to the Christian tradition.[27] Johann Baptist Metz marries a sometimes devastating critical analysis to an enduring optimism that political, social, and transformative praxis can offer, not simply to Christianity but to the world in general, a new hope in the face of the monumental suffering and evil of our times and of the modern world's bloody and divisive demise.[28]

Furthermore, to our already complicated picture one might add such further reactions to postmodernity and postmodern thought as liberationist postmodernisms, pluralistic, and (often more conservative in nature) post-liberal theories of postmodernism.[29] There are now many ongoing discussions, of course, of all such "schools" of thought in reaction to postmodernity, from varieties of feminist thought, the liberal political to the critical theorists, the structuralists, through various developmental and reactionary stages to the deconstructionists.

---

civilization created by industrialization and democracy, still caught in the clash between contradictory forces, the domination of instrumental reason with its dehumanizing consequences and the movements of resistance based on the conviction, be it secular or religious, that humanity has an ethical vocation" (p. 9).

27. Boeve, *Interrupting Tradition*, especially chapters V and VI, and Part 3.

28. Johann-Baptist Metz, "Theology in the Modern Age, and Before its End."

29. In relation to these differing perspectives, relevant here also are Terrence Tilley, *Postmodern Theologies* (Maryknoll, NY: Orbis, 1998); Stanley Grenz, *A Primer on Postmodernism;* various sections of David Ford and Rachel Muers, eds., *The Modern Theologians* (3d ed. Oxford: Blackwell, 2005); Graham Ward, ed., *The Postmodern God* (Oxford: Blackwell, 1997); Laurence P. Hemming, *Postmodernity's Transcending: Devaluing God* (Notre Dame: University of Notre Dame Press, 2005). Nicholas M. Healy also discusses the contemporary situation vis-à-vis postmodernism and the various theories about it in *Church, World, and the Christian Life,* 111–16, 145, 158, focusing largely on those he terms "neo-Nietzscheans." Of course the literature in such fields is now immense, so only a few representative examples are offered here for further illumination. One prominent example of a theologian who has sought to engage with various postmodern scholars and theories is the aforementioned Graham Ward. His numerous works have also sought to chart the "varieties of postmodern theology." See, *inter alia,* his "Postmodern Theology" in David F. Ford, ed., *The Modern Theologians* (2d ed. Oxford: Blackwell, 1997) 585–99 (332–38 in the 3d. ed., 2005); his edited book, *The Postmodern God* (Oxford: Blackwell, 1997) and, more recently, his edition of the *Blackwell Companion to Postmodern Theology.* Concerning such "varieties" see also Kevin Vanhoozer, ed., *The Cambridge Companion to Postmodern Theology* (Cambridge: Cambridge University Press, 2003), and the selection of writings in John D. Caputo, *The Religious* (Oxford: Blackwell, 2002).

Theologies in and of Postmodernity

All these multiple approaches to the present have found willing dialogue partners in the discipline of theology itself.[30] Indeed, the complex series of interactions between theology and other forms of postmodern discourse can be illustrated very well in the area of feminist thought. No account of the age should in any way underestimate the achievements and influence of scholars whose work lies at various points along the road from the earlier feminist theoreticians and activists, via a number of generations and schismatic or counter/parallel movements, accompanied by, in dialogue with, and sometimes in opposition to womanist and *mujerista* theologies, down to the post-feminists. Nonetheless, as Mary McClintock Fulkerson illustrates, for all such forms of theologizing "postmodernism enters this theological discourse by providing resources designed to advance such liberative ends."[31] Thus "[w]hat we do find in liberation-focused feminist theologies are appropriations of philosophical forms of postmodernism, such as Foucaldian critiques of the modern subject and modern notions of power, Lacanian/psychoanalytic accounts of the desiring subject, and post-structuralist/deconstructionist thought, all of which articulate refusals of unified and totalizing modern accounts of reason."[32] And indeed, just as in other areas of theological engagement with postmodernity, so in the arena of feminist thought, non-religious feminist theorists are now turning to feminist theologians for inspiration, as Serene Jones has illustrated.[33]

30. Lewis Mudge has assessed and admirably summarized some of these approaches in an attempt to discern their applicability in an ecclesiological context: "The thinkers in question are also 'deconstructionist' to the extent that they self-consciously refuse the grammars of institution maintenance—particularly the economic logic—of late twentieth-century societies. They are 'nonfoundationalist' to the extent that they refuse the aid of philosophical visions of any kind that purport to ground theological reflection in broadly persuasive and legitimating reality propositions, metaphysical, scientific, or otherwise. They are 'postmodernist' to the extent that they make a point of functioning intellectually in a world without given institutional grammars and philosophical foundations, either to celebrate its freedom or to recover its ancient traditions, or both" (*The Church As Moral Community* [Geneva: WCC Publications, 1998] 40).

31. Mary McClintock Fulkerson, "Feminist Theology," in Vanhoozer, ed., *Cambridge Companion to Postmodern Theology*, 109.

32. Ibid., 100. On feminist ecclesiology in particular see Natalie Watson, *Introducing Feminist Ecclesiology* (London: Continuum, 2002) and her "Feminist Ecclesiologies," in Gerard Mannion and Lewis Mudge, eds., *The Routledge Companion to the Christian Church* (London: Routledge, 2007).

33. Serene Jones, "Companionable Wisdoms: What Insight Might Feminist Theorists Gather from Feminist Theologians?" in Ward, ed., *Blackwell Companion to*

Other approaches (some of which we shall encounter again along the way) include the various schools of hermeneutics and, naturally, the varieties of fundamentalism, whether they be religious, political, scientific, economic, or nihilistic.[34] Thus has emerged the genre of "postmodern theology" in its own right, with further subdivisions such as "theologies of communal practice," postmetaphysical theology, postphilosophical theology, "radical orthodoxy," deconstructive theology, reconstructive theology, restorationist theology, and various additional recent varieties of feminist theology.[35] To their number should be added approaches taken by scholars focusing on the areas of environmental theology, eco-theology, and queer theology. Of course, many theologies overlap several different subdisciplines at one and the same time, so any attempt to pigeonhole a given work should always be undertaken carefully and be open to the admission that such labeling must remain non-definitive.

Again, one single volume could not hope to engage with all such theological approaches in detail or to do justice to an account of all. Certainly, some approaches I have purposefully avoided because they

---

Postmodern Theology, 294–308, and also her *Feminist Theory and Christian Theology: Cartographies of Grace* (Minneapolis: Fortress Press, 2000).

34. Cf. various further accounts in Meynell, *Postmodernism and the New Enlightenment;* Terry Eagleton, *The Illusions of Postmodernism* (Oxford: Blackwell, 1996); Pauline Marie Rosenau, *Post-Modernism and the Social Sciences: Insights, Inroads, and Intrusions* (Princeton: Princeton University Press, 1992); Ann Wilde, *Horizons of Assent: Modernism, Postmodernism and the Ironic Imagination* (Philadelphia: University of Pennsylvania Press, 1987); Stephen Toulmin, *Cosmopolis: The Hidden Agendas of Modernity* (Chicago: University of Chicago Press, 1992); "Modernity and Postmodernity," chapter 4 of Leslie Paul Thiele, *Thinking Politics: Perspectives in Ancient, Modern, and Postmodern Political Theory* (New York: Chatham House, 2003); Steven Best and Douglas Kellner, *Postmodern Theory: Critical Interrogations* (Basingstoke: Macmillan, 1991), and also the same two authors' "Postmodernism," chapter 13 of Robert C. Solomon and David Sherman, eds., *The Blackwell Guide to Continental Philosophy* (Oxford: Blackwell, 2003) 285–308. Here see also Paul Lakeland, *Postmodernity: Christian Identity in a Fragmented Age.* Various further discussions and debates of relevance may also be found among the chapters of Vanhoozer, ed., *The Cambridge Companion to Postmodern Theology.* David Tracy's work, of course, is highly instructive here; for a short discussion of its relevance to the debates about postmodernity in general see, again, Gareth Jones, "Tracy: Halting the Postmodernist Slide."

35. Typologies described in both Vanhoozer, ed., *Cambridge Companion to Postmodern Theology* and Ward, ed., *Blackwell Companion to Postmodern Theology.* See also the very helpful discussion in Lakeland, "Postmodern Thought and Religion," chapter 2 of his *Postmodernity*, 39–46. See also Tilley, *Postmodern Theologies*, and David Ray Griffin et al., *Varieties of Postmodern Theology.*

seem ill-suited to the nature of the debates in this volume[36] or because they seem to be problematic in their response to postmodernity and either will merit attention in later work[37] or are deemed suitably challenged elsewhere and so need not detain us further in our debates here.

Postmodern theologies focus on a range of themes familiar to theology throughout its long story, but they obviously attempt to do so in a novel way, whether critical, reductivistic, constructive, or restorationist. More recently some thinkers have sought to clarify their own work as being not primarily "postmodern theology" *per se* (here seeking not simply to avoid the pejorative connotations that opponents attach to such a label, but also to provide methodological clarification), but more as theologians plying their trade in a postmodern world—trying to make sense of the tasks and challenges for theology in this postmodern context. They nonetheless are attentive to the valuable insights from and potential pitfalls of the postmodern*isms*. I would place this volume and my own work in general in this last group.

But one form of reaction to the contemporary era will occupy more of our attention than many others, owing to the prevalence of the varieties of this reaction spreading across the denominations of Christianity. Here I shall simply identify it as an approach that perceives a certain understanding of the Christian faith and church in superior terms to other quests for meaning, understanding, purpose, and fulfilment in life. It looks more inward (to the church community) than outward and inculcates a more separatist understanding of the relation between the church and the wider "world." In their most partisan forms such tendencies tend to champion a particular form and understanding of Christianity as the most "full," "complete," or even the only "true" way of life that may lead to ultimate salvation, fulfilment, etc. Such an understanding, in a Roman Catholic context, would appear to run counter to the intentions behind *Lumen gentium* §14–16, as well as other conciliar documents and subsequent teachings (chapters 3 and 4 explore these matters further).[38]

36. For example, they may warrant greater treatment in a volume on the Christian church in general or on postmodern theology in general, but not in a volume focused primarily on Catholic ecclesiological challenges in the postmodern era.

37. E.g., the work of Stanley Hauerwas and of some proponents of Radical Orthodoxy will form the focus of later writings in progress, although both, especially the former, are treated in brief in certain sections of this volume.

38. As Gregory Baum illustrated, this part of the document makes "strong positive statements on non-catholic christians, declarations which have never been made in any ecclesiastical document before." Furthermore it "acknowledged the action of the Holy Spirit even beyond our Christian family . . . [it acknowledges that] whatever is true and good among other religions is due, not simply to human effort, but to him who

This approach is similar in many respects to an ecclesial mindset that prevailed in earlier periods of Christian history (but was challenged on many fronts in the mid-to-late twentieth century in favor of more inclusive and pluralistic worldviews)—namely, what is usually referred to as "exclusivism."[39] Because of such similarities (notwithstanding important differences), I have called this group of contemporary ecclesial attitudes and their attendant practices "neo-exclusivism."[40]

In sum, then, it would seem that we thus tend to view our age as if it were an abstract work of art or even a hologram—each seeing something different from his or her own particular perspective. My subject matter in this book is the exploration of the notion, nature, and tasks of church in the present age. But I nonetheless think it *is* helpful to indicate, in a general sense, how that age is being understood by those in its midst, and in order to do so I think it is most helpful to speak in terms of this age as being "*post*-modernity." And, although here we cannot go into exhaustive detail concerning the varieties of thought evident in the genre of postmodernism itself, along the way I shall note where key elements of that thought are relevant to the themes of this book.

To elucidate our central question further, then, we turn next to outline some of the challenges of postmodernity and then identify some ecclesiological responses that many believe have not proved too successful in confronting three particular difficulties for the church in our times. Of course, such problems must be confronted. It is no use merely jumping onto the "postmodern bandwagon" and trying to grin and enjoy the ride. Postmodernity has brought many incisive and disturbing questions to the church today. But *how* we understand, interpret, and tackle them will illustrate whether or not we have fallen prey to a reductivistic postmodern agenda.

Challenges of Postmodernity

Here I wish merely to outline, in brief, the challenges posed to the church by the symptomatic features of postmodernism itself. Many of

---

enlightens all men that they may have life" commentary in *De ecclesia: The Constitution on the Church of Vatican II* (London: DLT, 1965) 29.

39. For various accounts of "exclusivism" see Gavin D'Costa, *Theology and Religious Pluralism* (Oxford: Blackwell, 1986), and John Hick and Paul F. Knitter, *The Myth of Christian Uniqueness* (Maryknoll, NY: Orbis, 1987).

40. Mannion, "Ecclesiology and Postmodernity," *New Blackfriars* 85 (May 2004) 304–28.

these trends are only relevant to certain societies, though forms of them have had an effect upon most, if not all, postmodern societies.[41]

Relativism and Emotivism

The dethroning of the "grand narratives," the overarching and universal explanatory hypotheses, has led to a process some have called "detraditionalization,"[42] a rise in relativism and indeed emotivism that has gone hand in hand with the ongoing march of individualism.[43] What this has meant, in effect, is not simply that absolutes are shunned, but that, for some, everything tends to be judged in relative terms and, indeed, in terms of individual preference and emotional bias. This has been influenced by a further process that emerged in the modern period and has, in turn, influenced the further collapse or effective "sterilization" of ethical frameworks in many societies. Indeed, commentators speak of the "fragmentation" of moral norms and patterns of moral guidance themselves.

Moral Fragmentation

The competing moral frameworks of modernity have been so challenged by the reductivistic postmodern theorists, the practical consequences of their ideas, and the trends of postmodernity in general that we have seen a fragmentation of morality.[44] In particular, moral absolutes

41. For a representative account of the perceived theological challenges of postmodern developments see Thomas Guarino, "Postmodernity and Five Fundamental Theological Issues," *TS* 57 (1996) 654–89, and Jack A. Bonsor, "History, Dogma, and Nature: Further Reflections on Postmodernism and Theology," *TS* 55 (1994) 294–313. In a more general sense Peter Hodgson lists five particular "crises" of the "postmodern" era for our world as a whole, namely: the cognitive crisis (in both technical and philosophical rationality), the historical crisis (the end of both religious and secular versions of history working toward some positive end such as salvation, progress, the dictatorship of the proletariat, etc.), the political crisis (shifts in ideologies, in the axes of power in the world, decline of support for the "social ideals generated by the Enlightenment"), the socioeconomic crisis (the dysfunctionalities of free enterprise capitalism and state socialism and the effects of what, in the years after the publication of Hodgson's book, came to be called globalization), and, finally, the religious crisis: Christianity's decline in "the West" and the attendant emergence of new forms of being religious. See Hodgson, *Revisioning the Church*, 13–16.

42. An informative collection of essays on this concept is Paul Heelas, Scott Lash, and Paul Morris, eds., *Detraditionalization. Critical Reflections on Authority and Identity* (Oxford: Blackwell, 1996).

43. See Boeve, *Interrupting Tradition*, 53ff.

44. For a range of perspectives here cf. Daniel P. Hollinger, *Choosing the Good. Christian Ethics in a Complex World* (Grand Rapids: Baker Academic, 2002); Linda

are shunned and the possibility of transferable ethical norms is either not considered achievable or is dressed up in political, legal, or emotive garb, such as certain conceptions of "rights" without due acknowledgment that even such a concept as "right" in itself presupposes the existence of an ethical framework and basis for moral thinking. The "pick and mix" relativistic mentality that dominates the "consumer explosion" of the postmodern age has done great damage to the very notion of morality, effectively turning Nietzsche's perspectival hypothesis about objective morals into a self-fulfilling prophecy. What matters for many individuals now is not what is seen to be morally right or wrong, good or evil, etc., but what is right or "best" for that "me" that sits atop the consumerist age like a new god, imprisoned in its own heaven by its own volition.

Such developments pose stark challenges for the church in our times, for they fly in the face of that "being-in-community" Christianity seeks to develop and encourage. The church's very business is a *communitarian*, i.e., a social priority. To paraphrase T. Howland Sanks' reflections on an oft-quoted phrase, it is not simply that we should acknowledge that the church *has* a social mission, but, indeed, to state that the church *is* a social mission.[45] He continues: ". . . the church has understood salvation to pertain not only to individual 'souls' but to the transformation of the social, political, and economic order, indeed to the whole cosmic order . . . ."[46] Being and community are two of the fundamental concepts of Christian ecclesiology, perhaps *the* two prime ecclesiological concepts, for Christianity bears witness to a God whose self Christians believe has been revealed as three coequal, coeternal, and codivine persons (or, perhaps better still, "modes of being") whose form of being is understood precisely as a perfect community.

Meaninglessness and a New Context for Theodicy

The processes above, along with the moral fragmentation and the spread, adaptation, and further development of the ideas of Friedrich

---

Hogan, *Confronting the Truth* (London: Darton Longman and Todd, 2000); Paul Heelas, "On Things not Being Worse," in Heelas, Lash, and Morris, eds., *Detraditionalization.* I explore these debates further in a forthcoming volume, *Ethics in a Transvalued Age: Morality in the Shadow of Nietzsche.*

45. T. Howland Sanks, "Globalization and the Church's Social Mission," *TS* 60 (1999) 626. To avoid potential misunderstanding here, note that, as will become evident in our two final chapters, I interpret this phrase in a very different sense to that provided in the work of Stanley Hauerwas.

46. Ibid., 626ff.

Nietzsche (whether one believes he desired that or not) has led from the path of relativism in the direction of nihilism, which in turn has led to greater meaninglessness and despair in the lives of countless individuals and even communities. If we wipe away the "horizon of meaning," as Nietzsche's madman said we had,[47] we can expect little else by way of result. For the church and theology in particular this means there is now a new context within which we grapple with the problem of human suffering and evil in the world. If trust in a living God and a sense of meaning, purpose, direction, and fulfilment are becoming increasingly untenable for many people, so too our theodicizing must be approached very differently than in previous eras.[48] As George Pattison has illustrated, the contexts of the varied responses to evil and suffering, increasingly characterized by "outrage" in the late post-enlightenment era, also confront Christian theology and philosophy of religion with more demanding challenges than logic or trust alone can answer.[49] It has been said that *all* theology is, in a sense, a grappling with the problem of evil.[50] If there is truth is this statement, and I believe there is, then that grappling faces a very different situation today—practically, epistemologically, as well as doctrinally—than in previous historical epochs.

"Consumerization" of the Church and Religion

Indeed, recent studies show that all the above trends have in turn had a similar effect on religion in general and the church in particular. No longer are they perceived in terms of obligation, but rather in terms of choice. The "pick and mix" individualistic mentality that is sweeping many societies is also applied to spirituality and even within the ecclesial setting in general. This is witnessed in a profound sense in the sphere of ethics and the churches' moral teachings. Peter Brierley has outlined this situation in relation to the Christian church in Britain:

> It has become acceptable to make our own choices about a wide variety of aspects of life that were not options for previous generations. This is expressed in all sorts of ways, from the consumerism that has spawned

47. Cf. Friedrich Nietzsche, *The Gay Science* trans. Josephine Nauckhoff (Cambridge: Cambridge University Press, 2001) no. 125.

48. George Pattison, *A Short Course in the Philosophy of Religion* (London: SCM, 2001).

49. Ibid. See especially chs. 8, 9, 10.

50. See also, for example, a study that specifically examines these issues in the context of postmodern theory itself: Walter Lowe, *Theology and Difference. The Wound of Reason* (Bloomington: Indiana University Press, 1993).

the phrase "I shop therefore I am," to changing sexual mores . . . . [T]he changing pattern of church attendance is probably at least partly to do with personal choice . . . [and p]eople within the church are also exercising choice—about what to believe, who to follow, which church to attend. We have all played musical chairs as children; people now play musical churches as adults. . . . This consumerist approach means that the whole culture in which the church and Christian organizations exercise their ministry is changing radically. . . . [T]he church is facing competition of a kind it has not had to wrestle before. Choice in itself is, of course, neither right nor wrong, but this consumerist culture impacts leadership in a huge number of ways. . . .[51]

Indeed, while certain such developments are welcomed by some, this overlooks the fact that this descent into consumerization, which has become the new postmodern "religion,"[52] despite what Bauman may say to the contrary, has brought about not real or greater freedom at all, but rather a new form of enslavement.[53]

Crises of Legitimation

All such factors have led to a situation whereby religion in general, as illustrated here with particular reference to Christianity and the Catholic Church in particular, has faced one specific dilemma in this era. That key challenge is to the *authority* of the church, hence the *legitimation* for its principles and moral guidance and so its *relevance* in today's world. By no means is this challenge limited to the more obvious forms and forces of secularization and secularism.[54] The challenge to religion and the church comes from myriad different sources. For example, there is the challenge posed to the authority of religion from those who reject the value, place, and validity of religion on atheistic grounds, in particular the so-called "new materialism" in science led by

51. Peter Brierley and Heather Wraight, "Christian Leadership in a Postmodern Society," in John Nelson, ed., *Leading, Managing, Ministering. Challenging Questions for Church and Society* (Norwich: Canterbury Press. 1998) 87–88.

52. Thus the "consumerist turn" leads to everything seemingly being geared toward personal satisfaction and even religion is now "packaged," organized, and even "marketed" as such because believers are treating religion as something they may take or leave, picking and choosing which aspects they feel will "work" for them.

53. See Zygmunt Bauman, "Postmodern Religion." For a recent study of this "consumerization" of the church see John Drane, *The MacDonaldsization of the Church* (London: Darton Longman and Todd, 2000).

54. On such forms and forces cf. Boeve, *Interrupting Tradition*, 37–40, and Graham Ward, "The Implosion of Secularisation," in idem, ed., *Blackwell Companion to Postmodern Theology*, xvi–xx.

figures such as Richard Dawkins who reject any positive role for religion in our societies today and who, instead, view religion as a pernicious influence and combat religion and theological inquiry at every level.[55]

But, of course, the theories and agendas of reductivistic postmodernism have not gone unchallenged. This is so in both a positive and negative sense. In a constructive sense, a few examples include those such as David Ray Griffin's attempts to construct a more positive and communitarian response to the present times[56] and David Tracy's attempts to "halt the postmodernist slide."[57] So too, as indicated earlier, Hugo Meynell has suggested that "a new enlightenment" has emerged to challenge the dilemmas of postmodernity and, in particular, to restate the case for ethics today.[58] Such an approach even has its precursors among the Frankfurt School, that most critical of judges of the Enlightenment project. As Gregory Baum has reminded ecclesiologically oriented observers today,

> . . . the Frankfurt philosophers strongly objected to the complete rejection of the Enlightenment by conservatives, existentialists and fascists in the 1920s and 30s—and by postmodern thinkers in the 80s and 90s. The Frankfurt School offered a passionate defense of the Enlightenment's ethical achievement, the human rights tradition, and dreaded what would happen to people if their human rights were no longer respected.[59]

55. Various works of the Anglican theologian Keith Ward seek to confront Dawkins' often rather shallow, idiosyncratic, and ill-informed notion of both theology and religion in general, as well as the challenges posed by similar contemporary, and supposedly "cultured" "despisers of religion" (to borrow from Schleiermacher). See, e.g., Ward's *Religion and Creation* (Oxford: Clarendon) 1966; *God, Chance and Necessity* (Oxford: OneWorld) 1996; *God, Faith and the New Millennium* (Oxford: OneWorld) 1999; and *The Case for Religion* (Oxford: OneWorld) 2004.

56. David Ray Griffin, William A. Beardslee and Joe Holland (eds.), *Varieties of Postmodern Theology* (Albany: SUNY Press, 1989). Griffin's approach is discussed in Terence Tilley, with Craig Westman, "David Ray Griffin and Constructive Postmodern Communalism" in Terence Tilley, ed., *Postmodern Theologies* (Maryknoll, NY: Orbis, 1996).

57. Gareth Jones, "Tracy: Halting the Postmodernist Slide," chapter 5 of his *Critical Theology* 113–34.

58. Meynell, *Postmodernism and the New Enlightenment*.

59. Gregory Baum, *Amazing Church: A Catholic Theologian Remembers a Half Century of Change* (Maryknoll, NY: Orbis, 2005) 142. Of course, Baum adds the caveat that a streak of pessimism nonetheless infected the School: they could not commit themselves to the hope that twentieth-century humanity had the necessary resources to rescue itself. But, as indicated earlier, rights still presuppose the existence of a broader moral framework of some sort. Also on the Frankfurt School see Baum's "Modernity: A Sociological Perspective," in Geffré and Jossua, eds., *The Debate on Modernity*, 6–7 and, on other responses to the "crisis of modernity," 7–9. As he explains, "in the course of the nineteenth century, the Frankfurters argued, Enlightenment rationality collapsed

Further examples of such alternative yet still constructive approaches are thinkers such as Paul Heelas, who challenges the prevalence of "detraditionalization."[60] I shall touch upon other constructive approaches in later chapters. Let me simply say here that a further positive and constructive response to the age comes from those who believe ecclesiology can and must continue to be developed in our era.

Globalization: a "New" Grand Narrative?

Karl Rahner famously spoke of the coming of a "global church." Already, at the council, just as in the teachings of John XXIII and Paul VI, the church was conscious of itself as part of a worldwide family. But this increasing consciousness of the interconnectedness of the human family across the globe has brought stark challenges to bear upon the church's mission today.

Although some of the reductivistic and deconstructionist postmodern theorists have tried to suggest that our era marks a shift from an emphasis on the universal to a greater attention being paid to the local and the particular, in many respects the exact opposite has actually been the case.[61] We now live in an era of "globalization" that already functions, in a variety of ways, as a new "grand narrative."[62] The local and particular is now directly affected by events and decisions that may originate, literally, on the other side of the globe. Social, economic, cultural, and political realities are interlinked and interdependent to an intensity hitherto unparalleled. Technology and the communications revolution have facilitated the development of this phenomenon. T.

---

into instrumental reason alone. The urgent task of the present, after recognizing the dark side of the Enlightenment, was not to reject it altogether, but instead to struggle for a cultural retrieval of substantive reason as a source of ethics, and simultaneously to denote instrumental reason from cultural dominance. Against existentialists and phenomenologists the Frankfurters defended the importance of the natural sciences, and against populists and Fascists, they defended emancipation and solidarity as the uniquely human destiny. The Frankfurt School called their critique of the Enlightenment 'dialectical', involving negation and retrieval, and opposed as dangerous for the human community any non-dialectical negation of the Enlightenment" (ibid., 7).

60. Paul Heelas, "On Things Not Being Worse, and the Ethic of Humanity," in Heelas, Lash, and Morris, eds., *Detraditionalization*.

61. For a brief and accessible discussion of further challenges to the once "prevailing" postmodern wisdom in its various forms, see the various essays in "After Postmodernism," the Forum section of *The Philosophers' Magazine* 20 (Autumn 2002) 34–50.

62. Indeed, globalization has emerged from other "grand narratives" and ideologies, not least neoliberal economics and political philosophy.

Howland Sanks writes that "for theologians, our growing awareness and analysis of this phenomenon [i.e., globalization] is part of the ongoing reading of the signs of the times. . . . We are faced with a new situation that calls for new analysis and conceptualization."[63]

However, the phenomenon of globalization and its attendant social and economic consequences has led to a decline in social networks, co-operation, and social "capital" in a number of societies. These changes represent a real and immensely powerful counterforce to the gospel culture and mission. Once again individualism, driven by materialism, triumphs over community. Many places have witnessed developments little short of the very *death* of community. How does one "do" ecclesiology against such a backdrop?

What aims will preoccupy us throughout the coming pages? Our outline thus far has indicated that our focus will be specific but will also embrace wider debates at large in theology and the church in general today. Peter Hodgson has suggested that "The new cultural paradigm calls for a new theological paradigm, a revisioning of the entire theological agenda, including questions of method, God, history, human being, ecclesiology, eschatology, and religious pluralism. Work on theological method must address both the cognitive questions raised by postmodernist criticism and the practical questions raised by liberation theology." As with our general argument here, Hogdson believes the various responses to postmodernity sit between two equally unhelpful alternatives: on the one hand an attempt to "turn back the clock," to return to pre-Enlightenment mindsets, "to traditional bases of authority and conventional forms of religious belief," and, at the other extreme, "a radical relativism in which nothing is known, believed, or acted upon . . . . the temptation here is to retreat into intellectual games and hedonistic play—a mask for despair, cynicism, nihilism. Ironically such play requires a stable order as its context, for it has no staying power against demonic absolutes and political oppression."[64]

This present work, then, explores various aspects of such a challenge but focuses in particular on questions of ecclesiology in the main, and of method, ecclesial and religious pluralism, God, and history to various supplementary extents. In many ways we can share in Hodgson's own aims "to take up the agenda of a new ecclesiology, a new theology of

63. Sanks, "Globalization and the Church's Social Mission," 625. See also Robert Schreiter, *The New Catholicity: Theology Between the Global and the Local* (Maryknoll: Orbis) 1985.

64. Hodgson, *Revisioning the Church*, 18.

the church—one that is nonhierarchical, nonprovincial, and nonprivatistic in its ecclesial vision, one that focuses upon the historicality as well as the spirituality of the church, recognizes its distinctive communal form, and thematizes its liberative praxis and ecumenical mission."[65]

But, nearly twenty years after the writing of Hodgson's book, the ecclesiological and theological contexts, not to mention the cognitive, historical, political, socioeconomic, and religious contexts have all moved on—some beyond recognition of the situation the church was faced with in 1988. And, of course, this volume addresses, in the main, the challenges facing one particular ecclesial communion, the Roman Catholic Church, whereas Hodgson's was written from a Reformed background and addressed to the Christian church in general. Much of what we discuss here is relevant to the church on the whole, but the dilemmas it seeks to address are first of all those (the "beam in the eye," if one prefers) besetting my own church. But, like Hodgson's, our efforts will only ever be provisional, part of a theological project that, as with all theological projects, "must remain incomplete and open-ended."[66]

In debating the future of the church we embark on a journey and engage in a program that involves a re-evaluation of aspects of the church's life and structures. Many have gone this way before at different times in the long and varied story of the church. Just as with such occasions in the past, for many Catholics, and especially for many church leaders, this may be an extremely difficult journey to undertake. If the church is to enjoy positive developments in its future, it appears inevitable that there must be fundamental root-and-branch changes in the very manner in which it is organized, structured, and led. Careful attention must be paid to the *how* of going about all this and also investigating ways of transforming a multitude of aspects of leading, managing, and ministering in the church. Naturally, we must engage in dialogue with the wider societies and the world in general, learning lessons and gathering inspiration for how we might take the church forward.[67]

---

65. Ibid.

66. Ibid., 19.

67. Hence these questions are explored further in Part III of this volume and also in my "What's in a Name? Hermeneutical Questions on 'Globalisation,' Catholicity and Ecumenism," *New Blackfriars* (March 2005) 204–15.

Chapter Two

Postmodernity and the Church

Each of the previously mentioned "types" of postmodern theology has, to some extent at least, a corresponding understanding of and vision/prognosis for the church—some, of course, much more developed than others.[1] In many ways the dilemmas facing the church local *and* universal in our current age mirror the postmodern dilemmas of our cultural and intellectual situations in general.[2] Maureen Junker-Kenny, a specialist in practical theology and ethics, interprets the church's dilemma in the current age thus:

> The churches are also subject to the same criterion of the question of their resources for overcoming the conflicts of modernity, which have been substantially accentuated by the instrumental realization of reason in the form of power. How can they make it possible to experience the Christian message in the changed conditions of individualization and tendentious syncretistic *bric à brac*, the de-traditionalizing and dedoctrinalizing, and introduce it into public decisions? Just as it is clear that two ways of mediation which were taken for granted, culture as a whole

1. For a more detailed consideration of such see Gerard Mannion, "Postmodern Ecclesiologies," in Gerard Mannion and Lewis Mudge, eds., *The Routledge Companion to the Christian Church* (London: Routledge, 2007). Roger Haight addresses the ecclesiological *context* of postmodernity in *Christian Community in History* (New York: Continuum, 2004) Vol. 1: *Historical Ecclesiology*, 57–58, although he writes (p. 57) "In this work postmodernity remains a context out of which the work is written; it is not explicitly addressed."

2. Somewhat unsurprisingly as some might say, but my point is that a realization of this is usually perceived in view of the church's relation to the "world" and cultures external to itself. Often such factors are overlooked with regard to the situation "within" the church itself.

and the family, no longer support religious socialization as they used to, so too it is possible to recognize clearly the needs for orientation, meaning, belonging and comfort, meeting which is the task of the church in society.[3]

It is certainly true, however, that many documents of the Catholic Church's teaching seek to confront the dilemmas of the present age and that the late Pope John Paul II has even been described as a "postmodern theologian" in his own right.[4] But I would add here that we need to take account of the fact that our conceptions of such features of church life and practice as ministry, authority, and leadership in the church today all too frequently—in effect—either take little account of the postmodern reality in which we now live and/or adopt counterproductive strategies in response to the dilemmas of the age. All too often (and at each and every level of the church from parish to universal and institutional) our conceptions of church and, likewise, of ministry, authority, and leadership are based on (now much challenged and dismissed) modern and even premodern frameworks that are no longer tenable.[5] But it need not and should not be so. As Junker-Kenny suggests, the church "can take up and encourage the desire to seek subjectively appropriate ways of relating to God and witnessing, *instead of preventing it* by its appearance and the forms of its communication and process of decision. The communitarian and even fundamentalist retreat into the enclaves of their own convictions and the refusal to collaborate and share responsibility in processes of counselling and legislation are not alternatives."[6]

---

3. Maureen Junker-Kenny, "Church, Modernity and Postmodernity," in Christoph Theobald and Dietmar Mieth, eds., *Unanswered Questions. Concilium* (London: SCM, 1999/1) 98. A wide variety of perspectives on the church vis-à-vis postmodernity have emerged in recent years. This volume does not seek to present an overview, but rather engages with certain representative, influential, and/or innovative elements of the various viewpoints currently in the arena of discourse.

4. Cf. David Ray Griffin, William A. Beardslee and Joe Holland, eds., *Varieties of Postmodern Theology*, and Janet Martin Soskice, "The Postmodern Pope," in Laurence Hemming and Susan Frank Parsons, eds., *Restoring Faith in Reason* (London: SCM, 2002).

5. E.g., *Christifideles Laici* appears to maintain that culture and family can/do still provide ecclesial enhancement in the *same* fashion as in past epochs of history, as if to ignore very different realities in our situation today. On similar themes see Paul Lakeland, *The Liberation of the Laity* (New York: Continuum, 2003); on *Christifideles Laici* in particular, 125–28.

6. Junker-Kenny, "Church, Modernity and Postmodernity," 98–99 (italics supplied). Here, I take it, Junker-Kenny is referring to *enclosed* communities. I think an open and dialogical communitarian approach still has much mileage to offer our

Thus our ecclesial and ministerial conceptions in the present age need to be formed through processes that are more genuinely dialogical, and in a way that takes full account of the *variety* of dilemmas confronting communities across the globe as a result of the dawn of postmodernity. Furthermore, they need to be truly empowering and, as best fits the age, fully respectful of the principle of subsidiarity. I hope that what I say in the remainder of this book will sufficiently expand on such a suggestion.

Just as the systematic and philosophical theologian's task in a postmodern age is to shape and nurture a role for her or his discipline in the wake of postmodernity's attacks on ontotheology and grand narratives alike, so too must any postmodern "ecclesiology" confront the challenges of the age in an open and positive fashion. Part of its task would be to influence the development of new and effective forms of ecclesial practice, organization, ministry, and leadership now that the old concepts of authority have died, authoritarianism (at least, in the minds of many) has proven to be unworkable (not that it *ever* tallied with the gospel), and detraditionalization,[7] moral apathy, and the fragmentation of ethics and ethical frameworks are daily realities with which we all must live.

With all this in mind, now let us turn to explore in a little more detail what might be the particularly pressing *ecclesiological* challenges in the present era. For it is not simply *historical* paradigms that concern us here but *ecclesiological* paradigms also, which are as subject to flux and change as their historical counterparts (and interrelated with them in a number of ways). As much of the work of Avery Dulles has illustrated, the self-understanding of the church in a particular era can often become so influential and authoritative that the operational "model" of the church itself also takes on the status of a paradigm. More often than not the most influential paradigms will be, not surprisingly, those espoused by the "official" or the "institutional" church authorities.[8] The

---

postmodern times, cutting across many divides and centuries as it does, thus lending itself to our current age of flux and change.

7. Again see Paul Heelas, Scott Lash, and Paul Morris, *Detraditionalization. Critical Reflections on Authority and Identity* (Oxford: Blackwell, 1996). Lieven Boeve uses the concept for theological purposes in his own work, such as his study *Interrupting Tradition* (Leuven: Peeters, 2004), e.g., 52–54.

8. Cf. Avery Dulles, *Models of the Church* (Dublin: Gill and Macmillan, 1988). In referring to paradigm Dulles is of course (as was Hodgson) using the work of Thomas Kuhn. Dulles' later work is more qualified and less conducive to the ecclesiological pluralism this volume seeks to commend.

problem as many perceive it today, in our "postmodern era," is one related to the very possibility or, indeed, desirability of the notion of an overarching, uniform, or "privileged" paradigm at all. Do we need, should we, and *can* we have an "official" ecclesiology today? If we can and should, then what form might it take to facilitate best the upholding of the values, principles, and mission(s) of the Catholic communities across the globe? Chapter 1 of *Lumen gentium,* of course, made clear that our understanding of the mystery of the church is *not* reducible to any one particular image, model, or account. But *subsequent* ecclesiological developments suggest that a different approach (or at least a departure from the post-conciliar *understanding* of that text) has come to the fore since the 1970s and 80s. The task of confronting such questions is inescapable for, as Roger Haight has argued, "[a]ll theology is bound to some culture and historical situation; no theology can prescind from it; every theology should explicitly identify its place in a context and the problematic that drives it. For a theology to pretend to be above culture or to claim that it can speak adequately for all cultures invites appraisal as either naïve or intellectually dishonest."[9]

So the majority of ecclesial discussions today acknowledge that the postmodern era has presented many challenges to the church and to each of those individuals who see themselves as belonging to the church. Among all the debates surrounding the present age, whether one labels it the "postmodern era" or not, the dilemmas to be faced are nonetheless real, whatever nomenclature is settled upon.

But did the church not attempt to confront the "signs of the times" and address the gifts and challenges of a new historical era before, as the twentieth century turned into its seventh decade? Indeed it did, but the point today is that much of the promise of that engagement remains to be fulfilled and, as we have seen, there are new "signs of the times" to be discerned that might well demand new ways of doing Catholic theology and of being church. Let us narrow our focus further still and set the Catholic context of the questions to be explored in the coming chapters.

Vatican II: An "Unfinished Building Site"

For many the Second Vatican Council (1962–65) marked a turning point in the history of the church and in ecclesiology—the self-understanding of the church. However, the irony is that just when the

9. Haight, *Christian Community in History,* 1:57.

church seemed finally to have opened its doors to the modern world it found that world was already fast becoming conscious of itself as the *post*-modern world.[10]

One of the main problems I wish to address throughout this book is fundamentally linked to Vatican II and its perceived agenda and implications for the church. A large body of opinion contends (from many differing and often competing perspectives) that the vision of Vatican II has yet to come to full fruition throughout the Catholic community and in the relations between the church and the (now *post-*) modern world. Indeed, it is Hermann Pottmeyer's assertion that Vatican II was primarily a *transitional* council, clearer about what it was moving away *from* than what it was moving toward. In a now-famous metaphor, Pottmeyer has suggested that "the work of Vatican II has remained a building site." He employs the image of the construction of the new St. Peter's basilica in the sixteenth century. Construction took place *around* the existing church at that time. Four pillars were first built up, and these remained incomplete until the church could raise the necessary funds to finish its task (and we know what pastoral, not to mention theological issues were raised in certain quarters of Europe in relation to some of the fund-raising activities employed by the church of that time!). Pottmeyer develops the image in relation to the church today:

> Alongside the old edifice of nineteenth- and twentieth-century Vatican centralization arise the four mighty supporting columns of a renewed church and a renewed ecclesiology: the church as people of God; the church as sacrament of the kingdom of God in the world; the college of bishops; and ecumenism. While the building erected by centralization awaits demolition, as the old St. Peter's Basilica did in its day, the four supporting pillars of a renewed church and a renewed ecclesiology wait to be crowned by the dome that draws them into unity . . . .[11]

If we wish to explore how the church might move forward toward completing the work of Vatican II, we are confronted by a multitude of further complications and it must be asked whether the church has the necessary ecclesiological, theological, and moral "funds" to complete

10. So also Paul Lakeland, *Liberation of the Laity* (New York: Continuum, 2003) 262–63, and famously Edward Schillebeeckx, as discussed by David Tracy in "The Uneasy Alliance Reconceived: Catholic Theological Method, Modernity, and Postmodernity," *TS* 50 (1989) 556.

11. Hermann Pottmeyer, *Towards a Papacy in Communion: Perspectives from Vatican Councils I & II* (New York: Crossroad, 1998) 110.

its new jewel, just as it experienced many tribulations in completing the new St. Peter's.

Indeed, as Paul Lakeland indicates, the situation is now more complex still, for so many of the issues Vatican II sought to address remain "live issues" in our postmodern world.

> The council documents stand, cannot be abandoned, and indeed are invoked by representatives of both more conservative and more progressive wings of today's church. But the council itself, as a papal initiative to let fresh air into the church and to reexpress the ancient faith in a new world, must be considered an unfinished project whose final outcome remains uncertain. A hundred years from now, it may be that Vatican II will be seen as a brief progressive interlude in the history of an inward looking church. It is my guess that if this is indeed the way that the early twenty-second century sees the church, then there will be little of the church left to appreciate. But this is by no means certain.[12]

And the "live issues" that remain unresolved since Vatican II are now compounded by the challenges of postmodernity, as we shall see. But the church struggles to find a common way forward because foremost among the difficulties facing our task today is a plethora of ecclesiologies, of visions and models and paradigms of the church that seem to be fundamentally incompatible.[13] And this notwithstanding *Lumen gentium's* commendation of the variety of traditions with the church and of legitimate difference or variety (ch. 2, §13, cf. also the variety of images of the church discussed in ch. 1 of the same document).

Indeed, some would wish to counter that *Lumen gentium* offers the church a vision for the future. But such an argument misses the point here. As Pottmeyer illustrates, the building site was left unfinished. The potential of *Lumen gentium's* ecclesiological vision has yet to come to fruition and even that vision, in the light of the very different world we now inhabit, requires further qualifications, supplementation and methodological development today. Even with regard to *Lumen gentium*, it would seem there are "rival" interpretations and understandings jostling for primacy in the church today. The *reception* of *Lumen gentium*, as with all conciliar documents, is thus obviously an issue of major importance. Hence a further preliminary consideration must be addressed.

---

12. Lakeland, *Liberation of the Laity*, 112.
13. And what needs to be discerned is whether the simultaneous presence of some of these differing and sometimes incompatible ecclesiologies is necessarily destructive for the church.

Competing Ecclesiologies in the Postmodern Era

Inherent to the church throughout the Christian centuries, but pursued with a renewed vigor and sense of urgency since Vatican II, is the quest for a vital, energizing, and sustainable way of being the community called church, at both local and universal levels. Naturally, to borrow from Max Weber's wise warnings concerning typologies,[14] we must realize the proper nature and function of our visions, models, and paradigms of the church. Weber warned us that "ideal types" serve a heuristic purpose (and Dulles added that ecclesiological paradigms also serve an *exploratory* purpose), but such "ideal types" do not really exist in pure form in reality. Ecclesiology diverges from Weber in being an *aspirational* undertaking, charged with eschatology and hope: the church sees its mission as being bound up with trying to build the community of justice and righteousness that Christians refer to as the Kingdom of God, hence Vatican II's image of a *pilgrim* church.

The problem arises when we are faced with competing versions of this very quest. There is a multitude of post-Vatican II ecclesiologies,[15] most notably the now legendary clashes between the various ecclesiologies "from above" and "from below," the wrangling over what constitutes an authentic ecclesiology of "communion," differences that might perhaps be termed the *Communio* and *Concilium* visions of the church (understood respectively as more conservative and progressive, although such terms are too descriptively limiting).[16] Or, as Eamonn Conway has termed it, there is an "essential faultline" in the church today that, despite dealing in ideal types, nonetheless does capture the two main "camps" within which most ecclesial and ecclesiological perspectives fall, namely *aggiornamento* contra *ressourcement* and correlation contra

14. I have briefly discussed Weber's typologies in relation to ecclesial authority in Gerard Mannion, "What Do We Mean by Authority?" in Bernard Hoose, ed., *Authority in the Roman Catholic Church: Theory and Practice* (Aldershot, England; Burlington, VT: Ashgate Press, 2002) 26–27, 31. See also Max Weber, "Power and Bureaucracy," in Kenneth Thompson and Jeremy Tunstall, eds., *Sociological Perspectives: Selected Readings* (Harmondsworth: Penguin for Open University Press, 1971), 67ff.

15. Indeed, just as Ernst Troeltsch charted the various social visions of the Christian churches, in our age we need to explore not simply the varieties of ecclesiology in existence across the Christian churches but also those *within* many of the differing communions.

16. Here, again I stress that we are dealing with heuristic and exploratory conceptual devices as opposed to hard and fast realities. See chapter 3, which discusses these differing ecclesiological approaches in more detail.

rupture.[17] Conway asks whether the divisions really go as deep as the level of truth itself or whether they are simply divisions in terms of ecclesial strategy. Of course, as he acknowledges, while it once was difficult to compartmentalize leading Catholic thinkers and church people along such lines in a rigid fashion *theologically,* it is valid to draw such distinctions in terms of ecclesial politics, and one "party" in particular has influenced Catholic theological scholarship to a greater extent than the other in recent years. Indeed, while agreeing that here we deal with ideal types once more, I do believe that increasingly Catholics do identify themselves with one camp or another, so that what were perhaps once convenient ideal type constructions have now become self-fulfilling realities. Furthermore, church documentation and increasingly polemical theological currents of thought in recent decades have actually helped such a dichotomy to become all the more real, as we shall see.

I am not unsympathetic to those who, like Nicholas Lash, despair of the stereotypical nature of the *communion/concilium* compartmentalization—after all, theologically speaking it is true that many important scholars would be difficult to place on either side of the divide.[18] Of course, given the cross-fertilzation and interdisciplinary nature of theological inquiry in recent decades it could not be otherwise. However, *ecclesiologically* it is not so difficult: in particular, one finds it relatively easy to place many of those same scholars and church people with regard to where they stand on the question of the *church-world* relationship and, dare one say, even more so on the question of the relationship between *nature* and *grace.*

So, with regard to the methodological nuances that separate an "ecclesiology from above" and an "ecclesiology from below," Roger Haight explains that the latter is equivalent to a "historical ecclesiology" and is analogous to the procedure of "Christology from below." The method of an ecclesiology from below is one that is, first, "concrete, existential, and historical."[19] Second, it takes a "genetic approach," being

---

17. Eamonn Conway, "Speaking a Constant Word in a Changing World. Recognising and Resolving Tensions and Tendencies in a Postmodern Context," *New Blackfriars* 87 (March 2006) 110–20.

18. Lash has made this point on many occasions. But perhaps a different and and more widely acceptable point he makes is that we should not seek to juxtapose *ressourcement* and *aggiornamento* in oppositional terms. See Lash, "The Second Vatican Council of Happy Memory and Hope?" Austin Vereigh (ed.), *Unfinished Journey: The Church 40 Years After Vatican II* (New York and London: Continuum) 2003, chapter 1.

19. Roger Haight, *Christian Community in History,* 1:4.

attentive to any particular ecclesiology's "origins as well as its journey from them to the present."[20]

This method also acknowledges that the church is an organization within which and upon which social forces have an impact. Thus we should use social and historical analysis to examine the church itself, for "the social and historical situation within which the church exists" is "crucial for understanding its full reality."[21] The fourth defining characteristic of this method is that an ecclesiology from below is nonetheless a *theological* discipline "and as such cannot be reduced to conclusions that can be generated by history or sociology alone."[22] Nonetheless, it is important to discern precisely how the historical and sociological aspects relate to the theological dimension of such an ecclesiology. For Haight this is because "this church is experienced religiously or theologically because in it and through it people recognize the presence and activity of God." Likewise, the ecclesiological employment of symbols "pointing and referring to God" displays the role of "theological imagination and judgment" in the process.[23]

In many ways parts of this present volume offer an example of "ecclesiology from below"[24] and it further draws on and utilizes other ecclesiologies of this genre. However, not least because it could not do otherwise in addressing the postmodern context, it also moves "beyond" historical ecclesiology and into the realm of what Haight terms "comparative ecclesiology," a further methodological distinction that will be explained in greater detail in Part III of this work. Here we can simply identify and note the importance of the fact that such a method seeks to engage with, learn from, and build on the positive achievements of a wide variety of ecclesiological approaches in the recent and present eras, and not simply Catholic ecclesiologies.

20. Ibid., 5.
21. Ibid.
22. Ibid.
23. Ibid.
24. Bearing in mind that, following Rahner, as well as the Liberation theologians' conception of a "monistic view of history," I do not believe there is any such thing as "ungraced nature," or, therefore, any such thing as *purely* natural theology, divorced from the self-communication (i.e., revelation) of God. See Mannion, "What Do We Mean by Authority?" 33–34. See, also, for respective examples, Karl Rahner, *Foundations of Christian Faith* (Kent: Burns & Oates, 1978) 151, and Gustavo Gutiérrez, *A Theology of Liberation* (London: SCM, 1974) 153ff. For this understanding of history see also, for example, José Míguez Bonino, *Revolutionary Theology Comes of Age* (London: S.P.C.K., 1975) 137ff.

For Haight the converse ecclesiological "ideal type," namely, an "ecclesiology from above" is marked by a (somewhat precritcal) attempt to offer an account of the "essential nature and structure of the church that transcends any given context."[25] Such an essence is thus perceived to "transcend [the church's] particular instantiations, and these can be grasped precisely by abstracting from those individualizing particulars which characterize the church wherever it is, but are precisely not its defining substance."[26] This method tends toward exclusivism because it entails "setting forth the limits or frontiers beyond which is nonchurch or a defective embodiment of it."[27]

And this exclusivistic tendency goes further, for the understanding of the church that emerges tends to define the embodiment of that church as the "true church." Furthermore, such an ecclesiology attempts to ground its validity in the highest authorities and therefore assumes certain ecclesiological doctrines, or rather interpretations thereof, as normative. In extreme forms such an ecclesiology places the church in juxtaposition to the "world" and human culture. "In contrast to the world in its secularity, the church defines the sphere of the sacred. In Catholic ecclesiology in the past, this polarity took the form of the supernatural over against the 'merely' natural, or the 'fallen' and sinful; the supernatural was considered as elevating and transforming the natural order. Implicitly, the church represented a social reality that was in some measure set apart from the world, usually in some sense 'above.'"[28]

As I will attempt to outline throughout this volume in general, but particularly in chapters 3 and 4, such an ecclesiological "mindset" has returned center-stage in many authoritative quarters of the church in recent decades and, indeed, across the various denominations. In fact, I would go much further here than Roger Haight, who certainly does not identify particular denominationally and theologically specific examples: this account of "ecclesiology from above" might admirably serve as an accurate descriptive account of the ecclesiological methodology and vision that prevails in the Roman curia and, indeed, in numerous writings of Joseph Ratzinger, now Pope Benedict XVI, and in the hearts and minds of the many throughout the church who share such an ecclesial "outlook" today.[29]

25. Haight, *Christian Community in History,* 1:19.
26. Ibid.
27. Ibid.
28. Ibid., 21.
29. Indeed, "out"-look is perhaps a misleading term here, as we shall see.

For Haight, ecclesiologies from above deal in "revealed," "super-natural," and doctrinal terms. Furthermore, a fourth characteristic is that such an ecclesiology will not admit a *critical* historical account of the church's origins, but rather tends toward an attempt to affirm and uphold an a-critical *doctrinal* account: i.e., in accord with certain teachings concerning the church's history: "God's providence in history led to the church; God more or less 'directly' founds the church in the work of Jesus Christ; and God as Spirit animates and directs the development of the church from its beginnings at Pentecost."[30]

Thus such an ecclesiology, such a self-understanding of the church,[31] takes on a special authority in its own right. It elevates itself above challenge and criticism. The appeal to authority is final, and therefore "historical consciousness is controlled by doctrinal understanding."[32] The fifth defining aspect of ecclesiology from above is its "Christocentrism." By this Haight does not mean to play down or criticize the importance of christology for ecclesiology—far from it, as his two-volume study demonstrates in its entirety. Rather, it is a *specific* "christology from above" and exclusivistic mentality he questions, namely one that feeds into a view that "the church, even when not considered constitutive of the salvation of all, is the summit of all religious forms, and the single, normative religion that is superior to all others because the church is constituted by Christ as its center. In short, in an ecclesiology from above christocentrism has a tendency to become ecclesiocentrism."[33]

Haight's sixth and final aspect of the methodology of ecclesiology from above centers around the hierarchical structuring and ordering of the church itself and of the ministries within it: "the levels of power and authority have their foundation in God, and they descend."[34] Such breeds a "hierarchical imagination" and the structures of ministries themselves are seen as "corresponding to the will of God."[35] This makes it very difficult for such an ecclesiology to adapt to changing circumstances and contexts; any church governed through such a determining vision finds it very hard to rise effectively, in accordance with the gospel,

---

30. Ibid., 21.
31. In contrast, as we shall see, to the vision of Paul VI's *Ecclesiam Suam* and numerous documents from Vatican II in general.
32. Ibid., 22.
33. Ibid., 23.
34. Ibid.
35. Ibid., 25.

to meet new challenges. Thus all "new ministries" will be "absorbed into traditional structures or patterns."[36]

Hence for the analysis that will be set forth in this volume, just as for Haight, the realities of the postmodern world entail that any ecclesiology from above that displays such features will be highly problematic. The world we live in cries out for an ecclesiology that is attentive to its "joy and hope," its "grief and anguish," in the opening words of *Gaudium et Spes*. As we shall seek to illustrate, such ecclesiologies from above appear to turn their back on the world. A world of religious, ideological, and cultural pluralism, and yet also a world of mass poverty, one where dehumanizing globalization rampages throughout every facet of present-day life, a world of ever more divisive and shocking conflict, a world where simplistic political and strategic analysis promotes both the reality and the perception of a "clash of civilizations": such a world is ill-served by exclusivistic, world-renouncing ecclesiologies.

In contrast, an ecclesiology "from below" bears the promise that, in its attentiveness to historical context and in its historical consciousness, it can better adapt itself to meeting the challenges of the postmodern age. Thus, as Haight argues, such an ecclesiology will be more readily responsive to the challenges posed by globalization and pluralism, to the reality and value of other churches, other religions, and the "world" beyond religions. It will be all the more able to hear and respond to the anguished cry of the unparalleled human suffering in the world today. It will listen to, learn from, and meet the challenges posed by the experiences of women, just as it will face the realities of rising secularization in many parts of the globe, as well as the rise in individualism.[37]

Thus, what I wish to raise here, in drawing our introductory considerations to a close, is a further problem this inharmonious situation of ecclesiological conflict presents to the church today, namely what *sort* of ecclesiological approach would best help address three particular sets of challenges: first, the postmodern situation; second, completing and building on the work of Vatican II; and third, the difficulties caused by competing and/or incompatible ecclesiologies in operation within the church at one and the same time. Here, then, I am in agreement with Nicholas Healy, who has argued against what he calls "blueprint ecclesiologies": "Ecclesiology is not about the business of finding the single right way to think about the church, of developing a blueprint suitable

36. Ibid.
37. Ibid., 26–35. I outline and discuss Haight's own ecclesiological vision in greater detail in chapter 7.

for all times and places. Rather, I propose that its function is to aid the concrete church in performing its task of witness and pastoral care within what I call its 'ecclesiological context.'"[38]

Institutional or Communitarian/Visionary Ecclesiology?

We are thus faced with the following questions: if postmodernity is characterized by the dethronement of the "grand narrative" and the attendant consequences such a situation brings (in epistemological, sociological, theological, and moral/pastoral fashions), then is one dominant, centrally shaped and "defended" "institutional" paradigm the best-suited ecclesiology for tackling the three problems identified above? Or would a more genuinely communitarian, indeed visionary form of ecclesiology serve the church better for our times? We are questioning whether *one* fairly rigid and institutional ecclesiological paradigm[39] is adequate to facilitate the mission and development of Catholic Christian communities in a postmodern world. By "institutional paradigm" I mean an "official" and centrally, i.e. *curially,* defined and promoted ecclesiology. A new situation exists for ecclesial identity, theology, ethics, as well as for the ecclesiology that draws all this together, and so this volume suggests that perhaps a different *sort* of ecclesiology is now called for. Would a different *form* of ecclesiological undertaking serve the church better today and help overcome ecclesiological differences as well as facilitating the fulfilment of the vision of Vatican II for the church and addressing the challenges of postmodernity itself?

Approaching such questions from a somewhat different ecclesial angle, Nicholas Healy has also argued that a very different *form* of ecclesiology should be allowed to develop further and flourish:

> In contrast to the structure and rhetoric of blueprint ecclesiology . . . theological reflection upon the church is in fact from the very outset a matter of practical rather than theoretical reasoning. The practice of ecclesiology arises out of ecclesial practices, and is ordered directly towards them. Moreover, judgments about the concrete church, however incipient or implicit, are necessarily a factor in the construction of every ecclesiology. . . . The

38. Nicholas M. Healy, *Church, World and the Christian Life* (Cambridge: Cambridge University Press, 2000) 38. See especially ch. 2.

39. Recent church documents (again, contra *Lumen gentium's* reservations here) would appear to endorse such a particular paradigm of what it is to be church, namely a version of the "*Communio*" ecclesiology (e.g., cf. *Communionis Notio* and *Dominus Iesus*). See chs. 3 and 4 below.

primary aim of ecclesiology ought not to be to explicate a "particular model," but to make sound judgments about "everything else."[40]

It is in this sense that Healy refers to the "prophetic task" of ecclesiology. But, although Healy has correctly identified so many of the challenges facing contemporary ecclesiology, and despite the erudition of his work and its impressive range of conversation partners across the denominational and theological divide, in effect (as Healy has since acknowledged), it offers only one more "blueprint ecclesiology" in place of those he criticizes. He is correct when he writes that "The tendency of modern ecclesiology . . . is to include little explicit analysis of the church's concrete identity and its context,"[41] and in his final chapter, as well as other parts of the volume (and in various articles published since), he begins to discern how we might go about rectifying this omission. Hence that final chapter offers some tentative "hints" toward an "ecclesiological ethnography" along with admittedly equally tentative analysis of the concrete identity and context(s) of the church(es).[42] We must thus await his forthcoming work with great relish!

This book will explore these and other questions for the church in our times. Vatican II heralded the need for change and development and suggested the primary ways in which the church might discern the directions in which to proceed and the *modus operandi* of procedure, but it did not provide conclusive guidance on the how and what and where, etc. Now is a turning point for the church, a "new paradigm" if one prefers. How might the church best face these challenges, and is it ready to deal with awkward questions? Doubtless a number of the questions for the church in our times that we will encounter along the way will be uncomfortable for many within the church. But if the church can face such questions openly and honestly, ecclesial communion will be all the more strengthened. Richard Gaillardetz has drawn attention to the late Pope John Paul II's call for Christians to examine their consciences in preparation for the millennium of 2000. Although such a call did not extend to the Catholic Church *qua* church, Gaillardetz suggests that "Surely the examination of conscience he called for must have a corporate and ecclesial dimension. It must be legitimate to ask

40. Healy, *Church, World and the Christian Life*, 46.
41. Ibid., 47.
42. In this work I neither seek nor claim to offer such a developed "ecclesiological ethnography," but rather to point toward instances of such in certain places as well as to highlight the promise of certain ecclesiological methodologies for those wishing to undertake such a task.

how we can, *as a Church* . . . strengthen the ecclesiology of communion and further the cause of Christian unity."[43]

In one sense many such questions deal with the "unfinished business" of Vatican II as well as with the competing ecclesiological visions of its true legacy. So here we will share the sentiments of David McLoughlin in perceiving an engagement with all such questions as a constructive, albeit at times painful ecclesiological undertaking. McLoughlin observes that "Congar suggests it takes fifty years for a council to deliver its fruits: if that is so then this generation of bishops have a key role in enabling that to happen. Present problems are the basis of future rich opportunities. The Holy Spirit was poured out upon the whole apostolic group; the call today is for the whole episcopate to work together, that the Spirit so richly visible in our time may not be frustrated."[44]

This volume will touch throughout on what some have called the "battle" for the vision of the council. We will explore debates about fundamental ecclesiological visions and seek to discern productive ways forward in such debates.[45] We will then turn in earnest to discuss the dialogical nature of Vatican II and suggest that the call to dialogue in charity perhaps best captures its lasting legacy. We will seek to discern how ecclesial "bridge building" might be profitably pursued today and conversations within and outside the church fostered. We will explore tentative steps toward shaping an "ecumenical intercultural hermeneutic." We will look at the promise of new ways of doing ecclesiology, particularly on a comparative basis, as well as learning from those in the church who have discerned that this postmodern era calls for an embracing of the pluralistic reality in which the church finds itself. Indeed, we will suggest that pluralism requires not simply recognition, but also celebration. Hence we will seek to map the theological, doctrinal, ecclesiological, and, indeed, the moral *necessity* of dialogue with those within and outside the church.

---

43. Richard Gaillardetz, *Teaching with Authority: A Theology of the Magisterium in the Church* (Collegeville, MN: Liturgical Press, 1997) 277, referring to *Tertio millennio adveniente,* especially §§ 34, 36. Bernard Hoose makes a similar point in his "Authority in the Church," *TS* 63 (2002).

44. David McLoughlin, "Authority in the Service of Communion," in Noel Timms and Kenneth Wilson, eds., *Governance and Authority in the Roman Catholic Church: Beginning a Conversation* (London: SPCK, 2000) 136.

45. Space has not permitted a more detailed treatment of further important areas of debate pertaining to the church in our times; in future writings I intend to pursue additional themes at greater length.

Finally we turn to suggestions of what an ecclesiology that is less fixed, determined, and imposed "from above" might look like today. We will seek to learn from the revival in virtue ethics to explore ways of shaping a true "virtue ecclesiology" that might help the church better harmonize its own act and being, where analogical thinking replaces dichotomous thinking as the *analogia ecclesiae* bears witness to the God who is Trinity—to the God who is a community of coequal, coeternal, and co-divine persons. Such an ecclesiology, then, might embrace mystery, sacramentality, and practice alike.

Jean-François Lyotard believed that the present era—"a period of slackening"—is marked by a retreat from experimentation, from "avant-gardism," to where some stability, some certainty, some fixed and totalizing ways of doing things must be discovered, rediscovered, or invented. This he described initially as happening in the arts, but everywhere else too.[46] Whether this is done "in the name of postmodernism" or to combat it, there is a restless "desire for unity, for identity, for security, or popularity" at large in our times.[47] The attack on experimentation is "specifically reactionary."[48] Do we witness analogous moves in the contemporary church and specifically in ecclesiological developments in our recent times? Are we in the midst of such a totalizing drive toward imposed unity despite all the lessons the twentieth century sought to teach us? Has the great era of theological and ecclesiological conversation, experimentation if you will, "avant-gardism" to its detractors, the era that brought us and helped to shape the Spirit-inspired Council and the subsequent ecumenical Spring been firmly brought to a close in the church? In all our grappling with these challenging questions and with the challenges of the postmodern age itself, all who love the church might gain much from a sustained reflection on the words of the Anglican theologian Keith Ward: "The Christian church takes as its supreme authority a radical and startling young Jewish man, who opposed the religious authorities and called for a revision of many traditional moral attitudes. The institutional church might well consider the extent to which its very structure engenders influences that mute the radical demands of gospel morality, and sustain social conventions that reinforce prejudice and bigotry."[49]

46. "Answering the Question: What is Postmodern?" Appendix to *The Postmodern Condition—A Report on Knowledge,* tr. Régis Durand (Manchester: Manchester University Press, 1984) 71.
47. Ibid., 73.
48. Ibid., 75.
49. Keith Ward, *Religion and Community* (Oxford: Clarendon Press, 2000) 233.

PART II

PROBLEMATIC ECCLESIOLOGICAL RESPONSES TO POSTMODERNITY

Chapter Three

From the "Open Church" to Neo-Exclusivism?

In future we must take the risk not only of a church with "open doors," but of an "open church." We cannot remain in the ghetto nor may we return to it. Anyone who experiences and endures the confusion, partly unavoidable, partly avoidable, in all dimensions of teaching and practice, which undoubtedly exists in the church, is certainly tempted to long for the church which older people among us knew under the four Pius's and up to the last Council. We are then tempted, in such movements as that "for Pope and Church," in what is in fact in the last resort a sterile pseudo-orthodoxy, to "purify" the church as rapidly as possible and by administrative measures to draw clear frontiers, to "restore" the old order: in a word, to enter on the march into the ghetto, even though the church would then become, not the "little flock" of the gospel, but really a sect with a ghetto mentality.[1]

In more recent times . . . in her pastoral care for souls, the church has thought it opportune to express in a more explicit way the faith of all time.[2]

---

1. Karl Rahner, *The Shape of the Church to Come*, translated and introduced by Edward Quinn (London: S.P.C.K., 1974) 93.
2. Joseph Ratzinger and Tarcisio Bertone, *Commentary On The Profession of Faith's Concluding Paragraphs*, 16 July 1998, §3, translation in *The Tablet* (11 July 1998) 920.

Problematic Ecclesiological Responses to Postmodernity

We have suggested that the ecclesiological responses to the dilemmas and challenges of the current age are many. Few doubt that there is a need for some response. Yet some responses appear to have compounded the difficulties for the church in this era. Here I wish to focus primarily on some aspects of the dominant "official" or institutional response and to identify some of the further concerns such a response has generated. In other words, we need to examine the problems posed by movements from *within* the church community itself in reaction against the ills of modernity and postmodernity.

This chapter will attempt to summarize the implications of a "paradigm shift" in ecclesial life, namely the emergence of "neo-exclusivism" across denominations, which is now prevalent throughout Christianity. The term, itself, is ugly but also, in a sense, onomatopoeic. In the main this chapter, in keeping with the volume's primary focus on the Catholic Church, will explore the Catholic variant of such a "paradigm shift." This in turn relates to and is, in many ways, a major formative influence on the current "official," "top down" version of *communio* ecclesiology that shapes contemporary Catholic teaching, mission, and policy. But what is the background to such a form of ecclesiology? Let us explore the parameters of this phenomenon in a little more detail before examining its particular Catholic forms and the consequences of such a development for contemporary ecclesiological engagement.

The account of the advent of "neo-exclusivism" given here[3] is part of a wider thesis that we are witnessing a kind of "trans-denominational" reformation in the Christian church at present, which should equally be understood as a series of developments motivated, in the main, by the need to react to the variously-perceived ills of postmodernity. That is to say that whereas fundamental differences between Christians (in terms of doctrine, ethics, worship, and, crucially, ecclesiology) once used to be primarily along denominational lines, such is no longer the case.[4] Indeed, it is far more likely today that one can have much more in common with groups of Christians of another denomination than with many within one's own Christian denomination. Hence, in so many ways, the lines of "division" among Christians are thus now

---

3. See, also, the summary of this particular Christian response to postmodernity in chapter 2 above.

4. Of course, the term "denomination" is a modern construct developed out of sociological reflection.

transdenominational rather than interdenominational, (i.e., across rather than between denominations).

Acknowledging that we are again working with something of an "ideal type" and the limitations of such, as well as recognising the various faults with the now somewhat dated typologies dividing Christian outlooks into the familiar categories of "exclusivist," "inclusivist," and "pluralist," I nonetheless believe we can come to better understand the shifting ecclesiological sands today if we engage in some form of analogous analysis for our times.[5]

Thus the phenomenon of neo-exclusivism is, to a large extent, a reaction to the rise of various forms of a "pluralistic outlook"[6] and to the perceived aims of "liberalism" in its various forms.[7] It is also a reaction to the perceived dangers of relativism. Christopher Duraisingh[8] helps us to understand this particular aspect of this "transdenominational" development, for he has recently described the "fear of pluralism" inherent in many Christian communities in the following terms: "Forms of pluralism are seen as dangerous to the very identity and integrity of the church; therefore, greater and centralized teaching authority and clearer and uniform formulations of truth are seen by some as urgent for the very survival of the church."[9] Indeed, he continues to say that even Christians who may believe they are open toward the pluralistic reality may be deluding themselves. Thus "even those of us who can tolerate a certain amount of pluralism often tend to speak of the Christian tradition as homogenous and value expressions of unity over diversity. Essentialist descriptions of reality and valorising the homogenous over the diverse seem to be significant features of much Western thought and culture. For can it not be argued that the dominant

5. On the typologies cf. Gavin D'Costa, *Theology and Religious Pluralism* (Oxford: Oxford University Press, 1986). Such typologies are critiqued by, among others, Nicholas Healy, *Church, World and the Christian Life: Practical-Prophetic Ecclesiology* (Cambridge: Cambridge University Press, 2000), who nonetheless could be said, in parts of that particular text, to remain a "prisoner" of the very typologies criticized.

6. And so in the Catholic Church I suggest that it is a conservative reaction to the dialogical and thus pluralistic legacy of Vatican II. Pluralism is here taken to refer to an open worldview that seeks to acknowledge and celebrate, as fully as possible, the diversity of human culture and community in our contemporary societies.

7. See Johann-Baptist Metz, "Theology in the Modern Age, and Before its End," in Claude Geffré, Gustavo Gutiérrez, and Virgil Elizondo, eds., *Different Theologies, Common Responsibility: Babel or Pentecost? Concilium* 171 (1984) 13–17.

8. He writes from an Anglican perspective and addresses the situation in Christianity in general.

9. Christopher Duraisingh, "Contextual and Catholic: Conditions for Cross-Cultural Hermeneutics," *ATR* 82 (2000) 680.

tendency in Western metaphysical and theological traditions has been to privilege and valorise unity, harmony, and totality and thereby to denigrate, suppress and marginalize multiplicity, contingency, and particularity?"[10]

So in many ways fluctuating attitudes toward various forms of pluralism (cultural, philosophical, religious, theological, ecclesiological) in recent decades lie at the heart of so many of the issues under consideration here. Pluralism, of course, is one of the quintessential and defining characteristics of postmodernity itself.[11] It marks a move away from "closed systems" and worldviews toward more open, fluid, and dialogical engagements with "the other"—the latter being conceived in both individual and collective terms.

The concept has figured prominently not only in philosophy and cultural and political theory in recent decades, but also in theology. The two giants of Catholic theology in the twentieth century, Bernard Lonergan and Karl Rahner, both explored the implications of pluralism for Catholic Christianity and Catholic intellectual inquiry in some detail.[12] And cultural and intellectual pluralism (or, if one prefers, "polycentrism") obviously leads one to address questions about the reality of religious pluralism—and vice versa. Although pluralism has its critics from every side, this book will continue to engage pluralism primarily in a positive sense, given its apt description of our postmodern reality and the fact that it represents one of the perceived "threats" some Christians associate with the postmodern world.[13]

10. Ibid., 680–81. We thus return to Lyotard's concerns in relation to the "end of experimentation" and the desire for enforced unity and certitude encountered in chapter 2.

11. For a brief sample of theological treatments see Peter Eicher, "Pluralism and the Dignity of Theology," in *Different Theologies, Common Responsibility: Babel or Pentecost?* 3–12. For an extended study see the aforementioned David Tracy, *Blessed Rage for Order: The New Pluralism in Theology* (New York: Crossroad, 1975).

12. We shall explore some aspects of the thinking of both on this subject in chapter 7.

13. Examples of surveys and studies of the questions pertaining to religious pluralism include "Theology Between Faiths," chs. 36–39 of David Ford and Rachel Muers, eds., *The Modern Theologians* (3d ed. Oxford: Blackwell, 2005); David Ray Griffin, ed., *Deep Religious Pluralism* (Louisville: Westminster John Knox, 2005); and, for an older discussion of the "classic" divisions on such questions, Gavin D'Costa, *Theology and Religious Pluralism*, although D'Costa's position has developed considerably since (some critics would say more in the direction of neo-exclusivism). For a representative sample of Christian thinkers who embrace religious pluralism see John Hick, *An Interpretation of Religion* (Basingstoke: Macmillan, 1989), and his *The Metaphor of God Incarnate* (London: SCM, 1993); see also Keith Ward, *Images of*

With regard to current developments in the Catholic Church, David Ray Griffin has described the stance of the institutional church in relation to the postmodern age as "reactionary conservative postmodernism."[14] His assessment is based on the teachings issued under the name of John Paul II, which naturally are shaped by and representative of the institutional and central church "powers" in general.[15] Griffin discusses such theologies developed in relation to Pope John Paul II's "cultural theology," such as that of George William Rutler's *Beyond Modernity*.[16] Although Rutler shares the concerns of more constructive forms of postmodern theology, Griffin believes this and similar theologies are more akin to Catholic *antimodernism* and really advocate a somewhat supremacist role for the Catholic Church, and the papacy in particular, in the future. In this chapter I suggest that such a "supremacist" reactionary postmodernism is by no means restricted to just a few Catholics, nor is it restricted to those within the Catholic communion alone.

Note, also, the particular relevance here of the concept of "detraditionalization"—i.e., the process whereby "traditions" become less significant influences and guiding frameworks in the lives of individuals and societies.[17] In one sense the ecclesiological responses considered in this chapter are distinctive attempts to counter "detraditionalization." Those engaged in such efforts believe that the "correct" response to postmodernity and the threats it poses to Christianity is a steadfast and largely uncompromising reassertion of what they perceive to be *the* Christian tradition. But, of course, most of what they say can frequently, in effect, develop into an attempt to absolutize a particular interpretation

---

Eternity (Oxford: OneWorld, 1993). We shall encounter further Catholic thinkers in relation to religious pluralism in chapters 6 and 7.

14. David Ray Griffin, William A. Beardslee and Joe Holland, eds., *Varieties of Postmodern Theology*, Albany, SUNY, 1989. For further 'surveys' of varieties of postmodern theology, see, also, the numerous references in chapter 1 of the present volume.

15. I do not wish to imply that Griffin would agree with the analysis offered here, but his terminology is helpful and his own analysis constructive.

16. George William Rutler, *Beyond Modernity: Reflections of a Post-Modern Catholic* (San Francisco: Ignatius Press, 1987).

17. Again see Paul Heelas, Scott Lash, and Paul Morris, *Detraditionalisation— Critical Reflections on Authority and Identity* (Oxford: Blackwell, 1996). Recall also Lieven Boeve, another contemporary theologian who has also used this concept in his work: see his *Interrupting Tradition: An Essay on Christian Faith in a Postmodern Context* (Leuven: Peeters; Grand Rapids: Eerdmans, 2003), as well as his essay "Beyond the Modern and the Anti-modern Dilemma: Theological Method in a Postmodern European Context," in J. Verstraeten, ed., *Scrutinizing the Signs of the Times and Interpreting Them in Light of the Gospel*, BETL (Leuven: Peeters) 2007.

of selected aspects of Christianity's rich "Tradition"/traditions. The aim here, then, is to facilitate a critical dialogue with recent prominent teaching documents of the Catholic Church, as well as to indicate, albeit briefly, parallel trends in non-Catholic circles.[18]

So let us now turn to examine the particular Catholic variety of this "transdenominational" development. The stance taken by the "institutional authorities" of the Catholic Church represents one major response to the dilemmas facing religion and the church in the postmodern era. This distinctive approach began to exert increasing influence in "official" Catholic teaching in the later years of Paul VI. It became the default ecclesial mindset under John Paul II, and one could not be surprised if it were implemented throughout the church universal with yet more vigor under Benedict XVI. In order to safeguard aspects of its rich doctrinal and moral tradition and to maintain its position of influence in shaping communities for the better, the church has adopted a marked degree of intransigence toward voices of dissent within its own ranks and, on occasion, toward critical voices from outside the confines of its tradition. Moderate commentators and critics alike describe this approach as characterized by authoritarianism, a renewed emphasis on the hierarchical structuring and governance of the church, and a renewed and ever-increasing centralization of power and decision-making in Rome.[19] Richard McCormick has labeled this latter development "restorationism."[20] To many this runs counter to the spirit and tone of the documents that emerged from Vatican II and the many theological and ecclesiological developments they inspired. Still more, for others such as, for example, liberation theologian Leonardo Boff,

---

18. E.g., the emergence of "Radical Orthodoxy" and the ecclesiology of Stanley Hauerwas.

19. On authoritarianism and how it is very different from genuine authority see again Gerard Mannion, "What Do We Mean by Authority?" in Bernard Hoose, ed., *Authority and Roman Catholicism—Theory and Practice* (Aldershot, England, and Burlington, VT: Ashgate, 2002). On discussions of ecclesial authority in general see the other essays contained in Hoose's volume and also Richard A. Gaillardetz, *Teaching with Authority* (Collegeville: Liturgical Press, 1997). For a broad range of essays on a number of relevant topics pertaining to such developments see also Gerard Mannion, Richard Gaillardetz, Jan Kerkhofs, and Kenneth Wilson, eds., *Readings in Church Authority: Gifts and Challenges for Contemporary Catholicism*, (Aldershot, England, and Burlington, VT: Ashgate, 2003). For a further collection of a wide variety of perspectives on this and like developments see Charles E. Curran and Richard A. McCormick, eds., *Dissent in the Church* (New York: Paulist, 1988).

20. Richard A McCormick, "Moral Theology 1940–1989: An Overview," *TS* 50 (1989).

it runs counter to any "pneumatological" understanding of the church.[21] In other words, there seems to be less room for perception of a church in which the Spirit is active, bringing vitality and diverse charisms to different parts of the church in distinctively different ways. For feminist, womanist, and *mujerista* activists and scholars this situation causes increased frustration as it serves to entrench anew the forces of patriarchy, and class divisions against which such servants of the church had tirelessly and with great success campaigned in preceding decades.

Certainly there has been ongoing reference to the "authentic" interpretation of Vatican II's teaching and legacy throughout the pontificate of John Paul II and now, in perhaps a still more concentrated focus, under Benedict XVI. The latter has even urged *all* Christians to "keep alive the Spirit" of Vatican II. However, his request that Catholics reread the conciliar documents is somewhat qualified by his remark in an interview that the "authentic interpretation" of such documents is provided in the various documents issued by his predecessor, John Paul II (on many of which Joseph Ratzinger, of course, had so marked an influence). The new pope, in a way that is symptomatic of his own concerns with the ills of postmodernity, commends a less "liberal" interpretation of the conciliar documents.[22]

But a recurring question that has been asked by critics and sympathetic commentators alike is: exactly *how* are the faithful now to discern the coherence and consistency of official church statements, not least those made by then-Cardinal Ratzinger, now Pope Benedict, with regard to such subjects as Vatican II and its "authentic" interpretation and implementation, as well as the proper understanding of the "right" relation between the church universal and local, episcopal collegiality, the teaching authority of episcopal conferences, the nature and purpose of the curia, and like subjects? The reason for such concern is, of course, that many of that pastor's later writings and pronouncements have called into question and even, in parts, contradicted statements he made (and thus also opinions and judgments he can be said to have respectively held and made) earlier.[23]

21. Cf. Leonardo Boff, *Church, Charism and Power* (London: SCM, 1985), and *Ecclesiogenesis* (London: CollinsFlame, 1986).

22. "Pope Urges Faithful to Read Council Documents," *The Tablet* (5 November 2005) 29.

23. Note that I do not mean to endorse the notion that the "younger" Ratzinger was the liberal forerunner of the conservative older man. I believe the younger and older men have far more in common. Yet where there are clear discrepancies between the two, for whatever motivating reasons, they relate in the main to the statements we

Indeed, there is a further problem that should be highlighted from the outset. It is the difficulties created in taking certain Vatican II sentiments or innovations, which were frequently and deliberately tentative, suggestive, or at best facilitating in tone and character (or many would not have been passed in session!) and abstracting from them an entire theology of this and that. The result is that Vatican II, primarily a pastoral council, but especially so oriented in the document that contains most of its explicit teaching on the church in our times, *Gaudium et Spes,* has certain elements of its teaching turned into later dogmatic formulations or at least the basis thereof. Here, for example, John Paul's teaching might appear to be one example with regard to the family. Another example is Joseph Ratzinger's writings on Vatican II's ecclesiology of communion.[24] What Vatican II intended to be guiding and facilitative teaching is turned into more rigid, fixed, and determined dogma. Of course, Vatican II produced two "dogmatic constitutions," but it defined no dogma, as such. Of course, *Lumen gentium* offered an attempt to delineate some criteria of ecclesial reality, but how such have been subsequently *interpreted*, supplemented, and perhaps even distorted in some quarters remains an area of lively discussion throughout the church.

Yet one of the foremost reasons why a neo-exclusivistic approach might not be the best ecclesiological strategy to adopt in response to postmodernity is that it leads to an attempt to retrieve something that may never have existed or—if it did—has been necessarily left behind as historical and contextual developments demanded, *for the sake of* the gospel and the church. This all relates to the notion of the opposite of "detraditionalization," namely *re-traditionalization*. Paul Morris helpfully describes both processes in relation to our contemporary attempts to define and understand what "community" is and might be in our times; hence his insights are naturally of ecclesial and so ecclesiological relevance.

---

have from Joseph Ratzinger during and immediately after the council. See John Allen's biography, which juxtaposes the statements of the "two" men in more vivid fashion than we could hope to in this particular context, especially "An Erstwhile Liberal," ch. 2 of *Pope Benedict XVI: A Biography of Joseph Ratzinger* (New York and London: Continuum, 2005) 45–88, especially 56–76, "How Ratzinger Changed." (The book was previously published in 2000 as *Cardinal Ratzinger: the Vatican's Enforcer of Faith.*) See also Paul Collins, *God's New Man: the Election of Benedict XVI and the Legacy of John Paul II* (London and New York: Continuum, 2005).

24. See the range of his writings cited in n. 48 below.

The parallel processes of detraditionalization and re-traditionalization allow us to grasp something of our contemporary ambivalence concerning community. The first refers to the complex process of the undermining of established communal authority, resulting in the dis-embedding of particular traditions and specific customary practices within the life of a given community. Re-traditionalization is the parallel process in which the "tradition" to be overcome (detraditionalized) is constructed in opposition to, and normally as an earlier stage of, the detraditionalized present. This redefining and reworking of the past actually creates that past. Community, whatever our understanding, in order to be community, must have duration and thus must necessarily entail some notion of tradition.[25]

Morris's own example involves the transformation of Jewish communities in the modern world as they gradually were granted citizenship across Europe. The past can be re-envisaged in either prejudicial or romantic ways. In both these "pasts" the tradition becomes "invented" ("re-membered") to suit the present. "These two intimately connected, and mutually constitutive, processes redefined a new mode of detraditionalized 'identity' *and* constructed a re-traditionalized model of the tradition that was to be 'overcome.'"[26] Indeed, Morris also concurs with those we discussed in chapter 1 who believe that modernity has been so reinterpreted and transformed in recent decades that it has undergone a process of "detraditionalization" in itself, and this as a result of widespread disenchantment with the negative aspects and consequences of modernity.[27] Postmodernity itself, then, is fundamental to such a process. Morris concurs with Zygmunt Bauman that if postmodernity is the "age of contingency" it is nonetheless equally the "age of community"—an age in which the lust for, search for, invention of, and imagining of community come to the fore.[28]

25. Paul Morris, "Community Beyond Tradition," ch. 12 of Heelas, Lash, and Morris, *Detraditionalisation,* 223–49, at 224.

26. Ibid., 225.

27. Again see Gregory Baum's assessment, particularly in relation to the intentions shared by the church and the critical theorists in recent years, as attested in ch. 1 of his *Amazing Church* (Maryknoll, NY: Orbis, 2005).

28. "Community Beyond Tradition," 225. See Zygmunt Bauman, *Modernity and Ambivalence* (Oxford: Polity, 1991) 246. Morris goes on to suggest ("Community Beyond Tradition," 232) that "Postmodern and post-structuralist theory has, in a sense, been the attempt to re-think community, although this has often been rather obliquely." (He then discusses, as an example, the work of Jean-Luc Nancy and the concept of *Mitsein,* ibid., 232–37, 239, 241). Note that I would take issue with some aspects of Morris's later theories concerning religious communities of descent and assent, the latter, for Morris, being typical of the idea of church. I question particularly

In an ecclesiological application, then, such theories lend themselves to the suggestion that the emergence of neo-exclusivism, however aimed at the perils of late modernity and postmodernity its proponents believe their efforts may be, is nonetheless fixated on a kind of "mythical" past, an invented understanding of certain fundamentals of "tradition" that really furthers the actual process of de-traditionalizaton itself. *Certain forms of ressourcement* theology would fit such a description, while the "restorationist" tendencies afoot in contemporary Catholicism, with its "official" or "authentic" ecclesiology of communion imposed "from above," might well serve as a classic example of such a development.

Indeed, I suggest, if this paradigm shift has indeed taken place, and across denominations, it has not simply been a result of the reaction of various Christians to the postmodern era in general; it has also, more specifically, been shaped by the recent and contemporary perspectives of major church figures and theologians on the relationship between the church and the world and that between "nature" and "grace." Let us explore the best-known Catholic form of such a paradigm shift in more detail, in an effort to discern why certain forms of "re-traditionalization" may eventually come to serve only the eventual triumph of detraditionalization.

The Hermeneutics of *Communio* Ecclesiology

As chapter 2 noted, Nicholas M. Healy has recently criticized the notion of "blueprint ecclesiologies"—those that seek to offer a universally applicable and tightly defined understanding of what it is to be church.[29] Even if Healy does go on to construct an example of the very form of ecclesiology he sets out to reject, his phrase is helpful in the context of our own concerns in this chapter, which seeks to outline and critique the prevailing ecclesiological "paradigm" that predominates

---

his assertion that such "assent" communities distinguish between religion and culture whereas descent communities allow the two to overlap and are "inherently pluralistic as identity does not depend upon ideology but upon descent," ibid., 238–39. Given that he suggests Jewish and Hindu notions of community are examples of communities of descent, while forms of intolerant fundamentalism and reaction against pluralism are as evident in parts of the Jewish and Hindu religious worlds as they are anywhere else, along with the inherent commitment to pluralism among various Christian communities (which sometimes exist within the same communities and denominations with Christian forms of that fundamentalist rejection of the same), his binary oppositional thinking here is too simplistic.

29. Healy, *Church, World, and the Christian Life.*

within the official Catholic Church in the present time. This "official paradigm" contributes to many of the pressing difficulties the Catholic Church is currently facing.

In the decades following the initial euphoria of Vatican II we have seen the emergence of a variety of debates throughout the church, funded by and yet symptomatic of differing or even *rival* ecclesiologies. In chapter 2 we noted the differences between various ecclesiologies that proceed methodologically "from above" and "from below." In many ways these two methods characterize two leading fundamental church visions, both of which claim to be the heirs to the Council's vision and program for the church.

Once again bearing in mind that we are to a degree dealing with "ideal types," crudely and broadly speaking we could say the *official* version of the *Communio* understanding of the church is one "from above." The *Concilium* understanding is one "from below."[30] These two terms are thus useful to us in distinguishing between two fundamentally different approaches in ecclesiology after Vatican II.[31] Indeed, it is the divide between these two "ideal types" relating to the operative reception and interpretation of the spirit and vision of Vatican II that equally, in effect, demonstrates a different understanding of the church-world relationship, of the relationship between theology and culture, and even in certain cases the relationship between nature and grace. They therefore exhibit different approaches to understanding the mission of the church vis-à-vis "our times." The *Communio* approach privileges one dominant theme witnessed at Vatican II, but then points it to definite, more characteristically "post-modern" ecclesial ends.

Thus for the sake of explanation we shall group various aspects of ecclesiological thinking under these two headings, while acknowledging that we do so for the sake of convenience, as both terms encompass a variety of ecclesiological approaches in their own right. The intention here, then, is not to engage in *polemics*, but rather in description that

30. On ecclesiology "from above" and "from below" see Roger Haight, *Christian Community in History*, vol. 1, *Historical Ecclesiology* (New York: Continuum, 2004), especially ch. 1, "Historical Ecclesiology." See also ch. 1 of this volume.

31. See also Joseph A. Komonchak, "Towards an Ecclesiology of Communion," chapter 1 of Giuseppe Alberigo and Joseph A. Komonchak, eds., *History of Vatican II* (Maryknoll, NY: Orbis, 2003) 4:1–93. On debates leading to the Council's final statements on the church see also further chapters in volumes of the same series, including Joseph A. Komonchak on the preparatory schema, "De Ecclesia," (1:311–13), Alberto Melloni, "The Beginning of the Second Period: The Great Debate on the Church," (3:1–115), and Giuseppe Ruggieri, "Beyond an Ecclesiology of Polemics: the Debate on the Church," (2:281–357).

might aid *understanding* and so in *comparison*. It should also be noted that many parishes and dioceses and wider groups throughout the church exhibit symptoms caused by conflicts that can be traced back to the divisions between these two prime visions of church and other ecclesiologies that have developed out of them.[32] Let us explore these terms in greater detail.

In a very general sense, then, the "official" version of the *Communio* model is to be contrasted to a vision that is not so much a definitive model itself as a way of embracing the diversity of visions Vatican II helped to inspire. Hence it is more accurate to speak of it as a method, a *modus operandi,* or, perhaps better still, an "ecclesial disposition." This is an ecclesiology, that is, an ecclesial vision, "from below," focusing on the church's transformative mission to and dialogue with the world. As diverse a range of theologians as Hans Küng, Karl Rahner, Edward Schillebeeckx, Gregory Baum, Elisabeth Schüssler Fiorenza, and Monika Hellwig, to name just a few examples, have adopted some form of this vision.[33] We might term it a "collegial" ecclesiology or an ecclesiology of *Concilium.* As the name suggests, it espouses a method that is conciliar and dialogical, in keeping with the vision of "the Council," Vatican II. So it is an understanding of the church that begins "from below," i.e., an "ascending ecclesiology" in this sense—beginning from the grassroots level of the church and engaging in dialogue "upward," so to speak. But it is also theologically "from below" in interpreting the church's place, role, and mission among human communities in their attempts to relate to each other and their God and to build the kingdom of love, justice, and righteousness to which the gospel calls them. Mindful of the sacramental nature of the church, it yet embraces a *diversity* of ways in which the church can aspire to be both the sign and the mediator of God's salvific self-communication to the world. Its adherents see their business as the full and ongoing *implementation* of Vatican II. Such a vision seeks to be constantly reforming, renewing, and reshaping the church. Many of the serious debates concerning how these tasks can be achieved have been reflected

---

32. For two highly readable and informative discussions of these ecclesiological "divisions" see the following works by David McLoughlin: "Authority in the Service of Communion" in Noel Timms and Kenneth Wilson, eds., *Governance and Authority in the Roman Catholic Church: Beginning a Conversation* (London: S.P.C.K., 2000) 123–36, and "*Communio* Models of Church—Rhetoric or Reality?" in Hoose, ed., *Authority and Roman Catholicism,* 181–90.

33. Although, as we shall see, Schüssler Fiorenza can also be bracketed as an "ecclesiologist of communion."

in the journal *Concilium: Theology in the Age of Renewal;* hence the name of such an approach.[34] The journal itself was established to encourage conversation within and outside the church on the fundamental themes pertaining to contemporary church mission and practice that Vatican II helped to identify.

This "model" or "paradigm" (if we may speak of it as such) draws much from the understanding of the church as the "people of God." This vision of the church seeks to find a way forward through the tensions between the respective priorities and concerns of the local and universal churches. We will encounter many further examples of ecclesiology "from below," along these lines, in the chapters that follow.[35]

Note, however, that this does not mean that such scholars would shun the *concept* of *communio* or communion; far from it. It is an integral concept in the ecclesiological thinking of many such theologians. But that thinking leads them in a very different way from what is laid down in the *official* form of *Communio* ecclesiology, as presented in recent official church documents and in the writings of certain curial officials.[36] What, then, is the exact nature of this contemporary vision of church?

"Foundationalist" *Communio* Ecclesiology in a Privileged Position[37]

In an initial and affirmative sense such an understanding of the church might begin with an emphasis on positive factors most ecclesiologists could agree about, such as the fact that the term comes to us

---

34. The first issue appeared in 1965. The developments in Catholic ecclesiology treated in this book have, to a large extent, been witnessed throughout and debated within the many volumes of this journal, along with its "rival," *Communio*. In the words of Hans Urs von Balthasar in the very first issue (1972) and of Joseph Ratzinger on its twentieth anniversary, *Communio* was self-consciously conceived and understood as a "program" (see Ratzinger, "Communio: a program" (Fall 1992). As such, it sought to counter-balance the post-conciliar emphasis upon the notion of "the people of God."

35. For further varieties of ecclesiology "from below" see Haight, *Christian Community in History,* especially vol. 2, *Comparative Ecclesiology* (New York: Continuum, 2004).

36. Hence I refer to the "official" version of this ecclesiology with a capital "C."

37. For a full and in-depth study of the notion of the ecclesiology of communion that goes beyond this "official" form discussed here see, Jean-Marie R. Tillard's *Church of Churches: The Ecclesiology of Communion* (Collegeville: Liturgical Press, 1992); Walter Kasper, *Theology and Church* (London: SCM, 1989), ch. 8, "The Church as Communion; Reflections on the Guiding Ecclesiological Idea of the Second Vatican Council," 148–65; Dennis M. Doyle, *Communion Ecclesiology: Visions and Versions* (Maryknoll, NY: Orbis, 2000), and Miroslav Volf, *After Our Likeness: The Church as the Image of the Trinity* (Grand Rapids: Eerdmans, 1998).

from Saint Paul (2 Corinthians) and relates to the early eucharistic celebrations. Most commentators also highlight the trinitarian and inter-ecclesial (horizontal and vertical) dimensions of the concept (in Greek, *koinonia*). In one recent church document the concept was outlined in the following terms:

> The concept of *communion* lies *"at the heart of the Church's self under-standing,"*[38] insofar as it is the Mystery of the personal union of each human being with the divine Trinity and with the rest of mankind, initiated with the faith, and, having begun as a reality in the Church on earth, is directed towards its eschatological fulfilment in the heavenly Church. If the concept of *communion,* which is not a univocal concept, is to serve as a key to ecclesiology, it has to be understood within the teaching of the Bible and the patristic tradition, in which *communion* always involves a double dimension: the *vertical* (communion with God) and the *horizontal* (communion among men). . . . The new relationship between man and God that has been established in Christ and is com-municated through the sacraments also extends to a new relationship among human beings. As a result, the concept of *communion* should be such as to express both the sacramental nature of the Church . . . and also the particular unity which makes the faithful into members of one and the same Body, the Mystical Body of Christ, an organically structured community, *"a people brought into one by the unity of the Father and of the Son and of the Holy Spirit"*[39] and endowed with suitable means for its visible and social union.[40]

As David McLoughlin indicates, the church is thus understood as an "icon of Trinitarian life." "Like the Trinity, the Church's reality lies in an essential orientation towards relationship. Our God is a being-in-communion. If we share *koinonia* with God in Christ then we will find ourselves in *koinonia* with each other."[41] McLoughlin summarizes the ecclesiology of communion thus: "The patristic writings refer to the reality of the church in its essential mystery as *koinonia/communio.* The term is used by St. Paul to describe our relationship to God through Christ and through the Spirit within the Eucharist. In order to acquire a richer understanding of *communio,* then, we need to reflect upon our

---

38. John Paul II, *Address to the Bishops of the United Sates of America*, 16 September 1987, n. 1: *Insegnamenti di Giovanni Paolo II* 10/3 (1987) 553.

39. Cyprian, *De Oratione Dominica*, 23: *MPL* 4:553; cf. *Lumen gentium*, n. 4b.

40. *Communionis notio* §3. This document is discussed in further detail below.

41. David McLoughlin, "Authority in the Service of Communion," 129.

relationship with God. The Church is called to be *communio* because that is what God is."[42]

In short, *communio* has become perhaps the dominant concept in recent decades.[43] But in those same decades the understanding of this fundamental ecclesiological concept has been the subject of many a dispute and certain interpretations of the notion of "communion" (i.e., *communio*) have proved controversial for many in the church (and across various denominations).[44]

However, many theologians would *not* describe their own ecclesiology as a "communio" ecclesiology if that label served to bracket their vision of the church with those of other more conservative voices in the church in recent decades. Instead, they would emphasize the notion of local churches existing in *collegiality* with one another (as, analogously, the universities of Cambridge and Oxford are made up of many individual colleges). Hence in such versions of this type of ecclesiology the local churches are seen as having great value in their own right. For example, for Richard P. McBrien, as for many other Catholic ecclesiologists, "collegiality" is another term for "communion" and Vatican II's teaching supports such an interpretation.[45]

But some recent versions of a *communio* ecclesiology, including some documents containing such a vision that have emerged from the Vatican, place more emphasis on the "official" or universal church as having primary importance, with local churches being part of the church only insofar as they are in good standing with and live as church according to the norms laid down by the central church authorities in Rome.

However, as McLoughlin puts it, there is now the need "To address a growing tendency in ecclesiastical documents to use theological models as though they somehow necessarily had a reference to the experiential life of the church, when in actual fact the reality is somewhat different."[46]

42. David McLoughlin, "Authority in the Service of Communion," 129–30. On the origins and development of the term see also McLoughlin's "*Communio* Models of Church—Rhetoric or Reality?" 181–89. Also see the brief summary by Richard P. McBrien in *Responses to 101 Questions on the Church* (New York: Paulist, 1996) 65.

43. David McLoughlin, "Authority in the Service of Communion," 130.

44. The quotation from *Communionis notio* above might be interpreted as espousing elements pertaining to ecclesiology "from below" as well as from "above." However, in practice this official version is primarily focused on the latter elements.

45. See McBrien, *Responses to 101 Questions on the Church*. McLoughlin's own writings would also support such an understanding.

46. McLoughlin, "*Communio* Models of Church—Rhetoric or Reality?" 181.

In the *Catechism of the Catholic Church* one also finds an ecclesiology that begins with reflection on the community between the persons of the Trinity and the relation of the Triune God to humans in their earthly existence. It is thus that all interpretation of that existence and the church's role within it is guided "from above." But certain quarters of the church have offered an interpretation of *communio* that shapes an ecclesiology very much "from above" in an *institutional* sense (i.e., "top-down"), or a "descending ecclesiology." So such an interpretation of this type of ecclesiology is also "from above" in a second sense: it is one officially sanctioned by the hierarchy, the official authorities of the Catholic Church. It is based on such a "top-down" understanding of the church and is really an attempt to offer a universally applicable interpretation of the nature, life, and mission of the church. So for its critics such an understanding of the ecclesiology of *communio* always perceives the concept of communion itself through the same prism, namely that of the institutional church. And as this is always a perception "from above," mainly serving institutional priorities and ends, it accentuates the primacy of the universal over the local. Such an approach, which stands in contrast with one of the main insights emerging from the postmodern age itself (i.e., the need for the local to be given due autonomy and freedom over the universal, over totalizing "master" narratives), again seems ill-suited as a solution to the more negative developments of the age. In practice this all leads to a predominant focus on vertical over horizontal dimensions of the church (i.e., hierarchical over local, universal over grassroots diversity. Indeed one could also argue that it might be contrasted with elements of *Lumen gentium*, e.g., chs. 1, 2, as well.)

This was obviously the preferred ecclesiological model of Cardinal Joseph Ratzinger while he was head of the Vatican's Congregation for the Doctrine of the Faith,[47] and no doubt will remain so throughout

47. The range and development of Joseph Ratzinger's ecclesiological thought can be seen in a representative sample of his works such as "Free Expression and Obedience in the Church," in Hugo Rahner, et al., *The Church: Readings in Theology* (New York: P. J. Kenedy, 1963) 194–217; "The Pastoral Implications of Episcopal Collegiality," in *The Church and Mankind. Concilium* 1 (Glen Rock: Paulist, 1964) 39–67; "What will the Church Look Like in 2002?" in idem, *Faith and Future* (Chicago: Franciscan Herald Press, 1971) 89–106; "Introductory Thoughts on the State of the Church," in *Two Say Why. Why I Am Still a Christian, by Hans Urs von Balthasar, and Why I Am Still in the Church, by Joseph Ratzinger,* trans. John Griffiths (London: Search Press; Chicago: Franciscan Herald Press, 1973); Interview with Desmond O'Grady: "The Ratzinger Round," *The Month* 6 (1973) 409–12; "Magisterium of the Church, Faith and Morality," *Problems of the Church Today* (Washington, DC: United States

his pontificate as Benedict XVI. Among its prime theological exponents was Hans Urs von Balthasar (1905–1988). Essentially this model *as it is interpreted* by those such as Joseph Ratzinger and likeminded church people could literally be described as a *conservative* model of the church, i.e., concerned with preserving and consolidating certain forms of ecclesial life believed to be under threat in our time.

So, too, such interpretations of the *Communio* model may be described as a "kneeling" ecclesiology (to borrow from the assessment of Hans Urs von Balthasar's thought as a "kneeling theology"). This relates to how ecclesial communication, relationships, and structures of organization, authority, and governance are understood: very much in a "top-down" sense.[48]

Catholic Conference, 1976) 74–83; "On Hans Küng's *On Being a Christian*," *Doctrine and Life* 30 (1980) 34–39; *Principles of Catholic Theology: Building Stones for a Fundamental Theology* (San Francisco: Ignatius Press, 1982); *The Ratzinger Report: An Exclusive Interview on the State of the Church*, with Vittorio Messori (San Francisco: Ignatius Press, 1983); *Church, Ecumenism and Politics* (Slough: St. Paul's, 1987); *The Nature and Mission of Theology* (San Francisco: Ignatius Press, 1993); *Called to Communion: Understanding the Church Today* (San Francisco: Ignatius Press, 1996); "Address to the International Convention on the Implementation of the Second Vatican Council, February 27, 2000"; "A Response to Walter Kasper: The Local Church and the Universal Church," *America* 185 (19 November 2001); *Truth and Tolerance: Christian Belief and World Religions* (San Francisco: Ignatius Press, 2004). A number of studies of Ratzinger's theology have been published in recent years, including Aidan Nichols, *The Theology of Joseph Ratzinger: An Introductory Study* (Edinburgh: T & T Clark, 1988). More critical portraits of the man and his *modus operandi* while at the CDF are provided by Harvey Cox, *The Silencing of Leonardo Boff: The Vatican and the Future of World Christianity* (Oak Park, IL: Meyer-Stone Books, 1988); Peter Hebblethwaite, *The New Inquisition? The Case of Edward Schillebeeckx and Hans Küng* (San Francisco: Harper & Row, 1980); and, more recently, John Allen's re-released biography *Pope Benedict XVI* (London: Continuum, 2005). A brief yet insightful portrait is Michael Fahey, "Joseph Ratzinger as Ecclesiologist and Pastor," in Gregory Baum, ed., *Neo-Conservatism: Social and Religious Phenomenon*. English ed. Marcus Lefébure, *Concilium* 141 (Edinburgh: T & T Clark, 1981). Ratzinger's position on the ecclesiology of communion has been widely analyzed. Two useful discussions are offered in Miroslav Volf, *After Our Likeness*, Part I. "Ratzinger: Communion and the Whole," 29–123, 130–31, 140–41, 155–56, 163–65, 200–201, and Dennis Doyle, *Communion Ecclesiology: Visions and Versions* (Maryknoll, NY: Orbis, 2000). Of particular relevance here are ch. 7, "Communion and the Common Good: Joseph Ratzinger and the Brothers Himes," 103–18; ch. 8, "Communion, Reform and Liberation: Hans Küng, Leonardo Boff and the CDF," 119–36; and ch. 11, "Touchstone for the Vision: Beyond Selective Readings of Vatican II," 168–80.

48. Some parts of the material in these pages builds on my earlier "A Virtuous Community: The Self-identity, Vision and Future of the Diocesan Church," in Noel Timms, ed., *Diocesan Dispositions and Parish Voices in the Roman Catholic Church* (Chelmsford: Matthew James, 2001) 79–130.

In Balthasar's writings[49] and the works of those influenced by him we have much discourse about the Petrine and Marian dimensions of church—that is, on the one hand the institutional structures and leadership roles mirroring the church's belief that a special role was accorded by Christ to Peter, and on the other, the notion that those of "lesser" prominence in terms of their position and role in the church, in particular the laity, mirror the model of humble servitude Balthasar believes Mary to have typified. Both profiles, then, very much accentuate the model of servitude within the church for those of "lesser prominence."[50]

And yet Vatican II seemed to shape a vision of the church that purported to affirm the mystical, sacramental, and historical elements of the church, that wished to see structures at the service of the community rather than the latter dominated by institutional concerns.[51] But it is one thing to espouse such an ecclesiological vision; the harder task is to facilitate and to live it: consequent of particular interpretations, an ecclesiology of "communion" can be just as authoritarian and life-denying as any political society and/or hierarchical model of yesteryear. The very particular interpretation of the teachings of Vatican II that informs the "official" version of *Communio* ecclesiology appears to run counter to many other interpretations of the Council's intentions. And yet Rome has reproached alternative interpretations as erroneous.[52]

The late, great, pioneering Catholic ecclesiologist Philip Murnion once provided an assessment of these developments by describing five typologies of "competing ecclesiologies." Among them was what he termed the ecclesiology of "The Roman Church," and it would be hard

---

49. See, for example, Hans Urs Von Balthasar, *The Word Made Flesh*, vol. 1 of *Explorations in Theology* (San Francisco: Ignatius Press, 1989), and *Spouse of the Word*, vol. 2 of *Explorations in Theology* (San Francisco: Ignatius Press, 1991). For a selection of essays exploring themes in the works of von Balthasar see Edward T. Oakes and David Moss, eds., *The Cambridge Companion to Balthasar* (Cambridge: Cambridge University Press, 2003), and John Riches, ed., *The Analogy of Beauty: the Theology of Hans Urs von Balthasar* (Edinburgh: T & T Clark, 1987).

50. Note that von Balthasar has also come to have a deep influence on non-Catholic Christian neo-exclusivists in recent decades.

51. This is not a contested point. See Paul Lakeland (in agreement with Dennis Doyle), *Liberation of the Laity* (New York: Continuum, 2003) 222–23, and also McLoughlin, "*Communio* Models of Church—Rhetoric or Reality?" and Komonchak, "Toward an Ecclesiology of Communion." Even some of Balthasar's own earlier writings expressed similar sentiments, e.g., "Who Is the Church" from his *Spouse of the Word* (San Francisco: Ignatius Press) 1991.

52. This appears in an extraordinarily wide variety of statements and documents but, as we shall see, most definitively in *Communionis notio*.

to give a better summary of its characteristics than his vivid and comprehensive description:

> Recently this has adopted or usurped the term "communion ecclesiology" as its own. It is the view of church that places its emphasis on the universal church, the Holy See and the magisterium, the catechism, and the authority of the church as located in the hierarchy. The local church, parish or diocese, is a subdivision of the universal church. As is true of both the cultural and the devotional [forms of contemporary ecclesiology], the emphasis is on the individual—the individual's relationship with God, the individual's relationship to the priest, the individual rite of reconciliation, the priest's individual relationship to the bishop and the church, the individual bishop's relationship to the Holy See. The sacraments are emphasized as effective rather than expressive, as the work of the priest for the sake of the people. The distinction between clergy and laity is quite sharp and not to be blurred. Emphasis is upon creed, code, cult vs. community, service, and social ministry. Catechesis is instruction. Community is valuable only in the sense of solidarity.[53]

Many Catholics in these postmodern times will find that such a description resonates with their own experience of the "official" church, its authorities, and its public pronouncements and teachings in recent years. Indeed, many theologians will find that Murnion's description above, and its continuation below, accurately map many of the areas of contention and controversy in contemporary ecclesiological debates. And yet Murnion is *not* describing an ecclesiology of yesteryear; he is very much seeking to elucidate a particular ecclesiology peculiar to *our* times.

> The organizations of the church and their clear Catholic identity and submission to authority are important—the parishes, schools, etc. This is a clerical church. Women are included and are in positions of governance of their own institutions but not in those that relate to sacramental, doctrinal, or canonical authority. Clarity is more important than nuance, coherence than diversity, doctrine than theology. There is an appeal to the devotional, especially to Mary. There is also a distance from any person or movement that challenges authority. Unity is the touchstone of this ecclesiology, a unity that easily slips into uniformity, for there is always some fundamental uniformity in any unity. Philosophical theology is more significant than biblical theology. There is strong emphasis on

53. Philip J. Murnion, "Beyond Competing Ecclesiologies," private paper for ecclesiological elucidation, *Queen's Foundation Working Party on Authority and Governance in the Roman Catholic Church*, July 1999.

hierarchy and office. Participation with officials is for consultation only, not for shared decision making. The Pope's role over the bishops, the bishop's role over the priests and people of the parish, the pastor's role over the parishioners are all kept quite clear. As is true at the other end of the spectrum, namely, the cultural approach, the emphasis is on the universality of the church and the place of the individual, now subject to the authority of the church.[54]

Murnion here aptly summarizes many of the "problematic ecclesiological responses" to the present (postmodern) age with which the present volume is concerned. Murnion's untimely death in 2003 robbed the church of one of those rare souls whose thinking and practice alike sought to foster the dialogue necessary to enable the church to transcend internal divisions, to engage in genuine intra- and extra-ecclesial conversation, and *at every level* to flourish in new times and in the face of new challenges.

Of course, competing ecclesiologies are nothing new in the church. But, as Thomas P. Rausch has suggested, the task is to find solutions to such pressing contemporary questions as "How can progressives and traditionalists, apologists and theologians, evangelists, catechists, and social activists learn to find the truth in positions of the other? How can faith be reconciled with critical reason and the understanding of our world that comes from contemporary science? Can we identify some principles that might help us discover some common ground in the task of theology?"[55] In other words, there is clearly a need to continue the work of Murnion and those like him in their efforts to find "common ground" among the diverse riches to be found in the church Catholic throughout the world today.[56]

To illustrate and explore all such issues discussed in this section further, we now turn to consider two particular official documents (from the CDF) that illustrate the developments mentioned here and the ecclesiological thinking that informs them. The first, which we consider in this chapter, relates specifically to and takes it title from that very ecclesiology, namely, *Communionis notio*—the letter to bishops

54. Ibid., Again we return to Lyotard's observations concerning the attempts to impose "unity" in the face of the perceived threat of postmodernity.
55. Thomas P. Rausch, *Reconciling Faith and Reason: Apologists, Evangelists, and Theologians in a Divided Church* (Collegeville: Liturgical Press, 1998) xiii.
56. We offer some reflections on ways to foster such ongoing conversation throughout this volume, but especially in chapters 5, 6, and 7 on the importance of bridge-building and dialogue.

on the "authentic" and "inauthentic" interpretations[57] of the ecclesiology of communion. (We discuss the second document in chapter 4.)

The method of procedure here, as throughout the volume, will be mindful that while some have chosen to focus on the fundamental doctrinal content of recent documents, others have indicated that attention to the nuances of these documents and the ecclesiology that informs them may be a more appropriate approach. Thus the tone, character, and rhetoric of the same documents might reveal more than a simple comparison with other documents of the magisterium, both recent and historical. Such is perhaps not quite that method of "deconstruction" lauded and detested in equal measure in our postmodern times, but it nonetheless aims at a *form* of deconstruction and certainly strives, however imperfectly, to be attentive to the "imperatives" of contemporary hermeneutical realities (if such could ever truly exist without being self-negating).

Communionis notio—A "Blueprint Ecclesiology?"

In 1992 the CDF issued "official guidance" on this particular vision of the church in a *Letter to the Bishops of the Catholic Church on Some Aspects of the Church Understood as Communion.*[58] In §1 it sets out its purpose as follows:

> The concept of *communion* (*koinonia*), which appears with a certain prominence in the texts of the Second Vatican Council,[59] is very suitable for expressing the core of the Mystery of the Church, and can certainly be a key for the renewal of Catholic ecclesiology . . . . However, some approaches to ecclesiology suffer from a clearly inadequate awareness of the Church as a *mystery of communion,* especially insofar as they have not sufficiently integrated the concept of *communion* with the concepts of *People of God* and of the *Body of Christ,* and have not given due importance to the relationship between the Church as *communion* and the Church as *sacrament.*[60]

57. That is, from a Vatican perspective.

58. This may be accessed at http://www.vatican.va/roman_curia/congregations/cfaith/documents/rc_con_cfaith_doc_28051992_communionis-notio_en.html. An abridged version appears in Mannion et al., *Readings in Church Authority,* 39–45.

59. Cf. *Lumen gentium,* nn. 4, 8, 13–15, 18, 21, 24–25; *Dei Verbum,* n. 10; *Gaudium et spes,* n. 32; *Unitatis redintegratio,* nn. 2–4, 14–15, 17–19, 22.

60. In ch. 8 we will explore an alternative Trinitarian ecclesiology, the *analogia ecclesiae* that might serve the combination of these elements better for our times.

We are left in no doubt, then, from the outset, that the document seeks to offer a corrective and to outline "the" correct interpretation of an ecclesiology of *Communio*. The document was issued under the name of then-Cardinal Joseph Ratzinger with the intention of clarifying, expanding upon, and further interpreting—some would argue reinterpreting—the ecclesiology of Vatican II. In 2000 the release of a further document, *Dominus Iesus,* would further this same task, as we shall see in chapter 4. In both we are given insight into the ecclesiological model that, according to some analysts, this theologian-bishop was formulating for the church as early as the immediate aftermath of Vatican II.[61]

Communionis notio espouses an ecclesiology of the church as the sacrament of salvation for humanity and asserts the priority of the authority of the *universal* church (seen by many interpreters as identified here with the institutional church). The emphasis is on unity and the *immediate* rather than mediated communion (i.e., not through linking mechanisms or processes or institutions) of all individual and local churches with the universal church (this being the means whereby they are to be considered a "church" at all).[62] Hence in §8 we read:

> The universal Church is therefore the *Body of the Churches.* Hence it is possible to apply the concept of communion *in analogous fashion* to the union existing among particular Churches, and to see the universal Church as a *Communion of Churches.* Sometimes, however, the idea of a "communion of particular Churches" is presented in such a way as to weaken the concept of the unity of the Church at the visible and institutional level. Thus it is asserted that every particular Church is a subject complete in itself, and that the universal Church is the result of a *reciprocal recognition* on the part of the particular Churches.

Here we see the familiar problem of the priority of the universal or local church again taking center stage. Indeed, this question became the increasing focus of Cardinal Ratzinger's writing, teaching, and speaking in the new millennium, as we shall see illustrated also in our consideration of *Dominus Iesus.* The document continues by rejecting such "ecclesiological unilateralism," i.e., by reasserting the priority of the universal over the local church:

> This ecclesiological unilateralism, which impoverishes not only the concept of the universal church but also that of the particular church, betrays

61. See Michael Fahey, "Joseph Ratzinger as Ecclesiologist and Pastor."
62. This all relates also to the status and authority of episcopal conferences and individual bishops.

an insufficient understanding of the concept of communion. As history shows, when a particular church has sought to become self-sufficient, and has weakened its real communion with the universal church and with its living and visible center, its internal unity suffers too, and it finds itself in danger of losing its own freedom in the face of the various forces of slavery and exploitation.

It is open to question whether this "living and visible center" refers to the papal ministry of unity or, as appears more likely, to the Vatican—i.e., the central Roman authorities—in general. The "various forces of slavery and exploitation" today are, of course, the challenges postmodernity puts to the church in general. Thus the letter is suggesting those who seek to give priority to the local succumb to the temptations of postmodernity. This document, which is addressed to all bishops (though not drafted in collaboration with them), is clearly promoting an "official" ecclesiology and encouraging bishops to act against those who proffer alternatives.[63]

Although we have noted how *Communionis notio* spoke of particular churches straying and "weakening communion with the universal church," our discussions here raise the question: who actually decides what constitutes such a "weakening of communion" and what is simply an instance of the exercise of legitimate subsidiarity?

The letter further states that it is through a commitment to and participation in the Eucharist (§11, 14) and the episcopacy (with the pope at its head, §12-14) that a local/individual church gains full communion with the universal church.[64] That is, Christian communities that do *not* have bishops or do not celebrate the Eucharist in a sacramental fashion analogous to that in the Catholic Church should not be understood as churches that are part of the universal communion of churches. This is because—according to this ecclesiological model— the office of bishop and the celebration of the Eucharist are two prime

---

63. Admittedly Ratzinger, in his disputations with Walter Kasper, did state that the centralization of authority in Rome has nothing to do with a *Communio* ecclesiology, but this puts the ecclesiological horse somewhat behind the ecclesial cart, since a very distinct version of this type of ecclesiology has indeed been used to justify and implement such renewed centralization.

64. Of course, as we shall see in the following chapter, the claim could be made that such sentiments simply echo aspects of documents from Vatican II. On the eucharistic theme cf. John Paul II's encyclical on the Eucharist, *Ecclesia de Eucharistia*, and Paul McPartlan, *The Eucharist Makes the Church* (Edinburgh: T & T Clark, 1993), and *Sacrament of Salvation: an Introduction to Eucharistic Ecclesiology* (Edinburgh: T & T Clark, 1995).

ways *in which the communion of local churches together in the universal church is brought about.* As the letter states: "Since, however, communion with the universal Church, represented by Peter's Successor, is not an external complement to the particular Church, but one of its internal constituents, the situation of those venerable Christian communities also means that their existence as particular Churches is *wounded.* The wound is even deeper in those ecclesial communities which have not retained the apostolic succession and a valid Eucharist."[65]

The document thus warns against *overt* claims to autonomy (i.e., self-determination, self-governance, and general independence in decision making and organization) and self-sufficiency in local/individual churches and seeks to set forth a definitive teaching on the respective nature and promotion of unity and diversity in the church (emphasizing the former, limiting the latter in certain respects). Such attempts to indicate "gradations" of an "authentic ecclesiology" further underline the imposed nature of this ecclesiology and, as we shall see in the next chapter, will buttress later attempts to underline the self-understanding of an "authentic church" vis-à-vis other Christian communities and other world religions in the postmodern world in the document *Dominus Iesus.*

As indicated, its critics saw *Communionis notio* as being indicative of a very different *sort* of ecclesiology from that which characterized Vatican II. Indeed, it is not difficult even to see why some would interpret the letter's ecclesiological stance as a *reversal* of the efforts of Vatican II's more open and, at least in effect, progressive legacy and a return to the Roman centralizing tendencies more resonant with the ecclesiology of previous decades and even right back to the nineteenth century and certain implications of Vatican I.

Nonetheless, the document does offer a definite "ecclesiology of communion" that both reflects and has in turn influenced much theologizing and teaching in the church in recent decades. Indeed, the exponents of the "official" *Communio* model proclaim this vision of the church as the *fulfillment* of Vatican II, claiming that such an emphasis on communion is central to that Council's teachings.[66] Although some doubt it was quite *the* central concept at Vatican II that certain current church leaders have proclaimed it to be, nonetheless, as the American ecclesiologist Richard A. Gaillardetz writes, "Even when the

65. Ibid., §17.
66. See again Joseph Ratzinger, *Called to Communion,* and *Communionis notio* §1, at n. 60 above.

term 'communion' does not itself appear, a careful reading of the principal conciliar documents suggests that the concept was among the most influential at the council. The council retrieved this notion of communion from the biblical and patristic concept of *koinonia,* or *communion.*"[67]

But, to reiterate the fundamental issues here, those who interpret more recent official ecclesiology as a "reversal" of Vatican II see instead an applying of the brakes against the ecclesially *transformative* vision advocated at the Council. They also detect a re-embracing of an emphasis on the more restrictive hierarchical aspects of the church that were thus challenged. Of course, the defenders of the ecclesial vision of *Communionis notio* would say the reverse is the case: that the alternative interpretations of Vatican II are incorrect: hence the heart of the ecclesiological matter lies in better discerning the collective *sensus ecclesiae* that emerged from the Council.

In particular, critics believe that in such interpretations diversity and contextual considerations (i.e., taking account of local and cultural factors) are increasingly sacrificed as this understanding of the church becomes a received, indeed often *imposed* model and, eventually, a paradigm of church. Furthermore, they believe that the ecumenical implications of the recent institutional interpretations of this model are potentially grave. Gaillardetz also writes that the Vatican II documents "reflect a move away from that preconciliar universalist ecclesiology that viewed the diocese as little more than an administrative subset of the universal church. Vatican II represented an at least tentative return to an ecclesiology in which the one universal church is manifested on the communion of local churches."[68]

For critics of recent developments this would be perceived to be at variance with aspects of the later "official" version of *Communio* ecclesiology, though Gaillardetz (somewhat foreshadowing later debates that we will mention in relation to the 2000 document *Dominus Iesus*), adds in a footnote: "I say tentative because the council was not always consistent in this matter. Often texts that supported a [positive and genuine] *communio* ecclesiology were simply juxtaposed with texts that continued a more universalist ecclesiology."[69] By "universalist" we here take Gaillardetz to mean an overarching and *universally* applicable

67. Gaillardetz, *Teaching with Authority*, 8–9; see also Joseph A. Komonchak, "Towards an Ecclesiology of Communion," *passim.*
68. *Teaching with Authority*, 15.
69. Ibid., 15, n. 23.

ecclesiology that puts great emphasis on the priority of the universal church (and so is more akin to the earlier *institutional* ecclesiologies). In this volume, of course, we have spoken now of "official paradigms" or, as Healy terms them, "blueprint ecclesiologies."

None of this, of course, is to deny in any sense the many, many positive dimensions of the notion of communion, but critics simply argue that there are also more *authoritarian* forms of such a model currently being employed in the church. However, one particular problem is that it does appear that many in the church today do, in fact, believe that the *Communio* model is now an "official" model that is often imposed on other areas of the church and in ways not always suited to them. As with, for example, *Mystici Corporis Christi* (and its language about the body of Christ and mystical and sacramental elements), the incredibly powerful, communitarian, and sacramental imagery that *could* flow from an emphasis on communion can actually be stifled by institutional and hierarchical elements and language.[70] Hence the very vitality of such a vision can be diminished by an incompatible authoritarian ethos that sometimes shapes the expression and implementation of such a vision. Furthermore, the eschatological dimensions (positive aspects concerning the future of church and world alike in God's plan of salvation) of *Communio* models can be rendered powerless by the institutional strictures and rhetoric surrounding them.

In more specific terms, Gaillardetz has criticized the offical version of the *Communio* ecclesiology because of its very attempts to give *priority* to the universal church over the local churches. Instead, Gaillardetz asserts:

> In this relationship between the universal and the local it should be apparent that neither can be given priority over the other. To grant the priority of the local church would be to suggest that the universal church is little more than a confederation of autonomous local churches. To give priority to the universal church is to risk reverting to a preconciliar ecclesiology that conceives of the church as an international corporation subdivided into ecclesial departments or "branch offices." Only by accepting the radically relational character of the one church understood as a communion of churches can these two extremes be avoided.[71]

The ecclesial seriousness of the situation vis-à-vis the problems caused by the imposition of this "official" interpretation of *Communio* ecclesiol-

---

70. Cf. Mannion, "A Virtuous Community."
71. Gaillardetz, *Teaching with Authority,* 6–17.

ogy is further emphasized by Paul Lakeland, who describes how "at no time in history has the institution [of the Catholic church] behaved more like a corporate giant than it does today, with head offices in Rome and branches throughout the world, staffed by local managers called bishops. This ecclesial vision is wrong. It contradicts Vatican II."[72]

Indeed, we may say that the prioritizing of *either* local churches or universal church, one over the other, would actually contradict the Christian Trinitarian understanding of God as a community of coequal, co-divine, and coeternal persons.[73] The relation of the three persons of the Trinity to each other is described as a "mutual indwelling" or "interpenetration" *(perichoresis)* whereby the being of each is fundamentally bound up with that of the others. Along similar lines, and also referring to such a Trinitarian parallel with ecclesiology, specifically in relation to *Communionis notio,* Gaillardetz adds: "A theology of communion cannot properly be Trinitarian if it gives priority to either the universal or the local; this would violate the perichoretic relationship of the particular churches as the manifestation of the universal church. *This is the principal shortcoming of the CDF instruction 'Some aspects of the Church Understood as Communion.'*"[74]

It is thus that commentators have been asking whether or not this is a true ecclesiology of communion—i.e., is it ecclesiological rhetoric or ecclesial reality?[75] Here I would add that any "imposed ecclesiology" might be incapable of serving as a truly *facilitating* ecclesiology whereby community can be enhanced for the local churches that try to live out such an official ecclesiology by putting the gospel into practice. That is a more telling lesson that can be learned from ecclesiastical history and, indeed, is a much more accurate example of "ecclesiological unilateralism" than the letter's suggested "local" infringements. Thus today we might say that a universalist ecclesiology dominating the church can only do so at the expense of genuine ecclesiologies of communion being allowed to flourish. The domination of one particular form of any ecclesiology, in fact, contradicts the very concept of *communion.*

Then there is an additional problem posed by such developments for, as earlier intimated, *Communio* ecclesiology is far from being the

72. Paul Lakeland, *The Liberation of the Laity,* 240.

73. We will return to these themes in our final chapter.

74. The reference is to *Communionis notio.* Gaillardetz, *Teaching with Authority,* 16, n. 29 (italics supplied).

75. See also the exploration of this question in David McLoughlin, "*Communio* Models of Church—Rhetoric or Reality?" 181–90.

sole preserve of the Vatican. Nicholas Healy, among others, has shown how many widely different ecclesiologies of "communion" there are in existence. It is, he claims, a concept embraced by those he terms "*ressourcement* theologians" such as the Catholic Jean-Marie Tillard[76] and the Orthodox John Zizioulas, by liberation theologians such as Leonardo Boff, feminists such as Elizabeth Schüssler Fiorenza, "liberal Protestants" such as Peter Hodgson, and Free Church theologians such as Miroslav Volf. Yet once one considers what each actually understands "communion" to mean, any pretense of consensus disappears rapidly. Indeed, its meanings in Tillard and Hodgson may well be in conflict.[77] And so, as Paul Lakeland writes, the reality is that "some expositions of communion are better than others."[78] If this be the case, even "ecclesiological unilateralism" on the part of the Vatican authorities is harmful to true communion if an imposed ecclesial model exhibits the faults and dangers thus far outlined. For Healy, however, there is a nuanced distinction to be made when confronted by this problem: "This does not condemn us to talk past one another endlessly. It means that, if we want to challenge one or other of these ecclesiologies, our argument would be best directed, not against the model itself, but against the construals that govern its use. For what is in dispute among the theologians is *not* the word "communion" but *everything that guides its use*."[79]

---

76. Note, however, that to label Tillard a conservative would do him an injustice on several fronts.

77. Healy, *Church, World, and the Christian Life*, 44.

78. Lakeland, *Liberation of the Laity*, 223. He offers us a brief yet incisive study of *Communio* ecclesiology vis-à-vis the contemporary era on pp. 220–27. Both Doyle, *Communion Ecclesiology* (see especially the Introduction, 1–10, and chapter 1, "What is Communion Ecclesiology?" 11–22) and Volf, *After Our Likeness (passim),* would concur with Lakeland's judgment.

79. Healy, *Church, World, and the Christian Life*, 45, (italics in original). Along similar lines, although addressing the Catholic situation in particular, see Doyle: "Communion Ecclesiology can provide a framework for theological discourse within which Catholics on all parts of the spectrum can feel that there are at least a few crucial things that are mutually understood. It values a variety of approaches, not polemics. It offers tools, not weapons. Communion ecclesiology expresses and brings together a range of elements of Catholicism, both mystical and practical, both old and new, that span some of the great divides that plague the church today. The label 'communion ecclesiology' will at times be misused by those who automatically co-opt any approach to serve their own narrow views; the true reality of communion ecclesiology, however, will always work to subvert and overturn such narrowness. The communion ecclesiology that has its roots in theologians such as Möhler, Journet, Congar, and de Lubac will serve as a tool for promoting the broad and inclusive Catholic vision expressed in the documents of Vatican II" (*Communion Ecclesiology*, 179–80).

Thus we must acknowledge that adherence to the concept of *communio* is not enough in itself. How we live as church, how church is organized and governed, and how we understand what the church is called to *do* are just as important. Here Lakeland takes us to the very heart of the matter: "We need to recognize that if communion is explicated in isolation from mission, then the particular mix of the mystical, the sacramental, the historical, and the social that appears in any given version of communion ecclesiology will simply be one theologian's favorite items from the theological buffet. What the church *is* is intimately connected to what the church *is for*."[80] And we shall return to this theme—the connections between what the church is and what the church is for, as well as what the church *does*—in a number of subsequent chapters.

The Church and the Churches

Where does our consideration of the dangers of imposing a single and "official" ecclesiology lead us? In one sense to the very core of ecclesiological thinking. There has long been a pressing need for a full and informed debate on the true relations between the local and the universal church. What is called for in such a debate, then, by way of theological as well as ecclesial response? The first requirement is an open and frank discussion of the ecclesiological intentions behind such documents as *Communionis notio*—which, being a letter to bishops on the right and wrong interpretations of the ecclesiology of communion, aptly—for some—illustrates the "imposed" character of the currently prevailing paradigm. Second, there is need for a "deconstruction" of further church documents and "pronouncements from the center," which might involve a sustained discussion of and reflection on the nature of episcopal collegiality, the *sensus fidelium* with regard to this, the ordinary universal magisterium, and their actuality, as well as the reality of the present understanding and exercise of the magisterium in general. In the chapters that follow we will seek to offer some tentative steps toward such ecclesiological engagements.

For regardless of the hierarchical position of those who give priority to the universal over the local, the reality is that many bishops disagree. More telling still, if one goes into parishes across the Catholic world today one may find only the most tentative sense of "belonging" between

---

80. Lakeland, *Liberation of the Laity*, 223.

the parish and the diocese.[81] The diocese should really serve much more as both an agent and a sign of communion (in addition to the ministry of unity of the papacy), and yet it is failing to do so: why? One can also often find evidence of the equally tenuous state of *genuinely* lived communion between those at the parish level and the Vatican—and all this despite the resources for communication at the universal church's disposal today. This suggests, at the very least, that something is awry in the form and extent of relations, of communion between the various Catholic Christian communities across the globe.[82]

In relation to both such needs the protracted debate between Cardinals Ratzinger and Kasper (a theme we again touch upon in the following chapter) can prove informative.[83] One only has to consider *Communionis notio* §9 to see the dividing lines between their thinking, as there we are perhaps given Cardinal Ratzinger's definitive understanding of the matter:

> In order to grasp the true meaning of the analogical application of the term *communion* to the particular Churches taken as a whole, one must bear in mind above all that the particular Churches, insofar as they are *"part of the one Church of Christ,"*[84] have a special relationship of *"mutual interiority"*[85] with the whole, that is, with the universal Church, because in every particular Church *"the one, holy, catholic and apostolic Church of Christ is truly present and active."*[86] For this reason, *"the universal Church cannot be conceived as the sum of the particular Churches, or as a federation of particular Churches."*[87] It is not the result of the communion of the Churches, but, in its essential mystery, it is a reality *ontologically and temporally* prior to every *individual* particular Church.

81. For example, in the UK context see the various findings of the *Queen's Foundation Study on Authority and Governance in the Roman Catholic Church*, as reflected on in Noel Timms, ed., *Diocesan Dispositions and Parish Voices*. See also Mannion, "A Virtuous Community," in the same volume.

82. This is not to say that there are not numerous manifestations of that communion, but one finds it in the most surprising of places—for example, in the support for Catholic international charities, in the shared worship of Catholics who find themselves abroad and, perhaps most of all, in the relentless and continued grassroots enthusiasm for ecumenism and interfaith dialogue in numerous countries.

83. See again Kasper, *Theology and Church*, especially 148–65.

84. *Christus Dominus*, n. 6/c.

85. John Paul II, *Address to the Roman Curia*, 20 December 1990, n. 9, in *L'Osservatore Romano*, 21 December 1990, 5.

86. *Christus Dominus*, n. 11/a.

87. John Paul II, *Address to the Bishops of the United States of America*, 16 September 1987, n. 3.

And here perhaps it serves the debate well to recall that Gregory Baum, writing in the immediate aftermath of the final promulgation of *Lumen gentium*, offered a very different interpretation of the Council's sentiments on such matters. Baum explained the thinking of that document on the issue thus:

> The very structure of the church is marked by the collegial nature of the episcopate. Chapter III [of *Lumen gentium*] explains that each bishop as successor of the apostles becomes the principle of unity, the voice of the gospel, and the source of liturgical life within his own people, thereby constituting them as a church, a local church, in the strict sense of the term. *His people do not simply constitute a diocese or administrative portion of the church universal, but they are a true embodiment of the church of Christ, that is, an assembly of the faithful made into God's people through gospel, sacraments and apostolic governance.* These episcopally governed churches are catholic or universal because they are in communion with one another, especially through their bishops who belong to the episcopal college. On account of this collegial structure, the church universal may not be conceived as a monarchical organization under a single ruler, the pope, but rather, *as a family or body of episcopal churches,* united among themselves and under the supreme coordination of the supreme bishop, the pope. In technical language the Catholic Church is "a communion of churches."[88]

Of course, now famously, another young theologian seemed to agree with such an interpretation of *Lumen gentium* at the time.[89] But Joseph Ratzinger has since offered a very different interpretation.

88. Gregory Baum, "Commentary," in *De Ecclesia: The Constitution on the Church of Vatican Council II* (London: Darton Longman and Todd, 1965) 36 (italics supplied).

89. As noted, John Allen's biography of Joseph Ratzinger, *Pope Benedict XVI,* illustrates the full extent of the supposed shift in thinking between the young Council *peritus* and the later professor, cardinal, and now pope. But I would again suggest (as Allen himself acknowledges) that the shift in actual theological position was not as marked as many believe. Joseph Ratzinger may have been carried along with the tide of opinion at Vatican II, not least with the official statements of Cardinal Joseph Frings, to whom Ratzinger was personal adviser at the Council. Still, there is a marked discrepancy between the ecclesiological position in some of his writings at that time and since. By the time we come to *Dominus Iesus* the position had, indeed, come full circle. The younger Ratzinger even coauthored a volume with Karl Rahner on *Episcopate and Primacy* (London: Burns and Oates, 1966), with Ratzinger authoring the middle section of three, entitled "Primacy, Episcopate and Apostolic Succession" (although Rahner contributed the lion's share of the work for the overall volume), which helped provide historical and theological underpinning for Rahner's collegial arguments.

Third, there should be an analysis of the wider ecumenical implications of the relation between the church*es* local and the church universal.[90] Obviously this is linked to the need for a full and honest debate across the churches on the broader ecumenical *sensus fidelium* with regard to the relation between the church local and universal.[91] In a single volume we can only touch on the initial parameters of such necessary debates to a limited extent. Indeed, first we must exercise caution, for in recent years the official church has itself revisited these very questions. And what outlook did the resultant document adopt? Anyone expecting a major *metanoia* here on the part of the curia's thinking will, I suspect, be disappointed.

This chapter has sought to identify various aspects of ecclesiological hermeneutics that are pressing in the Catholic Church today. We now seek to discern what might be gained from exploring these tasks in greater detail.

---

90. Two further scholars whose work is of much relevance here are Cardinal Avery Dulles and the late Roger Tillard.

91. The World Council of Churches' Faith and Order Commission is set to offer some indication of where ecumenical thinking on such a question stands with the release, in 2006, of a much-anticipated document, *The Nature and Mission of the Church*, described as "the *Baptism, Eucharist and Ministry* of the twenty-first century."

Chapter Four

The Church and Religious "Other": Hermeneutics of Ecclesial Identity in Postmodern Times

A Hermeneutical "Refusal"?[1]

A single declaration from the CDF, entitled *Dominus Iesus,* caused a great deal of controversy at the dawn of the third millennium. The resulting debate ranged over relations between the church universal and individual churches, not least other Christian communions, matters of interfaith relations, questions concerning the realities of pluralism, and matters of ecclesial authority and governance.[2]

Released on 6 August 2000, this text led to many disagreements about the interpretation of the Catholic Church's relationship with other faiths and with other Christian churches. Indeed, the document appeared to set further explicit and definitive limits to what actually enables a community to be called a church. Here we seek to highlight some of the fundamental issues that featured in many of the debates

---

1. On the concept of "hermeneutical refusal" see Werner Jeanrond, *Theological Hermeneutics* (London: SCM, 1994), 164ff. and Gerard Mannion, "Hermeneutical Investigations: Discerning Contemporary Christian Community," in Paul Collins, Gerard Mannion, Gareth Powell, and Kenneth Wilson, *Ecclesiological Investigations— Christian Community Now* (forthcoming, 2007).

2. Some of the material in this chapter draws on an account of the document and reactions to it I produced for the digest of the Queen's Foundation project on *Authority and Governance in the Roman Catholic Church* in 2001.

surrounding the text. Among the more prominent were questions concerning the nature and function of the CDF, the implications of the document for Catholic theology and theologians, and its implications for the movement toward greater Christian unity as well as for relations and dialogue with other faiths. More specific questions concerned how the document affects those actually *working* in contexts where interaction with other faiths and Christian denominations is a fact of daily life.[3] Many also asked how the document relates to the vision of Vatican II on ecclesiology and on interchurch and interfaith dialogue. All such questions lead us into a further realm of inquiry, namely the nature and scope of the magisterium today and the role and contribution of the laity, bishops, and theologians.

Dominus Iesus: Its Purpose and Message

The document itself was intended to be a resource for theologians and bishops charged with teaching and interpreting the Catholic faith. However, while many have pointed to this fact to suggest that it has been misunderstood when examined by audiences for whom it was not intended, it should be noted that the text itself also states that it is aimed at "all the Catholic faithful" (§3). As such it concerns itself with certain aspects central to the faith that the CDF deemed to be in need of reiteration. These relate to the uniqueness of salvation brought about through God's incarnation in Christ, the place of the Catholic Church in God's plan of salvation, and particular questions relating to religious and ecclesiological pluralism (hence, once again, postmodern issues and perceived challenges).[4] The text acknowledges that the tone of its language is intended to be "expository." Here we will be specifically concerned, for the most part, with the ecclesiological aspects and implications

---

3. Some commentators believed the document was written to address the needs of bishops working in certain Asian countries where the multifaith reality posed fundamental questions with regard to Christian mission in such contexts. See also Gregory Baum, *Amazing Church: A Catholic Theologian Remembers a Half Century of Change* (Maryknoll, NY: Orbis, 2005) 121–22, which sees the document as a confirmation of the somewhat surprising shift in emphasis from dialogue to conversion in John Paul II's Apostolic Exhortation, *Ecclesia in Asia* (released on 9 November 1999).

4. The threats of relativism and pluralism are closely linked by the document: "The Church's constant proclamation is endangered today by relativistic theories which seek to justify religious pluralism not only *de facto* but also *de jure* (or "in principle")," §4. Of course, the relevant issues of pluralism move beyond purely ecclesiological or even exclusively religious concerns.

of the document, although naturally doctrinal factors will need to be attended to along the way.

The prime target of this declaration was religious "relativism," which the CDF believed to be a standpoint that tends to perceive all religions as equally valid paths toward salvation. Thus the declaration sought to remind its readers of the importance of the "Unicity and Salvific Universality of Jesus Christ and the Church." The document begins in a seemingly positive tone, à la Vatican II, but it soon becomes clear that a different emphasis is being accentuated.

> In interreligious dialogue as well, the mission *ad gentes* "today as always retains its full force and necessity."[5] God "desires all men to be saved and come to the knowledge of the truth" (1 Tim 2:4); that is, God wills the salvation of everyone through the knowledge of the truth. Salvation is found in the truth. Those who obey the promptings of the Spirit of truth are already on the way of salvation. But the Church, t*o whom this truth has been entrusted,* must go out to meet their desire, *so as to bring them the truth.* Because she believes in God's universal plan of salvation, the Church must be missionary.[6] Inter-religious dialogue, therefore, *as part of her evangelizing mission,* is just one of the actions of the Church in her mission *ad gentes.*[7]

And this shift in focus—from dialogue back to evangelization (as opposed to the understanding of dialogue *as* evangelization that would emerge in numerous Catholic circles following Vatican II)[8]—was further

---

5. *Ad gentes,* 7.

6. *Catechism of the Catholic Church* 851; cf. also 849–56.

7. Italics supplied. Cf. John Paul II's encyclical *Redemptoris missio,* 55, and also the Apostolic Exhortation *Ecclesia in Asia,* 31.

8. Paragraph 22 of the document states that the church, although "guided by charity and a respect for freedom" (reiterating *Dignitatis humanae* §1) must be committed "to announcing the necessity of conversion to Jesus Christ and of adherence to the Church through Baptism and the other sacraments, in order to participate fully in communion with God, the Father, Son and Holy Spirit." An editorial in *The Tablet* sensed a shift in curial emphasis toward other faiths was afoot as early as the beginning of 2000. The focus was moving to a one-sided emphasis on the revelation communicated by Christ, at the expense of the future-oriented (and thus presently limited) understanding of revelation in the New Testament, as well as of Vatican II's acknowledgment that the church "rejects nothing which is true and holy" in other faiths. "Through a Glass Darkly," *The Tablet* (26 February 2000) 259. Of course, *Dominus Iesus* itself did not refute the Vatican Council sentiment here; it simply chose to give greater emphasis to less positive Catholic perspectives on other faiths. Interestingly, the same journal's issue of 5 November 2005 carried an article stating that the new Pope Benedict *commended* this statement from Vatican II. However, the commendation was used to append an exclusivistic christological qualification of interfaith dialogue.

marked by additional qualifications of the hitherto seemingly more open understanding of the church's position vis-à-vis other faiths.

> Equality, which is a presupposition of inter-religious dialogue, refers to the equal personal dignity of the parties in dialogue, not to doctrinal content, nor even less to the position of Jesus Christ—who is God himself made man—in relation to the founders of the other religions. Indeed, the Church, guided by charity and respect for freedom,[9] must be primarily committed to proclaiming to all people the truth definitively revealed by the Lord, and to announcing the necessity of conversion to Jesus Christ and of adherence to the Church through Baptism and the other sacraments, in order to participate fully in communion with God, the Father, Son and Holy Spirit. Thus, the certainty of the universal salvific will of God does not diminish, but rather increases the duty and urgency of the proclamation of salvation and of conversion to the Lord Jesus Christ.[10]

At a press conference to mark the document's release, then-Cardinal Ratzinger stated that it sought to challenge a "false concept of tolerance" in the field of religious pluralism. He further added that nothing contained in the document was actually new teaching.[11] However, many have since commented that its *interpretation* of fundamental Catholic teachings, in a post-Vatican II context, was indeed something novel (or even nostalgic—i.e., reminiscent of preconciliar ecclesial documents). Hence *Dominus Iesus* was concerned with attacking relativistic tendencies, i.e., viewing all paths to salvation, even those calling themselves "Christian," as equally valid and beneficial for their adherents.

> The Church's constant missionary proclamation is endangered today by relativistic theories which seek to justify religious pluralism, not only *de facto* but also *de iure* (or in principle). As a consequence, it is held that certain truths have been superseded; for example, the definitive and complete character of the revelation of Jesus Christ, the nature of Christian faith as compared with that of belief in other religions, the inspired nature of the books of Sacred Scripture, the personal unity between the Eternal Word and Jesus of Nazareth, the unity of the economy of the Incarnate Word and the Holy Spirit, the unicity and salvific universality of the mystery of Jesus Christ, the universal salvific mediation of the Church, the inseparability—while recognizing the distinction—of the kingdom

9. *Dignitatis humanae* 1. Compare the subtle shift in interpretation of this Vatican II document with Stanley Hauerwas' attack upon the same, (n. 36).

10. *Dominus Iesus* VI, §22.

11. This echoes the line taken by many bishops in response to another document that caused much debate, *Ad Tuendam Fidem,* a motu propio, released by John Paul II in 1998.

of God, the kingdom of Christ, and the Church, and the subsistence of the one Church of Christ in the Catholic Church.[12]

The text goes on to locate the source of the difficulties facing the church today in "relativistic attitudes towards truth itself," those who attempt to juxtapose "western" epistemological categories with those from the "east," overt "subjectivism," problematic interpretations of history that limit the universal significance of events at the core of Christian faith, and eclecticism in theological method. Finally, those who dare to interpret Scripture "outside the Tradition and Magisterium of the Church" are also blamed. In short, many typically postmodern trends and theories are seen to beset the definitive preaching of the gospel in our times.[13] Next, the document sets out the CDF's interpretation of why the Catholic Church holds a privileged position in the soteriological economy, along with those churches in "full communion" with it. The latter include the Orthodox and Eastern Rite and Old Catholics by dint of their holding to a valid episcopacy and celebration of the eucharistic mystery.

> Therefore, there exists a single Church of Christ, which subsists in the Catholic Church, governed by the Successor of Peter and by the Bishops in communion with him.[14] The Churches which, while not existing in perfect communion with the Catholic Church, remain united to her by means of the closest bonds, that is, by apostolic succession and a valid Eucharist, are true particular Churches.[15] Therefore, the Church of Christ is present and operative also in these Churches, even though they lack full communion with the Catholic Church, since they do not accept the Catholic doctrine of the Primacy, which, according to the will of God, the Bishop of Rome objectively has and exercises over the entire Church.[16]

12. *Dominus Iesus,* Introduction, §4. Note that all forms and degrees of relativism are thus presumably here grouped together.

13. Ibid. Again we might be reminded of Lyotard's warnings about the flight from experimentation and the contemporary desire to impose unity and conformity: "Answering the Question: What is Postmodern?" appendix to Jean-François Lyotard, *The Postmodern Condition—A Report on Knowledge,* tr. Régis Durand (Manchester: Manchester University Press, 1984) 71–82. In relation to the condemned "conviction of the elusiveness and inexpressibility of divine truth" one might here pause for thought, given that many of the church's great mystical theologians, not to mention the Angelic Doctor himself, might find themselves thus condemned!

14. Cf. *Unitatis redintegratio* §14 and §15.

15. *Communionis notio* §17: *AAS* 85 (1993) 848.

16. Cf. Vatican Council I, Constitution *Pastor aeternus, DS* 3053–64; Vatican Council II, Dogmatic Constitution *Lumen gentium* §22. *Dominus Iesus,* Chapter IV §17.

The text states that "ecclesial communities" that do not meet such criteria should not, therefore, be referred to as "proper churches."[17] Numerous commentators on the document thus became concerned to ascertain whether this marked a distinct shift away from the ecumenical thinking not simply of the various interchurch discussions of recent decades, but also from the spirit of dialogue at Vatican II that gave rise to them, and that of Paul VI , indeed even—it could be argued—of John Paul II.[18] Obviously the document's meaning here is clear: it is referring to the Protestant denominations and the Anglican communion.

> On the other hand, the ecclesial communities which have not preserved the valid Episcopate and the genuine and integral substance of the Eucharistic mystery[19] are not Churches in the proper sense; however, those who are baptized in these communities are, by Baptism, incorporated in Christ and thus are in a certain communion, albeit imperfect, with the Church.[20] Baptism in fact tends *per se* toward the full develop-

---

17. Ibid. See also "Note on the Expression 'Sister Churches,'" 30 June 2000, and Michael A. Fahey, "Am I My Sister's Keeper?: The Vatican's New Letter on Sister Churches," *America*, 28 October 2000.

18. A case established well by, among numerous others, Gregory Baum, *Amazing Church*, chs. 4 and 5, who sees *Dominus Iesus* as a reversal not simply of the open dialogical spirit of Vatican II but also of documents such as *Dialogue and Mission* (released by the then-named Secretariat for Non-Christian Religions, 1984) and *Dialogue and Proclamation* (Pontifical Council for Interreligious Dialogue, 1991), which along with teachings and pronouncements by John Paul II helped indicate that dialogue is always to be respectful and sensitive and, in the case of the latter document, even hints that in certain situations the church must limit its mission to dialogue rather than proclamation (although both are fundamental to the churches' evangelizing mission, ibid., 115). Note, however, that with Baum's help, in chapter 6 of this volume we make the case that dialogue *is* evangelization, i.e., proclamation. Baum's verdict on *Dominus Iesus* is: "We note that the dialogue blessed by Cardinal Ratzinger is quite different from the dialogue across boundaries fostered by John Paul II . . . . In today's ethical horizon, it would be immoral to engage in ecumenical or interreligious dialogue, based on trust and aimed at mutual understanding, in order to persuade one's partners to change their religion. This seems to me quite basic. Ratzinger's proposal reflects an ethical horizon that the Church has left behind. . . . to enter into dialogue for the purpose of proselytizing would instrumentalize dialogue and destroy its profound meaning" (ibid., 120). For a selection of essays on Joseph Ratzinger's views here and in relation to the subject matter of *Dominus Iesus* in general, see his *Truth and Tolerance: Christian Belief and World Religions* (San Francisco: Ignatius Press, 2004), Most of these essays are from the 1990s, thus also from the period when the curial thinking reflected in *Dominus Iesus* was in formation. Baum's study illustrates the ambiguities of how John Paul II apparently embraced religious pluralism and commended it to Catholics in many statements, and yet church teaching in the final decade of his pontificate was often out of step with such sentiments. See *Amazing Church*, especially ch. 5.

19. *Unitatis redintegratio* 22.

20. Ibid., 3.

ment of life in Christ, through the integral profession of faith, the Eucharist, and full communion in the Church.[21]

The text continues, working toward a now somewhat "infamous" passage where, through a selective highlighting of the more negative and conservative elements of earlier church teaching documents, other Christian communions are referred to as being "defective." And, although more conciliatory parts of those other documents are (somewhat unavoidably) included, the emphasis here nonetheless seems intentionally more negative in tone. The perceived inferiority of other Christian communities is not left in doubt:

> "The Christian faithful are therefore not permitted to imagine that the Church of Christ is nothing more than a collection—divided, yet in some way one—of Churches and ecclesial communities; nor are they free to hold that today the Church of Christ nowhere really exists, and must be considered only as a goal which all Churches and ecclesial communities must strive to reach."[22] In fact, "the elements of this already-given Church exist, joined together in their fullness in the Catholic Church and, without this fullness, in the other communities."[23]

The document continues in this manner and, perhaps owing to its method of taking sentences here and there out of their wider documentary and indeed ecclesiological context, it was taken by many as saying that the mind of the Catholic Church toward other Christians in recent decades has been somewhat different from the way it has been interpreted and understood by numerous Catholics and their ecumenical partners alike.

> "Therefore, these separated Churches and communities as such, though *we believe they suffer from defects,* have by no means been deprived of significance and importance in the mystery of salvation. For the spirit of Christ has not refrained from using them as means of salvation which derive their efficacy from the very fullness of grace and truth entrusted to the Catholic Church."[24] The lack of unity among Christians is certainly a wound for the Church; not in the sense that she is deprived of her unity, but "in that it hinders the complete fulfilment of her universality in history."[25]

21. Cf. ibid., 22; *Dominus Iesus,* Chapter IV §17. Note that in both this passage and that quoted immediately above it we hear echoes of *Communionis notio* (see our previous chapter). Indeed, n. 59 of this section of *Dominus Iesus* refers to that document.

22. Congregation for the Doctrine of the Faith, Declaration *Mysterium Ecclesiae* 1.

23. *Ut unum sint* 14 (*Dominus Iesus* §17).

24. *Unitatis redintegratio* §3.

25. *Dominus Iesus,* Chapter IV §17 (my italics).

One could, of course, make the case that Vatican II's own documents did, indeed, contain such sentiments: is not the *Decree on Ecumenism* here cited? But the protracted debates at the Council over such documents, not to mention the efforts on the part of such figures as Cardinals Bea and Suenens, along with theological advisers such as Yves Congar and the like, in ensuring that a more positive ecumenical vision emerged from the Council, as well as both the words and deeds of Paul VI, suggest that a primary focus on the more negative elements is somewhat misleading,[26] or at least does not constitute the full picture. The language of Vatican II's documents, reflecting the debates that led to their formation, is in general much more nuanced than that of *Dominus Iesus*.

But this tone and language were not reserved solely for fellow Christians. The document goes on to state that non-Christian faiths are thus rendered still further away from the church in the text's implied hierarchy of paths to salvation,[27] of which the Catholic Church is perceived to be the truest and fullest.

> With the coming of the Saviour Jesus Christ, God has willed that the Church founded by him be the instrument for the salvation of all humanity (cf. Acts 17:30-31).[28] This truth of faith does not lessen the sincere respect which the Church has for the religions of the world, but at the same time, it rules out, in a radical way, that mentality of indifferentism "characterized by a religious relativism which leads to the belief that 'one religion is as good as another'"[29] If it is true that the followers of other religions can receive divine grace, it is also certain that *objectively speaking* they are in a gravely deficient situation in comparison with those who, in the Church, have the fullness of the means of salvation.[30]

Note that the documents of Vatican II are less helpful in supporting this shift in soteriological thinking, given the more positive emphasis contained in numerous conciliar documents with regard to other faiths.[31]

---

26. We shall see this in ch. 5, which explores Vatican II, Paul VI and the importance of ecclesial dialogue. See also, a special issue of *Louvain Studies* on Congar, (vol. 29, 2004) which includes the essay by Alberto Melloni, "Congar, Architect of *Unam Sanctam*," 222–38.

27. Cf. Chapter V.

28. Cf. *Lumen gentium* §17; John Paul II, Encyclical Letter *Redemptoris missio* §11.

29. John Paul II, Encyclical Letter *Redemptoris missio* §36.

30. *Dominus Iesus* §22 (emphasis in original). Cf. Pius XII, Encyclical Letter *Mystici corporis*, DS 3821.

31. As were the conciliar debates themselves: cf. the speech on the Council decree on ecumenism, *Unitatis redintegratio*, by the Bishop of Cuernavaca, Mexico, Sergio Méndez Arceo, "The Church as an Open Community," in Yves Congar, Hans Küng, and Daniel O'Hanlon, *Council Speeches of Vatican II* (London and New York: Sheed &

So what did this declaration represent? Chapter I said it was offering a "remedy" to relativism—so should it simply be judged, as many did judge it, as a timely reminder and articulation of certain fundamental tenets of the faith? Does it claim no more, as many commentators suggested, than any other major religion, in perceiving other paths to salvation as being inferior to the Catholic? Is it simply a document addressing certain postmodern ills and seeking to combat them with the "truth" of the Catholic Christian faith? Or does it, subtly or otherwise, actually proceed in a manner that was indeed untimely? Was the document born of a fear of postmodern trends and so perhaps issued in haste and in a form that could prove counterproductive? Does the document simply reiterate aspects of the Catholic tradition with regard to revelation, salvation, christology, ecclesiology, the kingdom, mission, evangelization, and interchurch and interfaith relations, particularly drawing on Scripture, certain patristic texts, and especially Vatican II and the teaching of John Paul II? Or does it actually draw together, in an a-contextual and a-historical fashion, a disparate collection of texts and teachings that fit poorly with the thrust of this declaration? Does it seek to impose on this age a very particular interpretation of the significance of the Catholic faith, of God's plan for human salvation and, of course, of the church itself? Is it an example of the "neo-exclusivistic" tendency we spoke of? A consideration of what a variety of commentators made of the document may help us discern possible answers to such questions.

Reactions to the Document: Catholic, Ecumenical, and Interfaith

A wide variety of responses appeared in reaction to the document. Perhaps a useful analogy may be drawn here with a much more monumental (and controversial) turning point in the history of the church and its doctrine. As in the debates that raged over papal infallibility before, during, and after Vatican Council I (1869–70), Catholic interpreters of *Dominus Iesus* fell into many camps. Some felt the document was a "public relations disaster" *(The Tablet)* and many feared the damage it would do to the vision of Vatican II, which committed the church to dialogue with the contemporary world. Others within and outside the Catholic Church described *Dominus Iesus* in terms such as "offensive," "insensitive," "archaic and outdated." Catholics working in interreligious contexts conveyed their dismay.

Ward, 1964) 118–21. He urges that ecumenism and the desire for unity be expanded to include people of all faiths and none: see especially p. 120.

Other Catholics believed, like the Vatican I "inopportunists," that while they agreed the document said nothing new (it rather reaffirmed fundamental tenets of Christian doctrine, albeit in uncompromising terms), it was uncalled-for and unnecessary to issue such a high profile document of such a tone at that particular time. There were still other Catholics, however, who shared the fervor for all things Roman of the nineteenth century "Ultramontanists" and applauded the firm commitment to Christian fundamentals in the document, commending its unswerving and unambiguous guidance. Even some non-Catholic groups of a "conservative" persuasion welcomed the issuing of such forthright doctrinal statements.[32] The appeal here was the manner of the document's reaffirmation of Christian "fundamentals." And yet this marks a peculiar "alliance" between groups on certain issues who would otherwise perceive others' communities to be ecclesially inferior to their own community.[33]

For many the major concern was how the cause of ecumenism might potentially be set back by the fallout from the document's publication. Commentators wrote that many church leaders appeared exasperated by the effect the document had on hitherto harmonious dialogue.[34] Across the Catholic world, leading church figures fervently sought to qualify and/or tone down the document's language or at least to challenge the more negative interpretations of its intentions. For example, in relation to the church in England and Wales, the Archbishop of Westminster (now Cardinal) Cormac Murphy-O'Connor stressed that *Dominus Iesus* was not intended for an audience outside the episcopacy and the theological community (though, as we have already noted, the text itself casts its net wider).

32. This adds further credence to our suggestions about the advent of a "transdenominational reformation." Stanley Hauerwas, for example, praised the document in a letter to the Durham (NC) *Herald-Sun* and in numerous other places as well. The journal *Pro Ecclesia* gathered a symposium on *Dominus Iesus* in its edition of Winter 2001 (vol. 10/1).

33. This was the case not only with regard to some approving reactions from Protestant and Orthodox scholars; even some reactions from Jewish and Muslim conservative voices could accept that the document was simply a Catholic version of the salvific "supremacy" that certain forms of their own faith proclaimed.

34. This was a sentiment shared also by some who had worked in the Vatican curia itself: see, e.g., Baum, *Amazing Church,* 120, who writes that John Paul's own statements (such as a message to an interreligious conference in Lisbon that year (in addition to the statement we have considered with regard to the Anglican communion) was of a very different character from *Dominus Iesus.* He adds the name of Cardinal Arinze to our list of Cassidy and Kasper as "dissenting" cardinals with regard to the tone of the text: "These three defended the imperative of ecumenical and interreligious dialogue and argued that engaging in it demands humility of the church."

Cardinal Edward Cassidy, head of the Pontifical Council for the Promotion of Christian Unity at the time of the document's release, went to great lengths to try to repair some of the damage the reaction to the document was believed to have caused ecumenical relations. In a speech at Worth Abbey (Sussex, UK), nearly a year after the release of the declaration, he admitted that *Dominus Iesus* could have been drafted in a better fashion and lamented the fact that neither he nor Walter Kasper (his successor as head of the council) had been present when most of the discussions that went into the formation of the document took place. But such a response does raise further questions with regard to the *modus operandi* of the CDF and the perceived anti-collegial mentality that has recently prevailed there.

Other members of various other Christian denominations and world faiths responded with a mixture of surprise, hurt, and anger. Ecumenical organizations expressed shock at the language used in the document. For example, the general secretary of the Lutheran World Federation, Dr. Ishmael Noko, told of his "dismay and disappointment" that the document ignored the wealth of many years' positive dialogue between Catholics and the Lutheran Church, adding that it also overlooked the language used to describe Lutheran ecclesial communities in the 1999 Catholic-Lutheran "Joint Declaration on Justification," which refers to them as "churches." The World Alliance of Reformed Churches considered withdrawing from scheduled talks with the Catholic Church and protested in the strongest terms to Cardinal Cassidy. Some Jewish groups wanted to cease all interfaith dialogue with the Catholic Church. Muslims pointed to "double standards" and logical inconsistencies in the document, which saw Islam as somehow defective yet also a means to closer unity with God. Representatives of other faiths expressed concern that their religion had been misunderstood and misrepresented in the document.[35]

Of course, the document was open to much misinterpretation and even misrepresentation. Nonetheless, many commentators, including those in positions of ecclesial authority, suggested that most of the fault for that lay in the language, tone, and style used by the document's author (or authors—it is believed, however, that the Salesian Fr. Angelo Amato drafted the document). Much theological analysis suggested that

35. A further variety of official responses and interpretive essays, Catholic, ecumenical, and interfaith, has been collected in a very useful volume by Stephen J. Pope and Charles Hefling, eds., *Sic et Non: Encountering Dominus Iesus* (Maryknoll, NY: Orbis, 2002).

Dominus Iesus contradicted or undermined other church documents as well as pastoral and ecumenical ventures. Those who offered such an assessment argued that the document appeared to go against the grain of Vatican II's perspective on such relations, as contained in *Dignitatis humanae* (the Declaration on Religious Liberty) and *Nostra aetate* (the Declaration on the Relations of the Church to Non-Christian Religions), not to mention some variance from *Unitatis redintegratio* (the Decree on Ecumenism). But many others of a similar mindset to that portrayed in the document were happy to see such documents undermined—and not simply within the Catholic community.[36]

There were calls for church leaders to take action to try and limit the perceived damage many believed the document had done to ecumenical and interfaith dialogue. One English bishop gathered an enormous collection of negative reactions and presented them to the authorities in Rome. The CDF itself held press conferences and issued further "clarifications" of the text. Even Pope John Paul II stepped in to reinforce his traditional support for ecumenical ventures and their integral and indispensable place in the life and mission of the church. In a speech given in the presence of the British Queen, who visited the Vatican in October of the year *Dominus Iesus* was published, John Paul stated that there could be "no turning back" from the goal of full unity toward which the Catholic and Anglican churches were working.[37]

Throughout 2000 and 2001 *Dominus Iesus* was a frequent topic of discussion in ecclesiological circles. Here we are returned to an aforementioned "disputation" as well, for among the more prominent and vociferous exchanges to emerge from the period following the release of the document was a protracted debate between Cardinal Ratzinger of the CDF, on the one hand, and (then newly created) Cardinal Walter Kasper, now President of the Pontifical Council for the Promotion of Christian Unity, on the other. In a series of exchanges[38] the latter stated

36. Again we might take Stanley Hauerwas' approval of the document as a representative example. Along similar lines see also his highly critical discussion of *Dignitatis Humanae*, "Not Late Enough: the Divided Mind of *Dignitatis Humanae Personae*," ch. 6 of his *A Better Hope: Resources for a Church Confronting Capitalism, Democracy and Postmodernity* (Grand Rapids: Brazos Press, 2000).

37. See *The Tablet* (21 October 2000) 1423.

38. Note again, of course, that Cardinal Ratzinger, in the view of many many, had famously changed his mind on this issue, given the position he took in the very first issue of *Concilium*. With regard to this debate see Kilian McDonnell, "The Ratzinger/Kasper Debate: The Universal and the Local Churches," *TS* 63 (2002) 1–24; Robert Leicht, "Cardinals in Conflict," *The Tablet* (28 April 2001); Walter Kasper, "'*Dominus Iesus*,' Address to the 17th Meeting of the International Catholic-Jewish Liaison Committee,"

his belief that the CDF's teaching reversed the traditional order of priority between the local and the universal church (in constitutive terms). Cardinal Kasper asserted that: ". . . a local Church is not a province or a department of the universal church: it is rather the Church in that particular place."[39] The esteemed ecclesiologist, Cardinal Avery Dulles, joined the debate, supporting the priority of the universal church over the local.[40]

Theological Debate and Analysis

Among the multitude of theological assessments of *Dominus Iesus,* one of the most lucid and pertinent was that produced by Thomas Rausch, Marie Chiltern Professor of Catholic Theology at Loyola Marymount University in California.[41] He acknowledges that *Dominus Iesus* was "written primarily for theologians,"[42] but also believes that it has nonetheless caused a great deal of confusion not only throughout the church, but even among the theologians it was meant to guide. This is particularly true of those engaged in ecumenical discussions and research.

Rausch writes that the document seems to imply that theological debate is closed on matters that the magisterium, particularly Vatican II, had previously left open.[43] Passages that merit closer attention include §17, which states that "ecclesial communities" without both a valid episcopate and eucharistic celebration are not churches "in the proper sense." There is also the issue of the status of orders in the churches born of the Reformation. On this issue Vatican II is particularly non-explicit. As Rausch's analysis demonstrates, the Council may have hinted toward some statement of incompleteness in such orders. Rausch believes something of a consensus exists among scholars that Vatican II suggested such orders were "illicit but not invalid"[44] or, quoting Cardinal Kasper, they

---

New York, May, 2001; Walter Kasper, "On the Church," *Stimmen der Zeit* (December 2000), reprinted in *America* 184 (April 2001) and *The Tablet* (21 June 2001). See also Walter Kasper, *Theology and Church* (London: SCM, 1989), Part Two: "The Church as Sacrament of Salvation," 111–94.

39. Walter Kasper, "On the Church."

40. See Avery Dulles "Ratzinger and Kasper on the Universal Church," *Inside the Vatican,* June, 2001.

41. Thomas Rausch, "Has the Congregation for the Doctrine of the Faith Exceeded its Authority?" *TS* 62 (2001).

42. Ibid., 802.

43. This recalls the problems identified in ch., 2 in relation to *Ad Tuendam Fidem.*

44. Ibid., 807.

have "a lack, but not complete absence" of ecclesial form).[45] Yet, as Rausch again shows, recent interpretations and ecumenical discussions often tend toward interpreting this in the light of the absence of full communion throughout Christianity in general rather than as a simple rejection of any claims to validity of such orders in the Protestant churches.

I might add that the *interpretation* of the distinction between "ecclesial community" and "church" with which *Dominus Iesus* seems to be operating[46] might appear to be somewhat contrived, given the ethos of much Catholic ecumenical theology in the post-Vatican II period. That the CDF took the rare step of actually issuing a document to explain and justify the line taken in *Dominus Iesus* over a month *before* releasing the declaration itself is telling.[47]

Francis Sullivan believes that Vatican II, while it employed these two distinctive terms, did not offer any definition of what it meant by the phrase "ecclesial communities," although the fact that it refers to certain communities separated from the Roman Catholic communion can be inferred from the Council's Decree on Ecumenism, together with other clarifications that appeared during the conciliar proceedings.[48] But Sullivan also notes that *Dominus Iesus* seems to suggest that the church of Christ is actually also "more extensive," and so to be found outside the Roman Catholic Church, as it appears to imply that other communities that preserve the episcopate and a valid understanding of the Eucharist are understood in the document to be "true particular" churches.[49] So for Sullivan more positive conclusions might still be drawn, at least as far as the question of where the church of Christ might be found: "Vatican II explained that the universal church exists 'in and from' the particular churches.[50] It would seem, therefore, to be the mind of the CDF that the church of Christ consists of all and only those which it calls 'true particular Churches.' While not all of these are 'fully' churches, they all have the essential gifts of episcopate and Eucharist and while not all are

---

45. Ibid., 810.

46. This is true no matter how much the author of the document believes it is following Vatican II here.

47. See "Note on the Expression 'Sister Churches,'" 30 June 2000.

48. Francis A. Sullivan, "Introduction and Ecclesiological Issues," chapter 1 of Pope and Hefling, eds., *Sic et Non,* 53.

49. Ibid., 54. Sullivan infers such conclusions partly on the basis of the official interpretation provided by the CDF at a press conference following the release of *Dominus Iesus* (ibid., 53–54).

50. *Lumen gentium* §23.

in full communion, their actual unity is seen as sufficient to justify speaking of them all together as constituting the one Church of Christ."[51]

Thus Sullivan sees this as a "positive" assessment of some non-Catholic churches, albeit one balanced by the negative assessment of others that lack valid episcopal orders. He also reminds us that Vatican II, while referring to the latter as "ecclesial communities" as opposed to "churches," "never flatly declared that the ecclesial communities are 'not churches in the proper sense.'"[52] However, in the wake of *Dominus Iesus* he sees less room for ecumenical hope, as §17 of the latter now denies that such communities are churches "in the proper sense." In addition, Sullivan, like others, notes that *Dominus Iesus* fails to refer to any of the positive agreements reached between Catholics and either Anglicans or Protestants through extensive dialogue. In contrast to

---

51. Sullivan, "Introduction and Ecclesiological Issues," 54. To explain the significance of this further: in general, Sullivan notes that this document actually offers a different interpretation of Vatican II to that which the CDF provided fifteen years prior to the release of *Dominus Iesus* (in its notification concerning Leonardo Boff's *Church, Charism and Power*, 1985), particularly with reference to the understanding of the Council's famous statement that the church of Christ "subsists in" the Catholic Church (as opposed to *Mystici Corporus Christi*, which equated the two). In 1985 the CDF countered Boff's suggestion that the church of Christ might subsist in other churches by firmly stating that *only* "elements" of that church could be found outside the Catholic Church. See also Dennis Doyle, "Communion, Reform and Liberation: Hans Küng, Leonardo Boff and the CDF," ch. 8 of *Communion Ecclesiology: Visions and Versions* (Maryknoll, NY: Orbis, 2000), especially 124–36. Sullivan believes that *Dominus Iesus* can actually be initially read in a more positive light: *Lumen gentium* §22 used the term *subsistit in*. Sullivan had long maintained that this is best translated as meaning "continues to exist in." But *Dominus Iesus* §16, and n. 56, would appear to further qualify the interpretation of *Lumen gentium* by rejecting the view that the formula *subsistit in* could also mean that "the one church of Christ could subsist also in non-Catholic churches and ecclesial communities." To this Sullivan responds, "I would insist that this is true only if *subsistit in* [*Lumen gentium* §8] means what the CDF now agrees it means" ("Introduction and Ecclesiological Issues," 52). In other words, Sullivan believes that the question of whether "only" elements of the church of Christ, as opposed to a subsistence of it, exist beyond the bounds of the Catholic Church, a question the 1985 *Notification* had appeared to settle, may, in light of *Dominus Iesus*, now appear not to be settled after all. I am, however, inclined to believe that more continuity exists between the intention of the 1985 and 2000 documents than such exegesis might suggest. Indeed, Sullivan's own analysis continues in a vein that would actually support such a conclusion vis-à-vis the differences between the tone of Vatican II's documentation and *Dominus Iesus* in particular. As we see immediately below, both Sullivan and Komonchak lend support to the contention that the intention at the Council was primarily positive, whereas in the latter two documents it is more negative.

52. Ibid., 54.

Vatican II, then, the tone of the 2000 document is certainly more negative here.[53]

But Sullivan also believes that what *Dominus Iesus* recognizes for those churches deemed to be "proper," Vatican II's Theological Commission also claimed could be said "although with some qualifications" for other "ecclesial communities." The commission spoke of their "truly ecclesial character" and noted that "in these communities the one sole church of Christ is present, albeit imperfectly, in a way that is somewhat like its presence in particular churches, and by means of their ecclesiastical elements the church of Christ is operative in them."[54] Such a positive assessment, Sullivan continues, was actually confirmed in similar terms by John Paul II in the encyclical *Ut Unum Sint*.[55] Sullivan nonetheless admits that *Dominus Iesus* offers a more restricted understanding of the church of Christ, despite the fruitful dialogue between the Catholic Church and those it designates "ecclesial communities." However, at the very beginning of his essay he points out the very significant fact that *Dominus Iesus* was a document of the CDF, not of Pope John Paul himself, and so "on questions regarding ecumenism, it has less authority than . . . *Ut Unum Sint*."[56]

Returning to Rausch's anaylsis, we learn that the third major area in which the document appears to settle an issue that Vatican II had decided not to is that of the link between episcopacy and ordination—specifically whether only orders conferred by a valid bishop are actually valid.

Once again in relation to developing trends we encounter throughout this volume, Rausch further notes that other church documents in recent times have also exhibited such trends as those he has identified in the tone of *Dominus Iesus*. For example, we have already encountered

53. Ibid., 55. See also Francis A. Sullivan, "The Impact of *Dominus Iesus* on Ecumenical Relations," *America* (28 October 2000), available at www.americapress. org/articles/sullivan-DI.htm.

54. *Acta Synodalia Concilii Vacticani Secundi* III/2, 335, cited in Sullivan, "Introduction and Ecclesiological Issues," 55. Here Joseph Komonchak lends further support, reminding us that, according to its own doctrinal commission, Vatican Council II chose to employ the term *subsistit in* "so that the expression might better accord with the affirmation of ecclesial elements that *are present* elsewhere," *AAS* III/1, 178, 80; see Joseph A. Komonchak, "Towards an Ecclesiology of Communion," ch. 1 of Giuseppe Alberigo and Joseph A. Komonchak, eds., *History of Vatican II* (Maryknoll, NY: Orbis; Leuven: Peeters, 2003) 4:42.

55. *Ut Unum Sint* §11; see Sullivan, "Introduction and Ecclesiological Issues," 55–56.

56. Ibid., 47.

an attempt to privilege the primacy of the universal over the local churches in *Communionis notio.* One can also witness the return to a minimalistic application of the term "ministry" in connection with the laity—most prominently in *Christifidelis Laici*—and the subsequent 1997 instruction *On Certain Questions Regarding the Collaboration of the Non-Ordained Faithful in the Sacred Ministry of the Priest.*

Rausch implies that, if his analysis of *Dominus Iesus* is correct, the CDF has perhaps *exceeded its authority.* At the very least, he suggests, the CDF should have made clear whether or not it was actually foreclosing debates Vatican II had *deliberately* left open. He notes that there is a great deal of difference between what count as "central truths of the Christian faith" and what is simply theological opinion—"even if it is the opinion of members of the Congregation for the Doctrine of the Faith."[57] The problem with *Dominus Iesus,* as Rausch concludes, is that it is unclear which is which in its pages. Worse still, its ambiguity extends to the status its author(s?) intended its readers to afford the statements contained in the document.[58]

We may now make some remarks concerning the document and its relevance to the wider debates with which this volume is concerned. The evidence suggests that *Dominus Iesus* is but a further illustration of shifting sands in the definition and operative understanding of the magisterium, the CDF, the status of Catholic theology, and the role and task of the Catholic theologian today.

Concerning ministry in particular, while Rausch is correct to focus on the disjunction between *Dominus Iesus* and Vatican II, the discrepancies between the document and aspects of the wider magisterium, (i.e., beyond the confines of the CDF and its own recent somewhat narrower understanding of the official magisterium) do not end there. Rausch mentions further church documents and also hints at discrepancies between Pope John Paul II's own teachings on ecumenism and *Dominus*

---

57. Rausch, "Has the Congregation for the Doctrine of the Faith Exceeded its Authority?" 810.

58. Sullivan also reminds his readers that, with regard to *Dominus Iesus,* "Theologians must distinguish between statements in it which are already dogmas of faith, and other statements that enjoy various lesser degrees of doctrinal weight. At the same time, a document such as this cannot be immune from respectful critique on the part of Catholic theologians. They have an indispensable critical role to play, not only with regard to what other theologians are saying, but also with regard to statements issued with ordinary, non-definitive teaching authority. Much of the progress made at Vatican II would have been impossible if it had not been for the critical work done by Catholic theologians, often at great cost to themselves, in the decades prior to the council" ("Introduction and Ecclesiological Issues," 48).

Iesus, as well as the many challenges from the aspect of the magisterium that marks the contribution of academic theologians.

But it is the ecclesiological and, more specifically, the ecumenical implications of the document that obviously give most cause for concern. One might thus go further than Rausch and suggest that the document challenges the actual *lived* witness to the gospel, particularly in relation to ecumenical relations and practice. Indeed, as the late church historian Adrian Hasting, pointed out the year before his untimely death, *Dominus Iesus* poses a particular problem for Catholics and Anglicans in the United Kingdom. And yet, during John Paul's visit to Britain in 1982, the distinguished Anglican theologian and clergyman Henry Chadwick, who had done so much to organize and facilitate the Pope's visit (not least when the Falklands war threatened to force its cancellation), was presented with the gift of a stole by the Pope himself.[59]

Hastings wryly raises the question that naturally occurs in the wake of *Dominus Iesus:* how do we interpret the Pope's actions, his intentions, and their implications? Or, as Hastings more humorously puts it: "If the Pope gave Henry Chadwick a stole, the special symbol of the priesthood, was it in order for Professor Chadwick to celebrate an invalid Eucharist?"[60] Indeed, Hastings' analysis goes further: ". . . it is fortunate that beyond such powerful gestures we have also the explicit affirmation by Pope Paul VI when in 1970 he called the Anglican Communion 'ever-beloved sister.' Unlike the note on sister Churches issued by Cardinal Ratzinger's congregation, this remark of Paul VI was included in the *Acta Apostolicae Sedis.* Is the cardinal affirming that Pope Paul was mistaken in what he said?"[61]

On the same issue Francis Sullivan suggests something of a *via media* in that we focus not simply on the validity of such orders, but rather on the "evident fruitfulness" of their ministry:

> . . . there can be no doubt about the life of grace and salvation which has been communicated for centuries through the preaching of the word of God and other Christian ministry in the Anglican and Protestant churches. We have to keep in mind that the "fullness" which Vatican II and *Dominus Iesus* attribute to the Catholic Church is a matter of *insti-*

---

59. A similar observation is made by Nicholas Lash, "On Defending the Faith," *The Tablet* (18 July 1998) 938.

60. Adrian Hastings, "Sisters for All That," *The Tablet* (21 October 2000) 1411.

61. Ibid. Note here the significance of the fact that Cardinal Ratzinger's commentary on *Ad Tuendam Fidem* also singled out the orders of the Anglican communion.

tutional integrity: a fullness of *the means of* grace which is not the same thing as the fullness of grace itself. There is no question of denying that other Christian communities, perhaps lacking something in the order of means, can achieve a higher degree of communion with Christ in faith, hope and love than many a Catholic community. Means of grace have to be used well to achieve their effect, and the possession of a fullness of means is no guarantee of how well they will be used.[62]

In light of our foregoing considerations, by now it might seem somewhat obvious that one of the foremost problems with the document is its superior tone. A leader in *The Tablet* put it thus: "It is widely stated that the text contains 'nothing new' but the objections come not so much to what is said as to what is not said, and to the exclusive and triumphalist tone."[63] As noted, a great many of the voices commenting on this text at the present time are of the opinion that it was published at a most inopportune moment and was most clumsy in expression. For many this document is a further example of the attempt to reinterpret and, for its critics, to reverse the mind and spirit of the *consensus fidelium* witnessed at Vatican II and increasingly developed and lived in the life of the church thereafter.

In effect, *Dominus Iesus* is a very prominent example of a document emerging from *within* one section of a particular community that purports to engage in ecclesiological hermeneutics but that many critics would perceive to be an example of an actual *refusal* to engage in meaningful hermeneutics that take account of the pluralistic world in which we live in these postmodern times. Indeed, it would appear that this document results in an undermining and, in some cases, even negation of the many positive steps taken earlier by the Catholic Church in dialogue with other

62. Sullivan, "Introduction and Ecclesiological Issues," 56 (italics supplied). See also Gregory Baum, who goes further still in "The Pilgrim State of the Christian Church," in Giuseppe Ruggieri and Miklós Tomka, eds., *The Church in Fragments: Towards What Kind of Unity? Concilium* 1997/3 (London: SCM, 1997) 116: "Vatican II also left us confused in regard to the status of the Catholic Church as the one true church of Christ. While the Decree on Ecumenism acknowledges the means of grace and the life of grace in the other churches and honors their role in the economy of salvation, it continues to affirm the Catholic Church as the one church in which the fullness of truth and grace prevails. *Yet the decree does not explain what this means.* In fact it uses the term 'fullness' in two almost contradictory senses: it speaks of the fullness of truth, grace and the means of salvation present in the Catholic Church [*Unitatis redintegratio* §2], and at the same time of the fullness with which Christ wants his earthly body to be endowed, which fullness lies in the future and represents the aim of the ecumenical movement [ibid., §24]. *But if fullness is a Spirit-guided task to be achieved in future history, how can any church claim this fullness at the present time?*" (italics supplied).

63. "Damage Limitation Needed" (21 October 2000) 1402.

Christian, religious, and human communities in general.[64] The language and tone of this document have suggested, to many within and outside the Catholic Church alike, that neither a true hermeneutical engagement as demanded by our times nor any charitable spirit of dialogue could be detected in the thinking that lies behind the elements of the document perceived to be absolutist and exclusivist pronouncements. Indeed, according to such an interpretation this document performed a great disservice to ecclesial hermeneutics and religious dialogue in general.

Thus, for its critics, the challenge is to discern whether such a shift in the tone and nuances of official Catholic statements suggests that here we are again returned to the rise of a neo-exclusivistic ecclesial mindset and the worrying re-emergence of superiorist and supremacist language—witnessed not simply in such documents as *Dominus Iesus* but in a varied collection of scholars and traditions seeking to offer certitude and enclosed communal security in the face of perceived postmodern threats: in other words, the "transdenominational reformation."

Attention to Consultation and Method

But in the specifically Catholic context further questions emerge. These include how church documents of this nature are commissioned, researched, composed, and released. Furthermore, *Dominus Iesus* suggested to many that there is a need for wide-ranging transformation of the processes of communication and discussion within and outside the church. Related to the latter is the issue of how far the CDF attempts to consult widely in the field on which it releases authoritative documents: for example, how diverse a panel of experts on religious pluralism and ecumenism was involved in the production of this document?

This particular declaration also gives rise to questions concerning the role of other Vatican departments and councils in relation to the Congregation for the Doctrine of the Faith. Finally, the document also points us toward the need for an open discussion of the demarcation between fundamental aspects of Catholic Christian doctrine and theological and ecclesiological *opinion*. We cannot hope to cover all such areas of concern comprehensively in one volume, let alone one chapter—but we shall touch on some of the more pertinent issues in relation to the overall direction of inquiry of the present volume.

64. See Gregory Baum, *Amazing Church*, 114–34, where he contrasts much good work on dialogue done by other Vatican departments, inspired by Vatican II documentation, with the tone of documents such as *Dominus Iesus*, which counters such efforts.

To illustrate why questions of method and consultation are so important, given the authoritative tone adopted in *Dominus Iesus* and the requisite authority bestowed on it by the faithful within the church and by numerous commentators (perceiving it to be truly representative of Catholic beliefs in *all* its aspects rather than just with regard to certain fundamental beliefs), assessments by experts in other fields can prove illuminating. One particularly revealing analysis is by the biblical scholar Pheme Perkins. She examines the way in which the document pulls together various biblical passages and sentences and uses them in the service of the general ecclesiological and religious case it is making. She finds that the lack of due attention to biblical scholarship, to historical and textual context and, above all else, to the *eschatological* context of the New Testament texts used therein is cause for concern.

Echoing our earlier suggestions, Perkins suspects that behind the triumphalism of the document lies a deep-seated *anxiety* brought about by the vagaries of the late-twentieth-century and early-twenty-first-century postmodern context—in particular the impact of interchurch and interreligious dialogue on the identity of the Catholic Church. It is not that there are not many genuine questions to be explored in relation to the latter, but she is nonetheless moved to ask: "Are its authors afraid that we will not be able to find a faithful and credible witness for the so-called postmodern world?"[65]

But her main concern is where *Dominus Iesus* turns "defensive" and "confuses centuries of faithful testimony to the gospel of Jesus Christ with never being wrong in what one says that 'good news' implies in the concrete situations of history."[66] Perkins is especially alarmed by the document's statement that those are in error who tend to "read and interpret scripture outside the Tradition and the Magisterium of the Church."[67] Perkins is an esteemed biblical scholar of international and long-standing repute. So it would prove foolish to ignore her concern that "*Dominus Iesus* treats examples of scripture . . . as warrants for dogmatic assertions that exist without context, whether that be within the texts that make up the canon, as representative of developments in

65. Pheme Perkins, "New Testament Eschatology and *Dominus Iesus*," ch. 4 of Pope and Heffling, eds., *Sic et Non*, 82. She draws on the work of sociologist David Lyon to illustrate that the document portrays several symptoms of an institution that feels threatened by the postmodern age, despite the awareness of the realities of postmodernity found elsewhere in the document. See David Lyon, *Jesus in Disneyland: Religion in Postmodern Times* (New York: Polity, 2000).

66. "New Testament Eschatology and *Dominus Iesus*," 80.

67. *Dominus Iesus*, Introduction §4

which the people of God were addressing concrete situations, or as texts that have had a checkered 'post-history' in Jewish and Christian circles."[68] But Perkins is also concerned that it seems the document does not limit the a-contextual and a-historical use of sources to Scripture alone, further emphasizing, for the discussions underway in this volume, that the methodological implications of the document really do merit further scrutiny.[69] "Neither scripture nor tradition are permitted a voice except as they are employed by the magisterium, which to this untrained eye appears to be found in church documents that are also treated as though they enunciated universal, univocal propositions that have no need of context or argument. So even the exegete who agrees that much of what *Dominus Iesus* wishes to affirm is crucial to our Catholic identity, and even that it can be discovered in scripture and tradition, comes away feeling that she or he has been hit with a sucker punch."[70]

But perhaps the most significant trend Perkins detects in the document and the response to postmodernity that lies behind it is the fact that it has "no ear whatsoever for the eschatological tonality of New Testament texts,"[71] which means also that it robs itself of the possibility of being attentive to those in this world who most need the voice of the gospel and who bear a close resemblance in many ways to the people to and for whom the gospel was first preached. These are the "choiceless," those who today are rendered still more powerless by the postmodern evils of globalization, those David Lyon refers to as the socioeconomic "alter-egos" of the elites who have increasing privileges in terms of education, technology, trans-national movement, etc.[72] The gospel today, as then, gives hope to such groups. But it is hope in the "end" that the first Christians believed in. Perkins sees the dismissal of certain forms of "kingdom"-oriented ecclesiology—because *Dominus Iesus* perceives

---

68. "New Testament Eschatology and *Dominus Iesus*," 80. As just one example Perkins cites the use made in *Dominus Iesus* of the letter to the Hebrews concerning the "once for all sacrifice" of Christ. She notes that the document shows no regard to the *polemical* context of Heb 9:11-14 vis-à-vis the perceived inferior sacrifices of the Jewish cult at that time (ibid., 81).

69. Here I might also add, as a further example, section 2 of Joseph Ratzinger's essay entitled "The Witness of the New Testament Regarding the Origin and Essence of the Church," ch. 1 of his *Called to Communion: Understanding the Church Today* (San Francisco: Ignatius Press, 1996) 21–40. It seems to be less about the New Testament witness *per se* and much more about contemporary issues and divisions in ecclesiology, despite the fact that its composition does resemble an *ad fontes* form of procedure.

70. Ibid., 81–82.

71. Ibid., 83.

72. Ibid., 82–83; Lyon, *Jesus in Disneyland*, 145.

them as overtly separating the kingdom from Christ and the church—as a prime example of such a lack of attention to eschatology.[73]

Perkins reminds us that we must distinguish between the divine grace the church can communicate and "particular persons and circumstances that have been entrusted with ecclesial authority" and that, in contrast to the former that is forever united with Christ, "always stand under God's judgment."[74] She thus concludes that "*Dominus Iesus* speaks with the voice of the elites in the twenty-first-century global village, not with the voice of the pious, humble ones like Mary or Peter—not even with the voice of the divided, persecuted, yet growing church of the pre-Constantinian centuries. These Christians knew that but for God's sustaining power, they could be wiped out. They hoped for the coming of the Lord precisely because existence was so fragile."[75]

Perkins goes on to remind us that the New Testament addresses the whole subject of evangelization from a marginal perspective, as opposed to one from the "center of power."[76] The latter compounds the "triumphalist, over-realized eschatology" (particularly in over-identifying the kingdom with the church) of *Dominus Iesus*—ironic, given that the document cites Paul, who chastised the Corinthians for the very same, just as it compounds the document's seeming inattention to the humble, cross-centered nature of Paul's understanding of apostolic authority.[77] Perkins's forthright conclusion is that

> *Dominus Iesus* presumes that Catholics draw their faith neither from scripture nor from tradition but from the ecclesial documents in which catchphrases and references from the former are passed through as rhetorical ornaments. The consequences of such disregard for the sources of revelation is alienation between those in control of such documents and the rest of the faithful, so the church's legitimate concern about retaining basic concepts of Christian faith appears to be no more than a power play.[78]

Even if Perkins's forthright criticisms prove only partially correct, and I am inclined to agree with the majority of what she writes, does this not point toward further difficulties perceived in a neo-exclusivist approach to the postmodern world—that it lessens the power of the

---

73. And Perkins believes the author(s) of *Dominus Iesus* to be "no better at reading patristic texts than they were at reading the New Testament" (ibid., 83).

74. Ibid., 83.

75. Ibid., 83–84.

76. Ibid., 84.

77. Ibid., 85–86

78. Ibid., 88.

church to speak out on behalf of those for whom the gospel charges it to speak? At the very least, does it not suggest that the possible "fault lines" betrayed by the clashes between not simply theologies of liberation and the CDF in the 1980s (foreshadowed by investigations in the 70s), but also between the CDF and theologies of inculturation and contextualization, betray a much deeper divide concerning how best to confront the oppression that subjugates the least of Christ's brethren in these times?[79] And if the perception of the faithful can indeed be that *Dominus Iesus* and like pronouncements are a "power-play," as Perkins suggests, then have certain offices of the church in Rome failed to heed the warnings of Foucault with regard to the interplay of power and authentic human existence and community in our times?

At this juncture it remains to be seen whether this text will be embraced fully throughout the church as definitively authoritative or whether its critics will insure that it becomes embarrassingly confined to the dusty shelves, save for the eager attention of later students of ecclesiastical, ecumenical, and interfaith history (the fate of so many documents issued by ecclesial authorities). We shall see what judgment the passage of time brings for *Dominus Iesus*. In the future, the advent of yet another new papacy and/or an ecumenical council might greatly overshadow its impact and long-term significance.[80]

Nonetheless, the document would appear to represent both a symptom and a cause of the situation facing the church in the contemporary "postmodern" era. It illustrates a great number of the most pressing ecclesiological issues of concern today, and hence serves as an excellent case study for discussions among groups in the church, the wider Christian community, and among interested parties of all faiths or none in relation to the place and future of the Catholic Church in the postmodern context.[81] Increasingly central to such discussions will be the ecclesial agenda

79. See Gerard Mannion, "What's In a Name? Hermeneutical Questions on Globalisation, Catholicity and Ecumenism," *New Blackfriars* (May 2005).

80. One anticipates with much hope the discussions generated by the forthcoming document from the World Council of Churches, *The Nature and Mission of the Church*.

81. Examples of further noteworthy interpretations of and reactions to the document include John D'Arcy May, "Catholic Fundamentalism? Some Implications of *Dominus Iesus* for Dialogue and Peacemaking," in Michael J. Rainer, ed., *"Dominus Iesus" Anstössige Wahrheit oder anstössige Kirche?* (Münster, Hamburg, and London: LIT-Verlag, 2001); Christine Van Wijnbergen, "Reactions to *Dominus Iesus* in the German-Speaking World," *Concilium* 2001/3, 147–52; Richard McBrien, *"Dominus Iesus*—an Ecclesiological Critique," www.sedos.org/english/McBrien.htm; Francis A. Sullivan, "The Impact of *Dominus Iesus* on Ecumenical Relations," *America* (28 October 2000), see www.americapress.org/articles/sullivan-DI.htm; that particular

pursued by Pope Benedict XVI. And, of course, Joseph Ratzinger's vision of the challenges postmodernity poses to Christianity—in particular, the church's "Babylonian Captivity,"[82] a vision obviously shared by a large number of Catholics, is far from being unique when one considers parallel developments in other Christian communions.

In all, then, a very *postmodern* debate was indeed raging when *Dominus Iesus* was composed, released, and discussed. But the postmodern world itself has changed greatly since the document's release, with events such as 9/11, further atrocities across the globe, wars in Afghanistan and Iraq, and a terrible and seemingly endless spiral of violence and infringement of human dignity and rights that often masquerades as a war on terror (but often employs the most terrifying tactics in pursuit of its ends). In the midst of an increasingly polarized world, with its divisions along the lines of faith and culture driven by various forms of "fundamentalist" thinking (whether religious, political, scientific, economic, or otherwise), the perils of accentuating difference in a negative light at the expense of highlighting the necessity of dialogue and commonality were brought home to people of all faiths and none in a manner the intensity of which has not been seen since perhaps the atrocities of the twentieth century's world wars.

It also appears that on occasion Pope Benedict has sought to counter the evils that can emerge from such a negative accentuation of difference for, in a New Year message for 2006, he did seek to urge all to recognize that the whole world is but one family. And, of course, the ministry of unity of the servant of the servants of God is a very different undertaking to the role of being prefect of the CDF. Pope Benedict has declared that Christian unity is his foremost priority. Thus the following chapters engage in constructive criticism in an effort to serve such ends, in however small a way: to help foster conversation and dialogue throughout the human family and to further energize the Catholic contribution to this. For it is to such a mission that the church is called. Some would suggest that the fact that *Dominus Iesus* generated all the disagreement that it did, and that open discussion was able to take place, is a positive sign.

---

issue of *America* was devoted to discussions of the document and also contains articles by Michael A. Fahey, "Am I My Sister's Keeper? The Vatican's New Letter on Sister Churches," and Francis X. Clooney, "*Dominus Iesus* and the New Millennium," along with an editorial on "Ecumenical Courtesy"; John Prior, "*Dominus Iesus* or A Plea to Humility?" 10/11/2000, http://www.sedos.org/english/Prior_2.htm.

82. Joseph Ratzinger, "Introductory Thoughts on the State of the Church," in *Two Say Why. Why I Am Still a Christian, by Hans Urs von Balthasar, and Why I Am Still in the Church, by Joseph Ratzinger,* trans. John Griffiths (London: Search Press; Chicago: Franciscan Herald Press, 1973) 67.

The church might not be in so bad a state as to quell all disagreement and dissent.

But developments such as the perceived "subsuming" of the Pontifical Council for Interreligous Dialogue into the Pontifical Council for Culture, along with Pope Benedict's controversial "illustration" in his September 2006 lecture at Regensburg, which deeply offended many Muslims, demonstrate that there is still cause for concern on many issues.

The character and tone of *Dominus Iesus* and of the ecclesiology that informs it and that it reflects are, indeed, it would appear, distinct from the prevailing character, tone, and ecclesiology of the documents of Vatican II. In this final analysis, then, this can perhaps best be summed up and illustrated by quoting from Eugene D'Souza, the Archbishop of Bhopal, who addressed the Council during the debates on ecumenism:

> It is true that we Catholics need not cultivate an inferiority complex. But the time is long overdue for us to get rid of any superiority complex. And we must certainly do our best to root out that oversimplification: "We possess the truth; the others say the same things as we do or they are in error; therefore we need not listen to them except to refute them. Horace said "To learn from the enemy is legitimate"—*a fortiori* from brothers in Christ. For "catholic" means "universal." Just as Christ took to himself everything human, sin alone excepted, so Catholicism which is true to its name should take to itself everything which is Christian, leaving out negations. In actual fact, for the principal first fruits of renewal we are heavily indebted to others—for the biblical movement to the Protestants, and for the liturgical movement to the Orthodox. Relying on their help, let us abandon those traditions which belong only to a particular school of theology or national character or religious order and which we have repeatedly confused with Tradition with a capital T. Or let us make certain superficial and peripheral devotions give way to what is deep and central. All this can help us to grasp more perfectly the mystery of Christ and the Church.[83]

But here, then, let us reiterate that this present volume will be arguing that any move away from the notion of the "open church" that Vatican II helped give life to is most likely to lead to further frustration for the church in its task of fulfilling its gospel mission in our time. Better that, instead of allowing (in Lieven Boeve's terms) a "closed" narrative to prevail—what we have termed an imposed "official ecclesio-

---

83. Eugene D'Souza, "Intellectual Humility," in Yves Congar, Hans Küng, and Daniel O'Hanlon, eds., *Council Speeches of Vatican II* (London and New York: Sheed and Ward, 1964) 142.

logical paradigm"[84]—the church return once again to discerning the "signs of the times" in an open and constructive *as well as critical* perspective.[85] As Jean-François Lyotard said in response to the broader cultural, artistic, intellectual, scientific, and political reactionary forces at work in resisting "the postmodern," a response that, I suggest, would nonetheless appear to have very deep theological implications for our times, "the answer is: Let us wage a war on totality; let us be witnesses to the unpresentable; let us activate the differences and save the honor of the name."[86] Thus the church in our times needs to foster and develop its own ecclesiological "postmodern critical consciousness." Pheme Perkins believes that *Dominus Iesus'* inattention to eschatology could undermine the church's understanding of how Christ intended his disciples to bring his teaching to all nations. The earliest Christians, it seemed, knew better how to "evangelize a world full of competing religious traditions."[87] Boeve warns that "every (closed, master) narrative that aims at the authoritarian reduction of multiplicity on the grounds of its own premises (thus stripping the other of his/her/its otherness) is open to criticism. From the postmodern perspective it would appear that only those narratives which admit to the specificity and limitedness of their own perspective and which witness to the impossibility of integrating the remainder are worthy of any claim to legitimacy."[88]

The remaining chapters of this book will seek to chart what the church might gain from developing its own ecclesiological understanding for our times in the light of "postmodern critical consciousness."

---

84. See chs. 1 and 2 above.

85. Recall Baum's admiration, in *Amazing Church*, that the church of Vatican II not only learned well from modernity but also helped unmask its "sinister side," as well as the parallels he draws between the church of and post Vatican II and critical theory.

86. Lyotard, "Answering the Question: What is Postmodern?" 82. A reflection on his arguments regarding the theological connotations and implications on pp. 79–81 might also be instructive: here I am, of course, drawing parallels between his notion of the "unpresentable" and modern and postmodern transcendental thinking, as well as the recent revival in mystical theology, along with the great tradition in Christian theology (with analogous traditions in other world religions) of acknowledging that God, as God is in Godself, is ultimately beyond unaided definitive human comprehension and so representation.

87. Perkins, "New Testament Eschatology and *Dominus Iesus*," 88.

88. Lieven Boeve, *Interrupting Tradition* (Leuven: Peeters, 2004) 91.

PART III

THE SCIENCE OF BRIDGEBUILDING

Chapter Five

The Science of Bridgebuilding:
From Confrontation to Conversation

Thus far we have encountered a number of issues that have proved detrimental to the communion shared by Catholics in our times. We identified as particular difficulties developments such as the advent of neo-exclusivism, the attempt to impose a kind of official ecclesiology across the entire church universal, and the inward-looking, seemingly world-renouncing mindset that has set back ecumenism and dialogue with other faiths. Furthermore, we noted that the renewed and ongoing ecclesiological impasse concerning unity and diversity, along with the debates about the place of the local church in relation to the church universal, have had a profound effect on the life and harmony of the Catholic communion in recent decades. The need for a hermeneutical undertaking with regard to the Catholic Church vis-à-vis religious "others" was also identified. These things formed the basis of discussion in chapters 3 and 4.

We could go on to chart further developments such as the "creeping infallibilism" and absolutist tendencies of the magisterium in postmodern times, the intolerance of dissent from official pronouncements and the "demand" of obedience, and the issues pertaining to the nature, understanding, and exercise of teaching authority today and the role of the Catholic theologian.

But it would appear that one common denominator throughout is the simple fact that too many Catholics share a sense that many of those in positions of ecclesial authority, and particularly in Rome, do not appear to be listening very much to any voices other than those that are in agreement with themselves and their own ecclesiological "blueprint" and structural principles. There appears to be little genuine conversation between those in positions of high authority in the church and those over whom and, we must not forget, *on behalf of whom* such authority is exercised. Indeed, if one takes the example of an official document such as *Donum Veritatis* we see that voices that do not fall into harmony with such official opinions are not simply ignored as valid conversation partners; they are rejected out of hand as voices of *dissent*. And, lest we forget, it is not simply the laity or those deemed to be of "lesser" rank among the clergy and religious who have found a deaf ear frequently turned to their supplications. Paul Lakeland goes so far to state that the "greatest tragedy" of the pontificate of John Paul II "was the failure to make collegiality a living reality."[1] We have sought to suggest that something is awry here, and we have been concerned with exploring the reasons why such ecclesiological developments are not serving the church well in its bid truly to live out the gospel mission in a postmodern age. Time and again, the issues we have been considering have pointed in the direction of ecclesial conversation, of dialogue and the need for more and better forms of it.

Hence this chapter makes a case for the ecclesial, doctrinal, and moral *necessity* of genuine and wide-ranging dialogue among people within the Catholic Church, and also with those in other Christian communions, those of other faiths, and even with those of no faith. Vatican II sought to commend such an approach. Our foregoing chapters suggest that the church's call to encounter and dialogue has somewhat stalled in recent decades. Thus we consider how the church's mission in this regard might be revivified, focusing first and foremost on dialogue *within* the Catholic communion.

Note that here we are not so much concerned with the ongoing and most commendable work of those Pontifical Councils and bilateral and multilateral Christian and religious groups and committees who continue to pursue transformative and fruitful work in the field of dialogue.[2] Rather, we are focusing on the more general impasse that seems to have been reached throughout the church with regard to dialogue—an impasse that hinders and even at times contradicts much of the sterling

1. Paul Lakeland, *Liberation of the Laity* (New York: Continuum, 2003) 115.
2. See Gregory Baum, *Amazing Church: A Catholic Theologian Remembers a Half Century of Change* (Maryknoll, NY: Orbis, 2005), chs. 4 and 5.

work carried out by the aforementioned bodies. Furthermore, the very positive things that various departments declare about dialogue, along with similar sentiments even in papal statements, are usually concerned with ecclesial dialogue *ad extra* (i.e., with other Christians and faiths). *Contra* Pope Paul VI and *Ecclesiam suam,* as we shall see, such sentiments in recent times do not appear to be applied sufficiently to the Catholic Church *ad intra.* Indeed, as Pope Benedict's first encyclical conspicuously illustrates, divisions and disagreements quite obviously obstruct the very business of the church itself—its mission to preach the gospel, to put that radical vision of love into practice. Paul VI's remarks in *Evangelii nuntiandi* also make it clear that divisions stand in the way of evangelization (i.e., of preaching the gospel and putting it into practice). "The power of evangelization will find itself considerably reduced if those who proclaim the gospel are divided among themselves in all sorts of ways. Is this not perhaps one of the greatest sicknesses of evangelization today? Indeed, if the gospel which we proclaim is seen to be rent by doctrinal disputes, ideological polarizations or mutual condemnations among Christians . . . how can those to whom we address our preaching fail to be disturbed, disoriented or even scandalized?"[3]

Peter Hebblethwaite, commenting on this very passage, felt that the entire text of *Evangelii nuntiandi* constituted a "heartfelt plea" on the part of Paul VI "for unity within the church, without which the work of evangelization will not get off the ground."[4] Such sentiments marked an openness, an honesty, a willingness to engage that appeared to encapsulate the spirit not just of Vatican II, but of the age.

Now, of course, some might say that within the pages of this book we have leveled criticisms that are uncharitable, and that we have raised issues in a fashion that may be polarizing. Some might question the "tone" of the criticisms here. Certain proponents of such a response, it must be said, might appear swayed by the recent climate of ecclesiological amnesia and ecclesial revisionism in the church today. But, and of greater concern, this is also a familiar response on the part of those within the church today who wish to see no criticism of the official authorities, but rather would commend a blind and obsequious obedience regardless of the implications of certain teachings and actions by those holding positions of ecclesial power and authority. To such a charge I would respond that, in contrast to Paul VI's "heartfelt plea" for unity,

---

3. *Evangelii nuntiandi* §77.
4. Peter Hebblethwaite, *The Year of Three Popes* (London: Collins Fount, 1978) 18.

in recent decades, as we have earlier noted, there has been a systematic attempt to quell disagreement with the official church authorities in a fashion that has been heavy-handed, exceeding the limits of the official magisterium, and the antithesis of the spirit of charity and dialogue that, as we shall argue, were the true missionary and ecclesiological legacies of both Vatican II and the pontificate of Paul VI. In other words, both a challenge and a plea must be made to those who, for whatever reason, either see no need for or even allow obstacles to stand in the way of genuine dialogue, or who dismiss out of hand all forms of what is termed "dissent," and this must be done on moral, theological (including doctrinal), evangelical, and ecclesiological grounds.

The writings, letters, sermons and addresses of both John Paul II and Benedict XVI (the latter both before and after his election) contain numerous references to dialogue. And all in the church should be grateful that dialogue remains a theme in recent papal pronouncements. But if such sentiments are to bear lasting fruit and to avoid being viewed with not a little irony and also avoid being characterized primarily as rhetorical statements with other ends in mind, much more still needs to be done to facilitate genuine dialogue within and outside the church. Such is the concern of this chapter and the next.

Here I wish to argue that dialogue *within* the church is as important as dialogue with others beyond the Catholic communion. Indeed, unless true dialogue exists and flourishes within the church, how can its members hope to engage in fruitful and lasting dialogue with others? It is to the credit of many within the church that such ecumenical dialogue has prospered and continues to prosper despite the paucity of intra-ecclesial dialogue within Catholicism. Here, perhaps, we might take soundings to learn from successful ecumenical conversations and apply their methodology to the efforts to foster greater dialogue "closer to home." In turn, of course, the flourishing of such dialogue will feed back into ecumenical and interreligious and global conversations *ad extra*.

How might one settle on a different approach in relation to these issues in a more positive fashion? What methodological principles might be discerned in order to begin such a task? First, recent research suggests that one must embrace a *conversational* method.[5] But a *true* conversation

5. For example, the various research projects, conferences, and publications undertaken by such ventures as the UK Queen's Foundation Working Party on Authority and Governance in the Roman Catholic Church; the Common Ground Initiative, USA; *Reflexiones Sobre La Autoridad Y Su Ejercico En La Iglesia Catolica* at the *Centro Bellarmino* in Santiago, Chile; and the Authority and Governance Seminars

can never be one-sided. There is a need to flesh out what a systematic and conversational method for dialogue might look like.[6] In such an undertaking one may both learn from ecumenical ventures and help make some contribution, however small, to such ventures in the future. How can the many necessary conversations the church is crying out for in our times be facilitated? Such questions will form the focus of this chapter.

The "Legacy" of Vatican II?

A further fundamental area of impasse—related to all the issues mentioned above that we have encountered in differing forms along the way, concerns the legacy of Vatican II. Much disagreement exists over the "true" ecclesiological vision and legacy of the Council. From Cardinal Ratzinger to the theologians of liberation to the respective

---

at the Jesuit Institute, Boston College, USA, which has also recently launched its wide-ranging and impressive initiative "Church in the Twenty-first Century" under the direction of Timothy Muldoon. Paul D. Murray's project exploring "Receptive Ecumenism," based at Durham University, England, offers much promise here also. On the last, see the reports on the hugely significant gathering at a colloquium in honor of Cardinal Walter Kasper, "Catholic Learning: Explorations in Receptive Ecumenism" 12–17 January 2006, *The Tablet* (21 January 2006). See, also the forthcoming volume on this theme edited by Murray, *Catholic Learning: Explorations in Receptive Ecumenism* (London and New York: Oxford University Press, 2007). On the concept of a dialogical ecclesiology see also the impressive study by Bradford Hinze, *Practices of Dialogue in the Roman Catholic Church: Aims and Obstacles, Lessons and Laments* (New York and London: Continuum, 2006). In this book I present a case for the pressing need for a dialogical ecclesiology and suggest ways in which a methodology might begin to be developed. Both the volume edited by Murray and that authored by Hinze further explore the methodological aspects of what is needed to further dialogue.

6. Here, note that the document issued in September, 1970, by the Secretariat for the Promotion of the Unity of Christians, namely, *Reflections and Suggestions Concerning Ecumenical Dialogue*, the result of various consultations from 1966 onward, does *not* appear in *AAS*. The document, sought "to offer some orientations for an important modern phenomenon (the development of dialogue in the modern world, and especially among Christians)" in light of Vatican II and related teachings of the era. See the text of the document in Austin Flannery, ed., *Vatican II: the Conciliar and Post-Concilar Documents* (Dublin: Dominican Publications, 1992) 535–53. It contains sections on the "Nature and Aim of Ecumenical Dialogue," the "Bases," "Conditions," and "Method" of dialogue, as well as its "Subjects" and "Forms." It states that the document "seeks to indicate pastoral orientations which have doctrinal foundations," ibid, 537. Here also we see reiterated the theological *necessity* of dialogue. See also later curial documents, including in particular *Dialogue and Mission*, issued by the Secretariat for Non-Christian Religions (1984), and *Dialogue and Proclamation*, issued by the Pontifical Council for Interreligious Dialogue (the secretariat was given this new name in 1988) (1991). These are discussed by Baum, *Amazing Church*, ch. 5.

adherents of *Communio* or *Concilium* approaches to the church—all claim to be the "true heirs" of the Council.

But I wish to argue that those who seek any "definitive" ecclesiology in a fixed sense in the documents of Vatican II are looking for the wrong thing and in the wrong place. This notwithstanding *Lumen gentium's* rich discussion of the various images and visions of the church, culminating in the notion of "the people of God." Instead, I would suggest that the enduring legacy of Vatican II, in accord with John XXIII's call for *aggiornamento,* is its unswerving commitment to *dialogue* among the human family. Hence in a postmodern age and an age of globalization, when all manner of conflicts take on previously unprecedented global relevance, such a vision remains as cogent and as hope-filled as ever. To this we now turn focusing, in particular, upon the conciliar document that articulated the notion of dialogical ecclesiology throughout.

Vatican II was not a council where such definitive and fixed agreement could be achieved, given the differences of opinion represented there. Indeed, the council fathers quite wisely avoided definitive pronouncements on a wide range of issues where they realized that dialogue was to be preferred, quite literally, to pontification. It has somehow become popular to castigate *Gaudium et Spes* in recent years, or to subordinate its significance relative to a particular reading of *Lumen gentium.* Indeed, ecclesial critics from the most rigidly conservative to the most fervently radical have suggested that it is now hopelessly out of date and so has little to offer us today. Others seek to perceive its "faults" as being the result of too much "optimistic" French influence at the expense of more "pessimistic" German input (perhaps overlooking that such debates were had at the time).

But aside from the fact that such criticism may be dependent on a distant memory of what the text of that document actually contains, it also demonstrates a fundamental misunderstanding of the *type* of document *Gaudium et Spes* was. Of course there are sections of the text that outline certain social, political, and ecclesial aspects of the 1960s. Quite naturally, these will now seem out of date. But by far the greatest portion of the document is concerned *not* with offering specific descriptive, prescriptive, and definitive teaching, but with something very different.

It should be remembered (because many do seem to forget the actual implications of this fact in recent years) that *Gaudium et Spes* was not a *dogmatic* constitution, but a *pastoral* one. It was concerned with offering general guidelines, encouragement, and methodological pointers toward how people in the church could best discern the now famous "signs of the times" and so live out the mission of the gospel anew in their day. Remember, also, that the title should really be translated into English as the Pastoral Constitution not on the church in the "modern world"—which would now seem quite dated to those shaped by cultures all too aware that modernity has, in many respects, passed on (to be supplanted by postmodernity, the end of history, a "brave new world order," or whatever may suit their particular outlook). The Latin text and most other translations speak of the church in *contemporary* times, or of the church in the world of *today*.[7] The title of the document is thus better rendered as "The Pastoral Constitution on the Church *in Our Times*."[8]

If one reads the whole document in that light, one will see that so much of it is as relevant, resourceful, and energizing today as it was when first promulgated in those hope-filled days toward the end of the Council. Because it is a pastoral constitution its teaching is less concerned with the detailed substance than with the pastorally-empowering *form* of ecclesiological vision and mission. In this sense it is in marked contrast to any determined and deterministic, any "official" or "blueprint" ecclesiology. *Gaudium et Spes* offers a vision that is primarily concerned with discernment; therefore subsequent generations can learn much from it. So in one sense much of what it teaches has a timeless quality—it will always address the church in "our times"—and whether those times be the modern world, the postmodern world, or the ages yet to come, *Gaudium et Spes* will have much to teach Catholics and others concerned with justice, freedom, peace, and love, that is to say, with human fulfilment and salvation, both individual and

7. See the informative treatment of the background to the constitution in general and this phrase in particular in Richard Schenk, "*Officium signa temporum perscrutandi:* New Encounters of Gospel and Culture in the Context of the New Evangelisation" (in papers collected from *Call to Justice—Gaudium et Spes 40 Years On*, www.stthoma.edu/gaudium). Schenk also reminds his readers that the document opens with reference not just to the "joy and hope" but also to the "grief and anguish" of the world. See also Giuseppe Alberigo and Joseph A. Komonchak, eds., *History of Vatican II* (Maryknoll, NY: Orbis; Leuven: Peeters) particularly the sections by Claude Soetens, 3:402–15 (2000), and Norman Tanner, "The Church in the World (*Ecclesia ad Extra*)," 4:270–331 (2003).

8. Of course, it is a much debated issue whether the constitution and even the Council itself were too preoccupied with the fast-fading concerns and mindset of *modernity* as opposed to being conscious of the actuality of a world already in the throes of what became known as "postmodernity." Nonetheless, this does not detract from its positive legacy in many areas.

social.[9] And, I suggest, above all else it is in its call to open and empowering *dialogue* of such wide-ranging and diverse forms that *Gaudium et Spes* both encapsulates the spirit of the Council *and* hands on something to later generations far more precious than any fixed and determined dogmatic principles that may actually be simply the contextually and temporally determined expressions of a particular understanding of the faith.

So let us first recall that call to dialogue and then explore how we might best carry on that crucial aspect of mission in our postmodern times, both within and outside the church, today.

Dialogue and the Priority of Love

First we recall one of the most famous passages of all from the Council texts and one that is so inspired by the vision of John XXIII in calling the Council:[10]

> By virtue of her mission to shed light on the whole world the radiance of the Gospel message, and to unify under one Spirit all men of whatever nation, race or culture, the Church stands forth as a sign of that brotherhood which allows honest dialogue and gives it vigor. Such a mission requires in the first place that *we foster within the Church herself mutual esteem, reverence and harmony, through the full recognition of lawful diversity.* Thus all those who compose the one People of God, both pastors and the general faithful, can engage in dialogue with ever abounding fruitfulness. For the bonds which unite the faithful are mightier than anything dividing them. Hence, *let there be unity in what is necessary; freedom in what is unsettled, and charity in any case.*[11]

Few passages can have been so often quoted from the Council and yet few have been ignored in practice across so many aspects of ecclesial life in recent decades. Herman J. Pottmeyer, commenting on this very passage, highlights the novelty of this concept of dialogue as applied to ecclesiology and mission, "The word 'dialogue' as a description of communication within the church is new. It is not found in preconciliar

9. Here we offer a positive assessment of *Gaudium et Spes* in relation to its call to dialogue but do not intend to suggest that the document is without faults. Nor would one wish to overlook fundamental aspects of the critique offered by those such as Johann Baptist Metz who criticize the document and Vatican II in general for displaying too bourgeois an outlook.

10. This is true notwithstanding its use of language that today would be deemed non-inclusive!

11. *Gaudium et Spes* §92 (italics supplied).

ecclesiology whose key words were 'jurisdiction' and 'obedience.'"[12] (Of course, we have since seen such terms return "center stage" in numerous church documents).

And this Pastoral Constitution is not alone in commending the grace of dialogue to the church. Indeed, the Council promulgated a number of documents concerned with aspects of what we might here term relational and dialogical ecclesiology (i.e., relations between the church, and other Christians, faiths, and peoples).[13] Above all else it is important to reiterate that the Council deemed *love (caritas)* was to take priority in all attempts at such dialogue, with those within the church, those of other Christian denominations, other faiths and indeed, all persons in the human family, regardless of their race, creed (or lack thereof), or color.[14] Thus the call to dialogue runs throughout the pages of this document, expressing its vision of the church's mission in a tone hitherto unprecedented in church documents in its openness and conciliatory sentiments.[15]

Significantly, this call to dialogue-in-and-through-love was set out in clear terms even before the completion of *Gaudium et Spes* by Paul VI himself in his first encyclical, *Ecclesiam suam* (1964).[16] Here Paul VI also commended the priority of love *(caritas)* in the church's dialogical mission. "Charity is the key to everything. It sets all to rights. There is nothing which charity cannot achieve and renew. Charity

12. Hermann Pottmeyer, "Dialogue as a Model for Communication in the Church," in Patrick Granfield, ed., *The Church and Communication* (Kansas City, MO: Sheed and Ward, 1994) 97–103, at 97. (Also published in *Catholic International* 12/4 [November 2001] 41–43 and now also available online at www.religion-online.org/showarticle.asp?title=275).

13. The documents that do this most overtly include *Dignitatis Humanae* (Declaration on Religious Liberty), *Nostra aetate* (Declaration on the Relations of the Church to Non-Christian Religions), *Unitatis redintegratio* (Decree on Ecumenism—i.e., unity among the churches), *Orientalium Ecclesiarum* (Decree on the Catholic Eastern Churches), and *Gravissimum educationis* (Decree on Christian Education).

14. See *Gaudium et Spes* §92. Of course, such sentiments would feed into ecclesial efforts to articulate the "preferential option for the poor" as well as those to develop ecclesial dialogue in relation to other groups who are marginalized and oppressed, including women. As we have seen in ch. 4, *Dominus Iesus* appears to highlight a more negative and restrictive interpretation, seeming to embrace anew and even expand the more conservative qualifying clauses inserted in the conciliar documents at various stages.

15. See also, in Part One: §§1-5, 19; chapter II, *passim;* §38; chapter IV, *passim.* In Part Two: §§57, 62, 75-76; chapter 5, *passim,* especially §§77, 84, and 92.

16. On the connection between the two documents see Evangelista Vilanova, "The Intersession," in Alberigo and Komonchak, eds., *History of Vatican II,* 3 (2000), beginning at 413, and in particular the section "The Impact of the Encyclical *Ecclesiam Suam* on the Council," 448–57; with regard to the direct influence of the latter upon the former see especially 456.

'beareth all things, believeth all things, hopeth all things, endureth all things.'[17] Who is there among us who does not realize this? And since we realize it, is not this the time to put it into practice?"[18]

Indeed, *Ecclesiam Suam* fundamentally links such charity to the very mission of the church itself, and such love actually finds its expression in dialogue, thereby fulfilling Christ's bestowal of the apostolic task upon the church.[19] This document draws together key concerns for the church as Vatican II was about to embark on its final session. In it Paul VI and his advisers[20] attempt to outline their own "agenda" for the church of the future. In the encyclical we see those in positions of ecclesial authority being urged to help the church fulfill its mission both fully and truly. Central to the text, as enabling that mission, is an appeal to the value and necessity of a deeper self-examination for the church. Thus the encyclical would have a profound influence on the development of *Gaudium et Spes* in particular and the spirit of the Council in general.[21]

Three principal "policies" are advocated: first, that the self-awareness of the church be informed by the concerns of the age, leading to an ongoing and transformative self-understanding. A mature faith is seen as key to this greater awareness, a *Sensus Ecclesiae*.[22] Second, there is stress on the importance of renewal and reform for overcoming the church's shortcomings. This is not to be understood as reduction or compromise, but rather as a reflective engagement with the world and a *restoration* of the essential features of the church. Third is the importance of *dialogue,* seen as an all-embracing priority and as a method for

17. 1 Corinthians 13:7.

18. *Ecclesiam suam* §56. Norman Tanner notes that this encyclical raised "high hopes" for the draft schema for what would become *Gaudium et Spes*. See Alberigo and Komonchak, eds., *History of Vatican II* 4:270. Recall that Benedict XVI's first encyclical, *Deus caritas est,* released in January 2006, also focuses on the concept of charity in the Christian tradition. We may hope that this extended meditation on charity influences further developments in the Catholic Church in the years of his pontificate. *Ecclesiam suam,* somewhat surprisingly, given their shared themes, is not referred to in the encyclical. This raises the question: does the new encyclical represent a further example of Benedict's way of confronting the perceived threats of postmodernity in his own way, which is distinctive in comparison with the character and tone of Paul VI and the documents of Vatican II?

19. *Ecclesiam suam* §64.

20. Although it is believed that, somewhat unusually, Paul VI penned the entire document himself.

21. See, e.g., Evangelista Vilanova, "The Intersession," at 413, and again the section "The Impact of the Encyclical *Ecclesiam Suam* on the Council."

22. This concept is, I suggest, of great importance to the development of the "ecumenical intercultural hermeneutic" discussed in the following chapter.

the enhancement of the church and the human family. Hence dialogue is seen as the *practical extending* of Christian charity.[23] And the call to dialogue is one that throws open the doors of the church to the world. In a passage far removed from the tenets of what we have termed neo-exclusivism we see something of an early acknowledgment of and an embrace of the pluralistic reality now confronting the church:

> The Church must enter into dialogue with the world in which it lives. It has something to say, a message to give, a communication to make. (§65) . . . Here, then, Venerable Brethren, is the noble origin of this dialogue: in the mind of God Himself. Religion of its very nature is a certain relationship between God and man. (§70) . . . The dialogue of salvation was made accessible to all. It applied to everyone without distinction.[24] Hence our dialogue too should be as universal as we can make it. That is to say, it must be catholic, made relevant to everyone, excluding only those who utterly reject it or only pretend to be willing to accept it. . . . (§76)

Here we see the *theological* necessity of dialogue articulated: the very *notion* of God's Word is a call to dialogue in itself. *Ecclesiam suam* stresses the value and importance of Vatican II for achieving the aims set out throughout the text. The document presents an understanding of the church's *authority* to enter into dialogue, within and outside the Catholic Church, aimed at furthering the salvation of all humanity. It can be said that this openness and call to dialogue epitomized much of Paul VI's pontificate and was stifled only by the increasing and depressing retreat from the world foisted on Paul VI following the fallout from *Humanae Vitae,* the reassertion of curial dominance in the church, and the various ecclesial and political battles that engulfed the second half of his papacy. So, as Peter Hebblethwaite, the veteran observer of Vatican and ecclesial affairs, could observe in the immediate aftermath of Paul VI's death, "his vision reached out far beyond the church—and he echoed some of the themes of his first and most personal encyclical, *Ecclesiam Suam.* He saw in everyone a brother, to be helped if possible, perhaps to be saved, at any rate to be listened to and learned from. He moved easily and without strain from the dialogues with God in prayer to the more difficult dialogue with men who start from different premises."[25]

23. As the conclusion will seek to indicate, uniting the theoretical with the practical in the church's mission remains perhaps the single most difficult challenge for the church today.

24. Cf. Col 3:11.

25. Peter Hebblethwaite, *The Year of Three Popes,* 7.

If this captures Paul VI's most enduring legacy, and I believe it does to a large extent, then such a legacy was in certain ways "placed on hold" during the pontificate of the late John Paul II. But here we do not wish to underplay the very positive advances made during that pontificate. Certainly John Paul initially reached out to other Christians, other faiths, and the whole world in a spirit of dialogue.[26] But, despite a more general decline in the fervor of ecumenical and interfaith discussions at this time, the case can be made that from the early-to-mid-1980s onward, following the initial "spring" of the early years of his pontificate, dialogue descended into monologue, even if in later years— as many have suggested—the "voice" with which the church spoke would increasingly be one that originated from sources other than John Paul himself.[27]

So in moving toward suggestions for the beginnings of a conversational *method*, the importance of dialogue and the priority of love *(caritas)* are attested in much additional church and ecumenical literature. However, notwithstanding the commendable sentiments expressed in such documents as *Ut Unum Sint*, we must attempt to discern why that dialogical spring developed into an ecumenical winter. The reality has sadly been that the mechanisms for genuine dialogue are simply not in place, and the spirit and tone of the curial response to numerous petitions bears this out.

This may rightly seem perplexing, for much of the literature relevant to such debates indicates that authority is an interactive process, a two-way engagement that has communitarian implications and always requires assent. We have elsewhere argued that the reality within the church in recent decades (as in much of the church's past) has been something very different.[28] Thus our concern here, as elsewhere, is to emphasis the particular need for a dialogical and empowering paradigm of *authority* to come to the fore. As Pottmeyer writes,

> The transition from a style of authority that was part patriarchal and part authoritarian to a style of authority that is exercised in the form of dia-

26. Indeed, see again Gregory Baum, *Amazing Church*, chs. 4 and 5, which demonstrate a disjuncture between the attitude toward dialogue demonstrated by John Paul II and that of Joseph Ratzinger (as discussed in chapter 4 of this present volume).

27. This latter remark is now so widely believed and acknowledged that most, of whatever ecclesial outlook, would not contest it.

28. See Mannion, "What Do We Mean by Authority?" in Bernard Hoose, ed., *Authority in the Roman Catholic Church: Theory and Practice* (Aldershot, England; Burlington, VT: Ashgate Press, 2002).

logue creates difficulties for the church. The new awareness that "we are all the church" creates fear in some people. This is one of the reasons for the tendency to return to one-way communication. One indication of this is the emphasis in recent church documents on obedience to the hierarchical teaching authority and on the relationship between hierarchical superiority and subordination.[29]

The moral theologian Bernard Hoose summarizes this situation very well, acknowledging that in the past neither love nor reason appeared to persuade people; instead, they obeyed ecclesial authority out of *fear*. But the new reality is a situation in which people in the church no longer have that fear. Indeed, the predominant fear in evidence today, a fear of criticism and dissent, appears to be on the part of those in Rome, along with those in other ecclesial places of authority.[30] Yet the church cannot move forward unless this new fear is overcome. Here Hoose draws on a now-famous lecture by Archbishop John Quinn, given at Campion Hall, Oxford, in response to John Paul II's invitation in *Ut Unum Sint* for others to help him reappraise how the office of Petrine primacy might better serve the ecumenical cause in the present age. Quinn suggested that "any serious effort" to answer this plea would necessarily involve criticism.[31] Hoose offers a pertinent observation: "John Paul II has shown himself to be well aware of some legitimate criticism of authority in the church, and has used his position well to make formal and sincere apologies for mistakes made in times past. It is now our duty to overcome our fear of, and resistance to, criticism so that fewer such mistakes will be made in the future and fewer apologies rendered necessary."[32]

True dialogue, then, must always be open to the possibility of critique. Open and honest discourse could admit nothing less.

---

29. "Dialogue as a Model for Communication in the Church," 98.

30. The same has been true of those in secular positions of authority. This is a further symptom of a particular reaction to the postmodern world and its challenges, namely the so-called "Flight from Authority" that has led, in turn, to the emergence of an increasingly authoritarian backlash. See Jeffrey Stout, *The Flight from Authority* (Notre Dame, IN: University of Notre Dame Press, 1995).

31. John R. Quinn, *The Reform of the Papacy: The Costly Call to Christian Unity* (New York: Crossroad, 1999) 44.

32. Bernard Hoose, *Authority in Roman Catholicism* (Chelmsford: Matthew James, 2001) 13.

Authority in Dialogue

Hermann Pottmeyer stresses that dialogue is a "key to the ecclesiology of communion."[33] If such a claim is to be taken seriously, then internal ecclesial transformation must become reality sooner rather than later. Furthermore, as we will see, our understanding of the church-world relationship today requires a renewed acknowledgment of the pluralistic nature of that world. But if all this demands, first of all, some fundamental shift in the understanding of and exercise of ecclesial authority, what might a different model of authority look like?

A substantial amount of literature in recent decades has sought to demonstrate the need to reform the structures and aspirations of our churches and the models of authority and governance in operation within them.[34] The emergence of such should hardly be surprising for, as indicated, was not a primary aim of Vatican II the emergence of a critical self-awareness of the church and a move toward its renewal? If we can make our churches less authoritarian and develop communities where leadership—as in the gospels—is based on *service,* then we may learn lessons about greater equality and morality for our wider societies. This is because truly communitarian-oriented structures of authority and governance allow the voice of everyone to be heard and ensure that the rights as well as the duties of all are respected and observed.

The evidence appears incontrovertible that church authorities often appear unable or unwilling to listen effectively to or act upon the genuine concerns of the laity, or even of religious, priests, and bishops within the church. We have earlier mentioned the reaction of the church's institutional authorities toward dissenting voices in recent decades. And yet, as Pottmeyer reminds us once again, this goes against the grain of that transformative pastoral vision of *Gaudium et Spes,* and of the council in general, "This development concerns many Catholics. It makes dialogue in the church more difficult, and it can hardly be reconciled with the following recommendation of Vatican II: 'Let there be unity in what is necessary, freedom in what is doubtful, and charity in every-

33. "Dialogue as a Model for Communication in the Church." See also Hermann Pottmeyer, *Towards a Papacy in Communion: Perspectives from Vatican Councils I & II* (New York: Crossroad, 1998).

34. Again see Gerard Mannion, Richard Gaillardetz, Jan Kerkhofs, and Kenneth Wilson, eds., *Readings in Church Authority: Gifts and Challenges for Contemporary Catholicism,* (Aldershot, England, and Burlington, VT: Ashgate, 2003); Francis Oakley and Bruce Russett, eds., *Governance, Accountability, and the Future of the Catholic Church* (New York: Continuum, 2004); and Hoose, ed., *Authority in the Roman Catholic Church.*

thing' *(Gaudium et Spes* 92). Nor does it correspond to the actual position of the majority of the faithful today."[35]

Here Pottmeyer, echoing Hoose, reminds us of the new situation, beyond one in which fear and blind obedience dominated the response of the people of God to the church authorities, in contrast to the understanding and exercise of the magisterium in recent times:

> Their fidelity to the faith and their acceptance of the truths of the faith are based less on obedience to their pastors than on understanding and conviction. Such an approach also corresponds to what Vatican II called the "dignity of human persons and their social nature." Even in the area of religion, men and women attain to the truth through "right and true judgments of conscience" which are formed as a result of "free inquiry, carried on with the aid of teaching or instruction, communication, and dialogue" *(Dignitatis humanae* 3).[36]

Leading scholars—basing their arguments on sound discernment of Scripture, traditions, and the experience of Catholic Christians in many ages— have demonstrated that there is a legitimate place, and perhaps, indeed, a necessity for *dissent* in the church, even if that term is an unduly negative and sometimes unhelpful one to apply to the voicing of legitimate concerns. Others prefer to speak of "creative fidelity"[37] or "disagreement." In all there is a need for the church to learn to live with a greater variety of perspectives (one might say with a greater reality of living catholicity) than has been tolerated in recent times. As the Anglican theologian Keith Ward writes:

> The church can only be saved from its tendency to authoritarian moral conservatism by the careful safeguarding of radical and marginalized voices within its community. Individual conscience, when informed and carefully considered, must be followed. While the church has the right to formulate an "official" view, and this view must be correctly disseminated and carefully considered, one *must also preserve the right of Christians conscientiously to disagree.* This may be an uncomfortable position for those who would like to see complete uniformity of moral belief. But

---

35. Pottmeyer, "Dialogue as a Model for Communication in the Church," 99.

36. Ibid. It is analogous to the role of *intuition* in moral discernment. Cf. also Bernard Hoose's article on "Intuition," *TS* (forthcoming).

37. See Francis A. Sullivan, *Creative Fidelity: Weighing and Interpreting Documents of the Magisterium* (New York: Paulist, 1996).

*it is probably inevitable in the complex and changing world of which the
church is part.*[38]

Ward's analysis here again suggests that we should, in this postmodern
world, adopt such a positive outlook not only in our moral debates but
also in all our wider ecclesiological dialogues, and likewise all in the
church should seek to understand that *imposed* uniformity is a harmful
strategy that runs counter to gospel values.

Given the current situation in the church, then, it is not surprising
that many voices have made a convincing case for change. What is required is a genuine concept of authority-in-dialogue. Here I stress that
none of what has been said is a call to succumb to contemporary trends
or to reject or neglect the past tradition; far from it. It may be that it is
those of a neo-exclusivist tendency who actually do this. This ecclesial
mindset, along with the neo-dogmatism that often accompanies it, is
indeed a *passing* trend that can even undermine the gospel itself. It is
literally in danger of being *counter-evangelical*. As Christof Theobald
writes: "First of all to emphasize the 'irreformable' character of the
dogmatic formulations of our tradition (bound up with the cultural
context of ancient Europe without being totally subservient to it), or
even to urge the objectivity of a complex of doctrines which is definitively
to be held, is an approach which threatens to close the way to the recontextualization of faith and finally to prove contrary to the
gospel."[39]

So here we emphasize, while at the same time regretting the need to
remind ourselves of it today, that the gospel model of authority shows us
that its true purpose is to enhance justice, freedom, and love. If aspects
of church authority fail to meet such criteria, the church risks being devoid
of true authority.[40] Indeed, as Pottmeyer tellingly observes, "The manner
of reception in the early church was part of a process of communication
based on dialogue."[41] The community of faithful as a *whole* is the legitimate

38. Keith Ward, *Religion and Community* (Oxford: Oxford University Press, 2000)
233 (italics supplied). Linda Hogan's preference for what she describes as a "personalist"
account of moral theology throughout her *Confronting the Truth* (London: Darton,
Longman, and Todd, 2002) echoes aspects of what Ward writes here.

39. Christof Theobald, "The 'Definitive' Discourse of the Magisterium: Why be
Afraid of a Creative Reception?" in Mannion, et al., eds., *Readings in Church Authority*,
118.

40. Again see Mannion, "What Do We Mean by Authority?"

41. Cf. Rahner, who sensibly cautions against imagining that uniformity ever really
existed in the church or, indeed, was the preferred norm: "Dialogue in the Church,"

bearer of authority.[42] The pressing question for our new millennium is *how* to enable the enhancement of justice, freedom, and love, and hence community? Pottmeyer suggests the following: ". . . the consensus of the universal church regarding doctrinal decisions was, from the outset, the most important criterion in determining whether a doctrinal statement was to belong to the church's binding tradition of faith. This is linked to the idea that the church is a community in which all the members have joint responsibility. This is why canon law adopted the secular Roman legal maxim: *Quod omnes tangit ab omnibus tractari et approbari debet* ('What concerns all must be discussed and approved by all'). This idea is also the basic premise of communication that is based on dialogue."[43]

We might begin to construct a new, dialogical and empowering paradigm of *authority* itself by showing the importance and priority of pastoral vision and community enhancement. We should again here remember that John XXIII urged the council fathers at Vatican II to try to make the Council, above all else, a *pastoral* one. We see that similar sentiments toward the priority of pastoral care are expressed in many church documents since, and if one peruses many of the writings and sermons of Joseph Ratzinger, particularly since the late 1960s, one will observe a definite—one might say apparently pre-eminent—concern with pastoral matters throughout. But once again we must deal here in terms of ecclesial reality and honestly confront the issues that remain obstacles to the fulfilment of pastoral mission, for our wider ecclesial debates will always have an impact on the pastoral and spiritual welfare of Christians in every walk of ecclesial life.

Those in positions of particular influence and authority in the church need also to realize that their exercise of that authority, their governance of communities, local, national, and universal, must be shaped by a vision of the church, an ecclesiology that puts pastoral needs and community enhancement at the head of their priorities. It is those in authority who are entrusted with the tasks of facilitating religious liberty and enhancing community in the present age.[44]

Theological Investigations 10. *Writings of 1965–67 II* (London: Darton, Longman, and Todd, 1973) 110.

42. Again see Mannion, "What Do We Mean by Authority?"

43. Pottmeyer, "Dialogue as a Model for Communication in the Church," 101. See also Timothy Radcliffe, "How to Discover What We Believe," *The Tablet* (28 January 2006) 13.

44. On this notion see, for example, David McLoughlin, "Authority as Service in Communion," in Noel Timms and Kenneth Wilson, eds., *Governance and Authority*

Praxis, of course must always be the result of all method, and of every theology in general and ecclesiology in particular.[45] The key to real, positive, and successful praxis is the building and maintenance of partnerships, both within and outside one's own Christian, religious, or existential traditions.[46] In all, we can thus suggest that one fundamental priority should be to build a methodological basis for a conversational disposition to facilitate the dialogue of authority that the postmodern age cries out for. This would greatly help the church to meet the challenges outlined thus far. In doing so, it could offer an exemplary model of authority to the wider world in an age of renewed models and systems of domineering power and authority. This chapter offers but a tentative contribution in the form of various suggestions toward this methodological task. Here we draw on the wisdom of Bernard Lonergan, who also stressed that only genuine, authentic authority could truly serve the community: "Authenticity makes power legitimate. It confers on power the aura and prestige of authority. Unauthenticity leaves power naked. It reveals power as mere power."[47] Lonergan also supports our reminder that authority belongs to the community, its true bearer,[48] and so, in a passage of particular pertinence to the church in our postmodern times, with the myriad struggles surrounding power and authority (both secular and ecclesial), he continues

---

in the Roman Catholic Church: Beginning a Conversation (London: S.P.C.K., 2000) 123–36.

45. Notwithstanding Joseph Ratzinger's critique of liberation theology. As I have argued elsewhere, "[I]f theology is, with any credibility, justification and, most of all, *moral* authority to challenge a world or a church which does not always live up to its potential, then theologians who call themselves Christian must, as the gospel teaches us so definitively, put their theology into *practice. Theology which has no practical outcome is not really theology at all.* That practical outcome may take a multitude of forms" (Gerard Mannion, "The Role of the Theologian," *Readings in Church Authority*, 365; italics added). See also Duncan Forrester: "The practical theologian is concerned with various modes of practice. As theologian she is concerned with the practice of the triune God, with discerning what God is doing in the world; with human behavior considered theologically and with what God is calling us to do and be today; with the being and activity of the church; with the practice of Christians; and finally with what virtually monopolized the interest of practical theologians for far too long, the activities of the ordained ministry and other ecclesiastical agents" (*Truthful Action* [London: SCM, 2000] 7).

46. Again see Hinze, "Synodality and Ecumenicity." In what follows we will turn increasingly to how ecclesiological theory might be better channelled into transformative ecclesial practice.

47. Bernard Lonergan, "Dialectic of Authority," ch. 1 of *A Third Collection* (London: Geoffrey Chapman, 1985) 7.

48. Ibid. See also Mannion, "What Do We Mean by Authority?"

with a warning against illegitimate exercise of power without true authority (i.e., freely-given assent): "The fruit of unauthenticity is decline. Unauthentic subjects get themselves unauthentic authorities. Unauthentic authorities favor some groups over others. Favoritism breeds suspicion, distrust, dissension, opposition, hatred, violence. Community loses its common aims and begins to operate at cross-purposes. It loses its common judgments so that different groups inhabit different worlds. Common understanding is replaced by mutual incomprehension. The common field of experience is divided into hostile territories."[49]

Evidently, then, church leaders need to listen and learn from within and outside the church:[50] which brings us back to dialogue.

49. Lonergan, "Dialectic of Authority," 9.
50. Cf. Richard Gaillardetz, who concludes his study of the magisterium: "As a Roman Catholic theologian, I affirm the necessity of a doctrinal teaching office in the life of the church. But the nature and exercise of this doctrinal teaching authority must be governed by the gospel of Jesus Christ and the conception of authority that flows from the life of ecclesiastical communion" (*Teaching With Authority: A Theology of the Magisterium in the Church* [Collegeville: Liturgical Press, 1997] 293).

Chapter Six

Preliminaries for an Ecclesiological Methodology for Postmodern Times

First, how might we go about constructing that much-needed "dialogical model of ecclesial authority" in order to move toward a "culture of accountability" in the church? In relation to the present dilemmas pertaining to ecclesial governance and authority I never tire of quoting the dictum of the philosopher Peter Winch, that the most important fact for the church to realize and openly acknowledge is that, in all matters pertaining to the church, the issue is not *who* decides, but *what* is to be decided. This is a crucial factor to bear in mind, for in reflecting on this simple statement we can develop an understanding of what "true authority" can be.[1]

For laity and clergy alike the question (and a timely reminder for the hierarchy and exclusivistic groups within the church) should not be *who* decides or who has the say in the church, but *what* we need to decide and how we are to go forward in the postmodern age. So, for example, in relation to the notion of ministry today—and here perhaps is a lesson for *all* in the church—it is not a question of "me, too; *I*" want this or that sort of role. Rather we should be asking: "How may I best *serve* the community?"

All our ecclesiologies, our models and visions of church and of ministry need to be truly empowering and not geared toward the formation

1. Who, himself, was following de Jouvenal's *Sovereignty,* see Winch, "Authority," in A. Quinton, *Political Philosophy*. Oxford: Oxford University Press (1971) 106.

of new forms of hierarchy and new privileged elites or counter-elites. All such principles in reforming ministry and structure should be based on the fundamental gospel principle of love, *caritas,* without which we can never hope to know God truly.[2] Hence they must likewise be based on *dialogue* and not simply disgruntlement. In these chapters we begin to explore how such true dialogue *for our times* might be encouraged and facilitated.

We have yet to heed fully those wise words of Yves Congar, who urged the church to develop a "new style for her presence in the world"—less "of" and more "in" the world. For Congar such a new style meant a complete re-evaluation of the place of the clergy and laity in the church, along with the forms of ecclesial organization and governance:

> We are still a long way from reaping the consequences of the rediscovery, which we have all made in principle, of the fact that the whole church is a single people of God and that she is made up of the faithful as well as the clergy. We have an idea, we feel, implicitly and without admitting it, even unconsciously that the church is the clergy and that the faithful are only our clients or beneficiaries. This terrible concept has been built into so many of our structures and habits that it seems to be taken for granted and beyond change. *It is a betrayal of the truth.* A great deal still remains to be done to declericalize our conception of the church (without, of course, jeopardizing her hierarchical structure), and to put the clergy back where they truly belong, in the place of member-servants.[3]

Already we are beginning to discern that our many debates about the challenges postmodernity brings to the church return, time and again, to similar themes: namely questions of character and virtue, both in terms of ecclesial institutions and of individual church leaders. These are themes we shall increasingly encounter in the remainder of this book, before commending attention to ecclesiological virtues as the most fruitful path for the church of today and tomorrow. Here already Congar helps

2. Cf. *Christifideles laici* §41 on *caritas,* which appears to neglect the fact that charity must also be paramount, indeed above all paramount *"within"* the church itself (in the sense of relationships and governance of an intra-ecclesial nature). See also Gerard Mannion, "Charity Begins at Home: an Ecclesiological Assessment of Pope Benedict's First Encyclical" (*New Blackfriars* [2007], forthcoming).

3. Yves Congar, "By Way of Conclusion," in Gerard Mannion, Richard Gaillardetz, Jan Kerkhofs, and Kenneth Wilson, eds., *Readings in Church Authority: Gifts and Challenges for Contemporary Catholicism* (Aldershot, England, and Burlington, VT: Ashgate, 2003) 48. Original taken from *Power and Poverty in the Church* (London: Geoffrey Chapman, 1964; italics supplied). Note Congar's careful qualification concerning ecclesial hierarchy—no doubt to guard against the actions of some of those among the church authorities of the time, at whose hands Congar had earlier suffered.

us travel farther along this methodological and moral pathway: "Much remains to be done before we can pass from the simple moral plane where as individuals we act in the spirit of humility and service, albeit within structures of caste and privilege, to the plane of ecclesiological concepts. According to St. Paul, ordained ministers in the church are the joints or nerves on which the whole of the active body relies for its smooth working (cf. Eph 4:16); their role is 'the perfecting of the saints' (that is, of the faithful) 'for the work of the ministry' which is laid upon us all, whose end is the building up of the Body of Christ (v. 12)."[3a]

The recent crises relating to abuse in the church on every continent clearly demonstrate that we are still a long way from completing such tasks. To counter such a "betrayal of truth" founded on the continued tolerance and maintenance of what Congar termed a "haze of fiction," the church, above all else, must bring the light of *truthfulness* into every corner of its life.[4] This should be its guiding light in taking the people of God forward and healing their pain, developing their love and community anew. It requires real humility and, above all, "*epistemic* humility," i.e., what Margaret Farley has described as the "grace of self doubt."[5]

Speaking at St. Peter's in November 2000, Pope John Paul II told lay people that they have an "enormous mission" to fulfill in the church and he encouraged them to learn from the documents of Vatican II.[6] There assembled were representatives of various "selected" (read "officially approved" and endorsed) lay movements and associations. Addressing the Congress of Catholic Laity, also gathered in Rome at that time, the Pope urged all Catholics to seriously examine their consciences, to ask themselves: "What have I done with my baptism and confirmation? Is Christ really at the center of my life? Do I have time for prayer? Do I live my life as a vocation and mission?"[7] And yet he also spoke against "selective and critical attitudes among the laity" with regard to the magisterium.[8]

3a. Ibid.

4. See Mannion, "A Haze of Fiction." Francis Oakley and Bruce Russett, eds., *Governance, Accountability, and the Future of the Catholic Church* (New York: Continuum, 2003) 151–77.

5. Margaret Farley, "Ethics, Ecclesiology and the Grace of Self-Doubt," in James J. Walter, Timothy E. O'Connell, and Thomas A. Shannon, eds., *A Call to Fidelity: On the Moral Theology of Charles E. Curran* (Washington, DC: Georgetown University Press, 2002) 55–75.

6. *The Tablet* (9 December 2000) 1687.

7. Ibid.

8. Ibid. Again, Pope Benedict XVI urged the laity also to reengage with the documents of the Council, but then immediately followed this by stating that their "authentic" interpretation was to be found in the teachings of John Paul II.

But here we return to a focus on the magisterium: if one is following one's conscience, as the church says all must, then in speaking out against aspects of the exercise of the church's authority, we may be doing precisely what our conscience tells us we must. Indeed, if any layperson peruses the documents of Vatican II he or she will find much there to further inspire him or her to speak out against many practices in the governance and leadership of the church in our times. If the church is to move forward from the numerous painful crises that currently afflict it, perhaps a universal examination of conscience and act of penance and reconciliation by the bishops would be the most loving and symbolic first step. What better way to begin to embrace the truth and truthfulness for which the church in our times is crying out?

Fundamental to the church thus moving forward is, of course, its own notion of the laity and its understanding of their place and role in the church. We need, as much *in practice* as in doctrine and documentation, to reflect on the fact that the laity *are* the people of God[9] and enjoy considerable rights and are called to full participation in church ministry and governance as a result of their being so. Indeed, it would appear that, once again, we need nothing short of a "Copernican revolution" in our understanding of who the people of God are—one that will involve jettisoning every vestige of outdated and life-draining clericalism from the life of the church, so that the laity and the whole human family become the central focus of ecclesial priorities.[10]

9. On the emergence of the theme "people of God" at Vatican II see Joseph A. Komonchak, "Towards an Ecclesiology of Communion," ch. 1 of Giuseppe Alberigo and Joseph A. Komonchak, eds., *History of Vatican II* (Maryknoll, NY: Orbis, 2003) 4:1–93.

10. An interesting work that addresses the ecclesial centrality of lay people is Leonard Doohan, *The Lay-Centered Church* (San Francisco: Harper & Row, 1984). Of course, John Henry Newman's thoughts concerning the laity are also of great relevance here—most famously as set down in his 1859 article "On Consulting the Faithful in Matters of Doctrine." His ideas have received much attention in a wide variety of studies. Two representative examples are Samuel D. Femiano, *Infallibility of the Laity: the Legacy of Newman* (New York: Herder & Herder, 1967), and Ian Ker, "Newman on the 'consensus fidelium' as "the voice of the infallible church" in Terrence Merrigan and Ian T. Ker, eds., *Newman and the Word* (Leuven: Peeters, 2000) 69–89. For a Protestant perspective see Peter Hodgson, "Toward a Theology of Ministry in the New Paradigm," ch. 3 of his *Revisioning the Church: Ecclesial Freedom in the New Paradigm* (Philadelphia: Fortress Press, 1988) 97–102.

True Catholicity and the Dynamics of Tradition and Truth

The process we have in mind might best begin with some reflection on the nature of "*true*" catholicity and the *dynamics* of tradition and truth. The rise and importance of historical consciousness informs such a debate. As T. Howland Sanks argues, the social mission the church is/has "is and always has been socially and culturally contextualized,"[11] so the task to be addressed here is how the Catholic Church in particular, and all other churches in general, can go about facilitating *true* unity in diversity, in relation to the situation both within and outside the church.

Here we gain some hope from the WCC document, *A Treasure in Earthen Vessels*. It certainly has its faults, but the most constructive part of all is at the end: "The Church *as* Hermeneutical Community." This contains discussion of many of the most important ecclesial concepts for our times (or for any), namely ecclesial discernment, authority, apostolicity, shared accountability, and the extremely important idea of ecclesial *reception*. Here we see it proclaimed that *ecclesial formation* is a prime duty for the churches. We also see acknowledgment of the emergence (or, I would suggest, if perceived in terms of christianity being a universal church of local churches, the *re*-emergence) of an *inter*-ecclesial magisterium beyond denominational boundaries. "An ecumenical exercise of teaching authority is already beginning to develop in some respects. It is hoped that ways of common decision making can be developed, even as there is allowance for certain decisions a church must take without or even against the opinion of others."[12] Likewise, the *conciliar* tradition in Christianity is here celebrated also, but now within the hermeneutical context (§61).

For David Tracy "hermeneutics has been one major alternative to both foundationalism and relativism"[13] because it gives due attention

11. T. Howland Sanks, "Globalization and the Church's Social Mission," *TS* 60 (1999) 626.

12. *A Treasure in Earthen Vessels* §59. We shall shortly discuss Roger Haight's argument that there now exist within Christianity "many magisteria" that must be engaged; see ch. 7.

13. David Tracy, "Beyond Foundationalism and Relativism: Hermeneutics and the New Ecumenism," ch. 12 of his *On Naming the Present. God, Hermeneutics, and Church* (Maryknoll, NY: Orbis, 1994), originally in Norbert Greinacher and Norbert Mitte, eds., *The New Europe: Challenge for Christians, Concilium* (1992/2) 133–34. Tracy says it is thus little wonder that so much European thought by the 1990s was hermeneutical in origin (e.g., deconstructionism) or in intent (much of semiotics and structuralism) and especially so in the character of much continental philosophy. But in particular he believes that "Especially when hermeneutics is allied (see Habermas, Apel, Ricoeur) with some form of critical theory or some form of the 'new pragmatism,'

to historical consciousness yet resists any temptation to "yield" to relativism. Tracy also reminds us how the hermeneutical tide itself is shifting—from an emphasis on text to one on discourse, from historical context to social location.[14] Here, then, we should acknowledge that much ecclesiological work is yet to be done in our times if the Roman Catholic Church, in all aspects of its life and mission but not least in its official teaching and its pastoral awareness, is to become a *catholic* hermeneutical community.

The moral theologian Charles Curran has offered an extended reflection on a concept of catholicity that is truly ecumenical (hence truly "Catholic") and confronts the actuality of today's church-world relation in a positive fashion. He also argues that our understanding of catholicity must be one that is informed by *moral* considerations. Hence Curran, like others, contends that we must avoid identifying the church with any one particular culture.[15] Instead, we should conceive of catholicity as a "transcendent unity."[16] Following Avery Dulles,[17] Curran suggests that true catholicity *demands* that difference be acknowledged and embraced.[18] Likewise, Curran stresses the importance of conversation and how we can learn so much from those *outside* the church.[19] And I think we must join Curran in reflecting at length on the reality of just how much the sinfulness of the church *impinges* on its own catholicity.[20] Of course, Curran is far from alone in highlighting this ecclesial reality. As Karl Rahner here demonstrated, "the dialogue must constantly be conducted in the awareness that it is taking place in the holy church which is made up of sinners; that it is intended to conduce to salvation; that those participating in it will have to answer for the part they play in it before the judgment of God.

---

the hope for an intellectual position beyond both relativism and foundationalism is genuine" (ibid., 134). Paul D. Murray offers similar thoughts on the need for a *via media* in Catholic scholarship utilizing the new pragmatism in his "On Valuing Truth in Practice," *International Journal of Systematic Theology,* vol. 8, no. 2 (April 2006) 163–83.

14. Tracy, "Beyond Foundationalism and Relativism," 133–34.

15. Charles Curran, *The Church and Morality: An Ecumenical and Catholic Approach* (Minneapolis: Fortress Press, 1993) 22–23, 27, 36–37, and *passim.*

16. Ibid., 24.

17. Note, however, that the position of now-Cardinal Dulles has significantly shifted in recent years.

18. Curran, *The Church and Morality,* 19–20.

19. Ibid., ch. 4.

20. Ibid.

Once this is recognized it should be entered upon in the church with all boldness. For it is much needed today."[21]

In this era of what Pope John Paul II regularly denounced as dehumanizing globalization, the church should also learn to counter its *own* globalizing and universalizing tendencies. This in itself demands a renewed understanding of catholicity. For the Anglican scholar Christopher Duraisingh, here drawing on Roman Catholic scholarship,[22] this means revising our understanding of the relationship between the universal and the local, emphasizing the importance of the local, and understanding the church as the "mutual inclusion and communion that exist among the local churches."[23] Here he echoes sentiments expressed in our earlier chapters concerning the need to resist a universalist ecclesiology:

> Does not the very word catholic, *kata' holon*, imply this? As the word means "according to the whole," the wholeness is the communion that exists, comes to be expressed, among the locals. Of course, it does not mean that the federation or the organization that draws them together brings about the catholicity. The communion is in itself the expression of their catholicity. The fullness of the apostolic tradition-ing process is precisely expressed as the local churches share their contextual expressions of the faith out of every tribe and nation.[24]

Duraisingh shuns both "narrow parochialism" and "false universalism where the position of one, often the one who has the power, becomes the universal norm for all," as well as any attempt to perceive contextuality and catholicity as polar opposites. Instead he believes them to be "tandem concepts . . . inseparably related. One without the other makes no sense."[25] Duraisingh, who was previously Director of the WCC's Commission on World Mission and Evangelization, calls for "serious cross-cultural conversation and the use of a critical hermeneutics of difference" and, in a telling assessment of the failures of Christian communions genuinely to engage in such, he believes that

21. Rahner, "Dialogue in the Church," *Theological Investigations* 10. *Writings of 1965–67 II* (London: Darton, Longman, and Todd, 1973) 120.

22. Joseph Komonchak, "The Church Universal as the Communion of Local Churches," in Giuseppe Alberigo and Gustavo Gutiérrez, eds., *Where Does the Church Stand?* (New York: Seabury, 1981) 30, cited in Duraisingh, "Contextual and Catholic," 693.

23. See our brief account of the Ratzinger-Kasper debate on this issue in ch. 4.

24. Duraisingh, "Contextual and Catholic," 693–94. See also *Lumen gentium* on where the people of God are to be found, namely in all nations and at all times, §13.

25. "Contextual and Catholic," 694.

unless "the diverse cultural expressions of the Christian story everywhere are received as central elements in the tradition-ing process, we will not be liberated from a past which remains essentially European. Nor can we receive the stories of the good news in Christ in ever new and multifaceted ways relevant to our times."[26]

The interrelatedness between mission and evangelization and our debates here cannot be overstated. For Catholics in particular the work of Hans Küng, himself a victim of the forces against dialogue and dissent within the church, can be most informative.[27] His uneasy relations with the Vatican came to a crisis when he published a short text, *The Church, Maintained in Truth*, in 1979. In it he extolled the virtues of a teaching authority of the church that could admit it was fallible and live and learn by its failings. The CDF issued a declaration on 18 December that same year, stating that the book proved Küng had "departed from the integral truth of the Catholic Faith"; it went on to assert that Küng could no longer be considered a Catholic theologian or function as one in his teaching. Much controversy followed and many theologians rallied to Küng's defense.

The postscript to the English edition of Kung's book[28] was entitled "Why I Remain a Catholic." Composed in the aftermath of his curial censure, it is a sometimes impassioned defense of "Catholicity" and a dynamic sense of the church (catholic in time and space, i.e., across centuries of history and diversity, and in fellowship with Christians the world over). He attempts to answer the question "*Who* is a Catholic theologian?"

> Catholicity has two dimensions: temporal and spatial. First, *catholicity in time:* A theologian is Catholic if he is aware of being united with the whole church—that is, with the church of all times. He will therefore not describe from the outset certain centuries as "un-Christian" or "unevangelical." He is sure that in every century there was a community of believers who listened to the gospel of Jesus Christ and tried in one way or other, so far as it is possible for human beings in their frailty and fallibility,

26. Ibid., 682.
27. For various accounts of Küng's clashes with the church authorities see Küng's own *My Struggle for Freedom: Memoirs,* trans. John Bowden (London: Continuum, 2003), Peter Hebblethwaite, *The New Inquisition* (London: Fount, 1980), and John Allen, *Pope Benedict XVI: a Biography of Joseph Ratzinger* (London: Continuum, 2005) *passim,* esp. 92–94, 113–14, 127–30. Küng actually enjoyed a "cordial" meeting with the new Pope Benedict in 2005, although the issues over which he received censure, it was reported, were not discussed. Küng thought the meeting significant not least because Benedict's predecessor has ignored pleas for a meeting for twenty-five years.
28. Hans Küng, *The Church, Maintained in Truth* (London: SCM, 1980) 80–87.

to live according to his example. . . . Second, *catholicity in space*: A theologian is Catholic if he is aware of being united with the church of all nations and continents. He must therefore not orient himself only to the church of this country or to a national church and will not isolate himself from the church as a whole.[29]

This, Küng asserts, is what it truly is to be a Catholic, and a Catholic theologian in particular. Against "Roman imperialism" (perceived Vatican intransigence) the true criterion of catholicity is Jesus Christ himself. Thus the Catholic theologian must be evangelically oriented, just as Protestant (evangelical) theologians should be "oriented in a Catholic way." For Küng, catholicity is both a gift and a task. Above all, Küng maintains the principle that "Being Catholic, then, means being ecumenical in the fullest sense."[30] What might this mean in ecclesial practice?

Humility in Method: Learning to Listen, Informing the Debate

In the face of postmodernity and its challenges, and echoing our earlier reflections, it appears evident that all dialogue partners within the church should strive to avoid adopting an arrogant disposition or anything that encourages absolutism, and should shun attempts to promote the *imposition* of fixed views, ways, and answers. Rather, it is our collective task to try to *discern* the mystery Christians call God, and the mystery of human existence, and to discern the signs of our times as John XXIII and *Gaudium et Spes* urged us.

And humility—in face of the pluralistic reality within which we all live today[31]—is the most appropriate virtue to adopt in our encounters with the other (as Aquinas indicated, it is, after all, a "master virtue"). Humility draws together due attentiveness both to historical consciousness and to the reality of pluralism in which we live today. Humility encourages (critical) ecclesial self-awareness and the development of that *Sensus ecclesiae* of which Paul VI spoke. Roger Haight has explored the parameters of this issue over a sustained period of time and suggests the following:

29. Küng, *The Church, Maintained in Truth*, 85.
30. Ibid. See also idem, *Reforming the Church Today—Keeping Hope Alive* (New York: Crossroad, 1990).
31. See David Tracy, who speaks of a "new modesty" in celebrating difference and otherness amid a newfound communality; a new experience of the vital traditions of self-criticism and ethical universalism of rights and justice, which "Europe also means throughout the world": "Beyond Foundationalism and Relativism," 132.

the interiorization of historicity encourages a certain humility or modesty in the Christian witness to ultimate truth. This is not a modesty that stems from uncertainty and doubt: Christians know what they have experienced of God through Jesus Christ. But Christian experience of God is also characterized by mystery and unknowing. And Jesus is a particular, historically conditioned mediation of God. The Christian today should share a sense of the limitations and culturally conditioned character of the Christian tradition. The Christian should also be open to more and fuller dimensions of an encounter with the same God that is revealed in Jesus but also mediated through other religions.[32]

Thus awareness of historicity also points toward the manifold pluralism that marks our reality today in its religious, cultural, and intellectual forms alike.

The importance of *humility* in developing a method for dialogue (and in countering exclusivistic tendencies) relates to the wider issues pertaining to the nature and purpose of church authority. A return to a broader debate concerning the *Sensus Fidelium* and an appreciation of the *true* nature of authority should each be attended to as part of this task.[33] Such humility should feed into ecclesial structures, governance, and ministry also, so that those within the church *practice* as well as preach their moral vision. At Vatican II the Archbishop of Bhopal,

32. Roger Haight, "The Church as Locus of Theology," in *Why Theology?*, *Concilium* (1994/6) 19. In a more recent writing Haight states that "This bond to history attaches to all human knowledge and hence theological expression an acknowledgment that there is more truth in all domains than can be attained from a particular perspective. It encourages an openness to other points of view and achievements, an expectation that what is and will be discovered by others shares a validity that exceeds or adds to the cumulative knowledge up to this point, and hence, finally, a certain humility before the unknown that continually beckons from the future. Historical consciousness can exist in different degrees, but some level is necessary for an appreciation of the value of the truly other": "Comparative Theology" in Gerard Mannion and Lewis Mudge, eds., *Routledge Companion to the Christian Church* (London: Routledge, 2007). Note that none of this should be taken to diminish or misrepresent the wonder of the Incarnation. But, as Kierkegaard's *Philosophical Fragments* demonstrates, this doctrine nonetheless presents a paradoxical challenge to all Christians, and unless they embrace it in all of its paradoxical character (which, essentially, is what the Nicene-Constantinopolitan creeds commend Christians to do), the fullness of life in Christ remains elusive for them. Note also that embracing the mystery of God is not an intellectual "escape clause." Here one runs up against the limitations of human knowledge and experience alike. In mystery we see where world religions and philosophies come closest to one another. Thus mystery is a concept whereby divisions can be further transcended.

33. See John J. Burkhard, "*Sensus Fidelium*," in Mannion and Mudge, eds., *Routledge Companion to the Christian Church*, as well as his earlier volume, *Apostolicity Then and Now: An Ecumenical Church in a Postmodern World* (Collegeville: Liturgical Press, 2004) *passim*.

Eugene D'Souza, commended the virtue of humility to the church fathers, in particular intellectual humility: "Let us with sincere and truthful hearts direct our attention to those complementary truths which, as one of us has well said, our separated brothers sometimes emphasize better than we do. I want to insist on this point. Just as love is not perfect unless it is universal and total, so humility too should be total and should include what I call intellectual humility, or even doctrinal humility."[34] For Archbishop D'Souza ecumenism would thus contribute to the "doctrinal *aggiornamento*" of the church. And here I suggest that the postmodern *aggiornamento* of ecclesiology, of mission and practice, cannot be effectively achieved without ecclesial humility.

Humility, then, brings us to reflect on the doctrine of the Incarnation, one of the most fundamental aspects of our faith, and in particular on the kenotic aspects of that doctrine. It likewise enables us to appreciate once again that the church is always a community both of holiness and of sinfulness.

The Pope is known as the "Supreme Pontiff" and thus should be a master "bridge-builder," as the name suggests.[35] Both John Paul II and now Benedict XVI have made public statements declaring such "bridge-building" a central focus of their papal ministry. But, as we have seen, the reality in the church tells us that much work remains to be done here. In all, we are mindful of any pleasant "mist" created by language concerning "dialogue," "unity," "love," and "solidarity."[36] But if confrontation is to be resolved and more frequently transcended, some serious and sustained theological, particularly ecclesiological, and also ethical thinking and debate will be required. Where are our considerations leading us?

Ecumenics: "an attempt to think Christianity as a whole"

This was John Macquarrie's definition of systematic theology,[37] but from a methodological standpoint it could easily refer to theology in general. Indeed, it could—better still—describe the science of

---

34. Eugene D'Souza, "Intellectual Humility," in Yves Congar, Hans Küng, and Daniel O'Hanlon, eds., *Council Speeches of Vatican II* (London and New York: Sheed and Ward, 1964). See especially p. 141 for his remarks on avoiding a "superiority complex," quoted in ch. 4 above. This recalls Margaret Farley's understanding of "the grace of self-doubt."

35. *Ut unum sint.*

36. Here we take our lead from Gregory Baum, as discussed below.

37. *On Being a Theologian* (London: SCM, 1999) 35.

ecumenics: for no theological discipline is more totally systematic in its embracing of *every* aspect of the human quest for meaning and salvation we know as Christianity. Because theology can encompass such features of the lives of human individuals and communities alike (a *shared* quest), so it can help shape a *vision* for the *empowering* ecclesiology that is the goal of our quest. Where might the development of such a method lead us, and what is the end in itself to which this methodology might provide a means?

I suggest that much good may come from a close and critical scrutiny of the fundamentals of ecumenism, which was revived in the nineteenth century by different Christian denominations seeking closer unity. They can provide a model for our search for ecclesial alternatives and dialogue, and even for application within one particular communion. Ecumenism is the science of bridge-building, a science of dialogue across different groups. In our globalized, pluralistic world, as the church at Vatican II began to recognize and publicly acknowledge, the ecumenical task is now widened to include people of all faiths and none.

It is very evident in our postmodern times that there are wider questions relating to the divisions between all human communities, and the term "ecumenism" itself can now also mean dialogue and efforts at bringing about greater unity throughout the whole human family. As Paul A. Crow writes, "It seeks to overcome all things that divide the church as well as the human community; that isolate people, nations, and cultures; that break fellowship or separate persons from God and from each other."[38] This ecumenism requires a framework that allows us to unite and work together to realize common values without the danger against which Konrad Raiser (former General Secretary of the World Council of Churches) has cautioned us, i.e., dissolving our real differences into consensus. Let us turn to consider more substantive suggestions for ways forward and explore further the dialogical imperative in both its *ad intra* and *ad extra* ecclesial dimensions.

Tentative Steps Forward: Some Inspiring Ecclesial Visions

Charles Curran, with many others, has written that our times cry out for ecclesiologies that are not only dialogical but also prophetic in

38. Paul A. Crow, Jr., "The Ecumenical Movement," in Charles H. Lippy and Peter W. Williams, eds., *Encyclopedia of the American Religious Experience* (New York: Charles Scribner's Sons, 1988) 2:978.

character.[39] In a sense both the previous chapter and this one explore the methodological parameters of such ecclesiological thinking. We have been concerned with explicating the nature, value, and necessity of dialogue and we seek to examine, both here and in the following chapters, what a more fruitful ecclesiological method for the church in our times might be like. For the Irish theologian Eamonn Conway, we live in the midst of a "crisis in correlation," not simply in the church but also in culture. The challenge, he believes, is to find new models of correlation.[40] But our task is broader still: moving beyond correlation, and not just trawling for new models, but perhaps a rediscovery, reappraisal, and reappropriation of some older visions whose enormous ecclesial potential has yet to be fully realized.[41]

At this stage of our explorations let us outline a few of the more important aspects of this method, drawing on a few indicative scholars whose work has focused on the issues here in hand and who may help take our considerations farther still. We begin with Rahner and that "necessity" of engagement. By no means do I intend the selection to even closely approximate to an exhaustive list. Many will think of other scholars with like-minded ecclesial visions, but those discussed here and in chapter 7 appear to offer suggestive reflections on most of the main issues identified in this chapter.[42]

39. Charles Curran, *The Church and Morality: An Ecumenical and Catholic Approach* (Minneapolis: Fortress Press, 1993), ch. 4. Similar themes occur in, for example, Nicholas Healy, *Church, World, and the Christian Life* (Cambridge: Cambridge University Press, 2000) and, of course, numerous feminist scholars: see Natalie Watson, *Introducing Feminist Ecclesiology* (London: Continuum, 2002).

40. See Eamonn Conway, "Speaking a Constant Word in a Changing World. Recognising and Resolving Tensions and Tendencies in a Postmodern Context," *New Blackfriars* 87 (March 2006) 110–20.

41. This is not meant in the sense developed by certain proponents of the *ressourcement* movement in Catholic theology. I have in mind a more constructive reappropriation. Thus engagement with aspects of the rich traditions over the centuries might go hand in hand with unlocking the stultified potential of, for example, the legacy of Vatican II and of liberation theology in particular. Further examples might include the ecclesiological potential of the thought of Antonio Rosmini-Serbati and certain elements of the Catholic modernist movement, whose works were read with great interest (despite being prohibited) by the young Angelo Roncalli, later Pope John XXIII.

42. Aside from those discussed in this chapter and throughout the rest of this volume, there are a great many other contemporary scholars, a detailed account of whose work would enhance the discussions here, but for the limitations of space. In particular, the great potential offered by recent ecclesiological engagements with the social sciences and ethnography is one very exciting area of ongoing and future development. I hope that what is included at least provides food for thought and fires further discussion and debate on a number of the most pertinent issues today with regard to building constructive ecclesiologies for our times.

The Necessity of Dialogue

Karl Rahner perhaps epitomizes this "dialogical spirit" of the Council more than most: Little wonder, given his influence on numerous documents, not least *Gaudium et spes.*[43] We are reminded of the *necessity* of dialogue by Rahner's important essay, "Dialogue in the Church," written in the midst of disputes concerning the Council's true legacy.[44]

> It may be that it is only through such a dialogue that [the church] can attain to that particular concrete historical form of the abiding truth which is to be the basis for her activity in hope and love, and which has to be worked out by herself in the particular circumstances of the present if she is to proclaim the gospel of God in Christ effectively to her own age. . . . When we speak of dialogue and the necessity for it here, then, we mean dialogue to the extent that *it arises from a specific contemporary situation and is rendered necessary by this.*[45]

Here we see further illustrated just how fundamental is dialogue to evangelization. Rahner here draws together and encapsulates so much of the discussion outlined thus far in our chapter. Discerning the "signs of our times" leads to such a conclusion. Furthermore, Rahner fundamentally links such necessity to the pluralistic reality of the late twentieth century. Here he addresses the issue with respect to intellectual pluralism, but I suggest one cannot discuss even this in isolation from other forms, most notably religious and cultural. "Dialogue is necessary in the church because of the situation of a pluralism of ideas within the church. In order to achieve a still clearer view of this necessity it must

43. Cf. Norman Tanner, "The Church in the World *(Ecclesia ad Extra),*" in Alberigo and Komonchak, eds., *History of Vatican II,* 4:270–331 (2003).

44. Karl Rahner, "Dialogue in the Church," *Theological Investigations* 10. *Writings of 1965–67 II* (London: Darton, Longman, and Todd, 1973). See also his "Perspectives for the Future of the Church" in *Theological Investigations* 12. *Confrontations II* (London: Darton, Longman, and Todd, 1974), and *Theological Investigations* 20. *Concern for the Church* (London: Darton, Longman, and Todd, 1981). On Rahner's ecclesiology in general see the other essays contained in *Theological Investigations* 10 (on ecclesiology, sacraments, eschatology, and church and world); *The Shape of the Church to Come* (London: S.P.C.K., 1974); "On the Structure of the People of the Church Today," in *Theological Investigations* 12; *Theological Investigations* 14. *Ecclesiology, Questions in the Church, the Church in the World* (London: Darton, Longman, and Todd, 1976); "The One Church and the Many Churches" and "Is Church Union Dogmatically Possible?" in *Theological Investigations* 17. *Jesus, Man and the Church* (London: Darton, Longman, and Todd, 1981). An impressive study is Richard Lennan, *The Ecclesiology of Karl Rahner* (Oxford: Oxford University Press, 1995).

45. Rahner, "Dialogue in the Church," 104–5 (italics supplied).

be pointed out that neither the teaching authorities nor the pastoral authorities of the church can, by their own act, supply any substitute for this dialogue."[46] Indeed, perhaps *the* most positive aspect of postmodernity is the inescapable awareness of the pluralistic reality in which we live. Postmodernity offers pathways that can lead to the intellectual, cultural, and social liberation of human beings from the many existentially draining struggles for uniformity.

Let us attempt to outline in greater detail the *necessity* of dialogue for the church. First, it is doctrinally necessary (and we have already encountered some aspects of why it is necessary in a *theological* sense). Christianity believes that God uttered forth the Word, and what followed was creation.[47] The definitive expression of God's word was in the Incarnation—the person, work, and enduring presence and significance of Christ. The word of God also lives on in Scripture and tradition, and in the church itself, understood as the body of Christ, the "*logos* of God." The very nature of doctrine also demands dialogue. Doctrine emerges from lengthy processes of reflection on and discussion and even disagreement about revelation—God's self-disclosure—and on human experience in relation to this. Doctrine develops. Its explanation and articulation, by necessity, change and adapt according to the requirements placed on such articulation by contextual and cultural considerations. The concept of catholicity itself, understood across time and space, acknowledges this.[48] Thus without dialogue, doctrine does not really exist. Stale dogma, in the pejorative sense of that word, is all that can, at best, emerge where there is no dialogue. The creeds would not be with us today in the form that they have without the dialogue that was deemed necessary in the church of the early Christian centuries.[49]

So we understand that God addresses humanity—"dialogues" with the world, if you will—for God does not simply address; God desires a response. God calls humanity to dialogue in love—with one another

46. Ibid., 110.

47. This is not to understand God's utterance and creation as *event*, rather it is an analogical summary of both the logos christology tradition and much interpretation of the doctrine of the Trinity. As in so many areas, we can learn much clarification here from theologians "of the East." Here cf. also, Gregory Baum, *Amazing Church*, 38–39.

48. Recall our earlier discussions on catholicity above. Cf. also the relevance of the Orthodox theological concept of *sobernost*, as elucidated in the works of Aleksei S. Khomiakov in the nineteenth century. Here, for example, see Robert Murray, "Collegiality, Infallibilty, and *Sobernost*," *One in Christ* 1 (1965) 19–42.

49. See Roger Haight's summary, "Comparative Ecclesiology," in *Routledge Companion to the Christian Church*.

and with Godself. Dialogue brings union and draws us closer to atonement and to communion with God's very being. One here recalls the importance, for Rahner, of God's offer of self-communication to human persons, so central to his early work, *Hearer of the Word*,[50] and definitively articulated in his later *Foundations of Christian Faith*.[51]

Second, dialogue is *ecclesially* necessary (and many of the fathers at Vatican II, as well as the Paul VI of *Ecclesiam suam*, not only came to realize this, but also came to celebrate it). Communion cannot be genuine, nor can it flourish without true dialogue. Whenever the church ignores the necessity of dialogue, or even stifles conversation, it fails to be church truly. The church is called to embrace diversity, to acknowledge a variety of gifts and ministries, to listen to and engage with all humanity both within and without the church.

Third dialogue is *morally* necessary. The essence of the gospel is love—a radical love that transcends boundaries, partisan and selfish concerns and lifeless dogma and religiosity. It reaches out to every corner of society and demands that we do not withhold love and justice from any. In one sense, then, one of the most fundamental elements of the moral vision of the New Testament and its later articulation in the church, might be called a "dialogical imperative."

Gregory Baum—"Wider Ecumenism" and the Church as Hermeneutical and Transformative Agent

Thus our reflections here on dialogue really return us to a consideration of the reality of the church-world relationship today. In this sense Gregory Baum, perhaps more than most, epitomizes and articulates the necessity of dialogue. He does not just link dialogue and evangelization, he believes that the two can actually be equated. Baum does not agree with those who would perceive the church's mission simply in terms of "service to the world," but his identification of dialogue with proclamation is all the more profound and transformative for that. The church in our times must understand proclamation anew. For many, Baum is a prophet for our times.

In terms that anticipate much later thought in the fields of religious studies and, later still (as we shall see), comparative theology, as well as anticipating the dilemmas posed by many of the divisions and neo-exclusivistic tendencies we have earlier considered, it is thus that

50. Karl Rahner, *Hearer of the Word* (New York: Continuum, 1994).
51. Karl Rahner, *Foundations of Christian Faith* (New York: Crossroad, 1978).

Baum suggests that the church's mission must be defined in terms of proclamation.

> But what is the church's message to the world, understood in the light of the new focus? The church is destined to engage in dialogue with other people, with their religions and ideologies: in this dialogue the Gospel is sounded. In this dialogue the church listens to the convictions of others and expresses her own faith in Jesus Christ in terms accessible to her partners. What is the purpose of this dialogue? Is it to convert others to the Christian Church or is it an intellectual effort to supply better information to the participants? It is neither one nor the other. Dialogue in which the Gospel is sounded is a truly redemptive ministry, thanks to which both partners enter more deeply into what is God's will for them. Dialogue is mission. Dialogue is a new way of proclamation.[52]

Reflecting on part of the above statement, Rebecca McKenna has argued that "There is probably no other term Baum used more frequently in relation to the church and its mission than 'dialogue.' . . . Throughout Baum's writings, dialogue has continued to be an important dynamic that explains the challenge and gift of the church in relationship to the world."[53] In recent years, in contrast to the at times seemingly ambivalent attitudes of John Paul II and the Roman Curia to other churches and other faiths, Baum asks whether the church believes religious pluralism is part of the divine plan for the world, and he thus commends the need for a "kenotic ecclesiology" that facilitates harmonious dialogue, collaboration, and coexistence. Baum argues that *this* is the best way to ward off divisive tensions of the postmodern world and the threat of secularizing and anti-religious tendencies.[54] For Baum, dialogue can be transformative and enriching both for those conversation partners with whom the church engages *and* for the church itself. With regard to the latter, Baum continues, in and through dialogue "the church, too, enters more deeply into what is God's will for her. Listening to others in the light of the gospel, the church will be able to detect the presence of God's Word in the convictions and aspirations of other people. Since God's Word is present not only in scripture and tradition but also in present history, the church that seeks to submit herself totally to the Word of God is in

52. Gregory Baum, *Faith and Doctrine* (New York: Newman Press, 1969) 116.
53. Rebecca McKenna, "The Transformative Mission of the Church in the Thought of Gregory Baum," *TS* 59/4 (December 1998) 613.
54. Gregory Baum, *Amazing Church*, passim, but especially ch. 5.

need of dialogue with the whole world. *The church needs the world to become truly church.*"[55]

Baum thus offers a vision of church-world relations that is a far cry from that espoused by neo-exclusivistic ecclesiologies in the present era. Indeed, as dialogue is so central to the varied and enormous output of works Baum has bequeathed not just to the church, but to the human community in general (as McKenna has shown), we can learn much from his own methodological thinking and from his personal conduct in living out such a "mission" of dialogue. Indeed, not only was Baum a key theological adviser *(peritus)* at Vatican II, he was also highly influential upon the composition of the Council's Decree on Ecumenism, as well as that of the text on relations with non-christian religions. Furthermore, Baum founded *The Ecumenist,* a journal aimed at promoting ecumenical dialogue, and went on to initiate and coordinate a wide variety of ecumenical, interfaith, and inter-community ventures in dialogue and research.

For Baum the church, at Vatican II, transformed its understanding of the tradition in relation to inter-church and interreligious dialogue so dramatically due to reasons that were of a fundamentally *moral* nature: "the emergence of a new ethical horizon, associated with democracy and pluralism and sustained by commitment to freedom, equality and participation."[56] McKenna's incisive study of Baum's work brings to the fore the prophetic and constructive nature of his work and thereby demonstrates the promise of his tireless efforts for contemporary and future ecclesiology and ecclesial life in general. She also quite rightly highlights how much Baum later drew upon the further documents of Vatican II in shaping his own understanding of dialogue, although he also was concerned that the Council, while acknowledging a "plurality of missions," had failed to harmonize its understanding of "traditional mission" (evangelization) with this new, wider understanding of its "radical openness to the world."[57] Nonetheless, McKenna also notes how §92 of *Gaudium et Spes* "challenged Baum to extend his definition and aspirations regarding ecumenism."[58] Henceforth he spoke of a "wider ecumenism" that embraces the entire human family.[59] McKenna

55. Baum, *Faith and Doctrine,* 117 (italics supplied).

56. Baum, *Amazing Church,* 104. See also Edward Schillebeeckx, *Interim Report on the Books Jesus and Christ* (New York: Crossroad, 1981) 78.

57. McKenna, "The Transformative Mission of the Church," 614.

58. Ibid., 615.

59. Gregory Baum, "Ecumenism After Vatican II," in Wilhelm Kantzenbach and Vilmos Vajta, *Oecumenica: An Annual Symposium of Ecumenical Research* (Minneapolis:

defines this as an ecumenism "that focuses on contemporary issues and the unity of all peoples."[60] What better approach for a globalized world and for meeting the challenges of a postmodern era?

McKenna goes on to chart the journey Baum's thought and life has taken, from his doctoral studies and work in ecumenism and Jewish-Christian dialogue to his engagement with a wider humanistic agenda, to studies in psychotherapy, to his embracing of the moves toward political theology and the attendant critique of church and society that brought with it.[61] I would add that his many works have also embraced the social sciences, debates concerning the future of Canadian society and, coming full circle, contemporary ecclesiology once again.

Nonetheless, dialogue does not come cheap and can even be painful. As Harold Wells has observed, for Baum dialogue can bring both sorrow and joy. Nonetheless, the latter is truly great, for when we are confronted by different truths we are also opened up to the presence of God's word. Dialogue is truly revelatory.[62] Baum is certainly not blind to the danger that dialogue can be an excuse to avoid real change, or that it can be usurped for darker purposes. There are some, including certain value systems, with whom dialogue would not only be fruitless but wrong. At times even the church must engage in conflict and even requires a "theology of conflict."[63] Applying these insights to the inner life of the church, Baum speaks of "institutional illness" and "ecclesial pathologies."[64] McKenna again summarizes his thinking at this time most succinctly: "The church, like every other group (and individual), needs confrontation and conflict in order to move from false consciousness toward transformative, liberating

---

Augsburg, 1967) 149–58 (see 157), cited in McKenna, "The Transformative Mission of the Church," 614 n. 26.

60. McKenna, "The Transformative Mission of the Church," 614 n. 26.

61. Ibid., 609. See Gregory Baum, "A Response to Haight, Hutchinson, Simpson, and Rotstein," *Toronto Journal of Theology* 2 (1987) 203–208, and Mary Jo Leddy and Mary Ann Hinsdale, eds., *Faith that Transforms: Essays in Honor of Gregory Baum* (New York: Paulist, 1987). I was fortunate enough to be in attendance at the special seminar, "The Work of Gregory Baum: An Appreciation," at the 2002 Annual Meeting of the *American Academy of Religion*, held in Toronto, 25 November 2002. Baum was present and provided the response to the papers himself.

62. Harold Wells, "Gregory Baum's Early Ecumenical and Dialogical Theology," paper given at the seminar "The Work of Gregory Baum: An Appreciation," Toronto 2002.

63. McKenna, "The Transformative Mission of the Church," 620. Recall Quinn and Hoose on the inescapability of criticism in genuine dialogue, chapter 5, above.

64. Ibid. See Gregory Baum, *The Credibility of the Church Today: A Reply to Charles Davis* (New York: Herder & Herder, 1968).

truth. The church would only become free of its ideological blindness and become truly church to the degree to which it responded to the conflicts and questions raised by ordinary people."[65]

Baum came to understand that first conflict and struggle were necessary, and then *true* dialogue could prosper.[66] Unity should no longer be the central focus of ecumenism.[67] "Universal solidarity" should be the prime focus, and the church's core mission is to the whole of humanity,[68] joining with others in a broader movement for solidarity.[69] This echoes sentiments expressed by David Tracy, who believes that "love as real other-regard will not shrink from the necessary moments of confrontation, conflict, argument demanded by all serious conversation on the fundamental questions of existence in the situation and the fundamental responses of every religion."[70]

Indeed, Baum has argued that the tensions that beset the church— between the logic of mission and the logic of management, between adapting to new social conditions and conservative attachments to "old ways," between "the objectification of faith in doctrine and ritual and the existentialist quest for the personal meaning of faith" and, finally, between ecclesial centralization and the freedom of local communities[71]—are all tensions that will never be overcome but rather must be engaged in charity in each and every ecclesial generation. "These dilemmas cannot be resolved in permanent fashion: they keep on creating tension, conflicts, disappointments and frustrations. Organized religion can thrive only through a series of successful compromises. The larger the ecclesiastical body, the greater the need for mediating positions acceptable to the members for the sake of social

---

65. McKenna, "The Transformative Mission of the Church," 621.

66. Ibid., 622.

67. Ibid. See Baum, "Unity or Renewal," in *The Ecumenist* 13, 1 (1974) 5–9, at 7–8.

68. Ibid., 628. See Baum, "The New Ecclesiology," in *Commonweal* 91 (Oct. 31, 1969) 123–128, at 124.

69. Ibid., 630. See Baum, "Faith and Liberation: Development Since Vatican II" in Gerald Fagin, ed. *Vatican II: Open Questions and New Horizons* (Wilmington, DE: Michael Glazier, 1984) 75–104, at 103–4. (Republished in Gregory Baum, *Theology and Society* (New York: Paulist Press, 1987) 3–31. McKenna's citation can be found here at 29–30).

70. David Tracy, *The Analogical Imagination: Christian Theology and the Culture of Pluralism* (New York: Crossroad, 1981) 447; see also 453.

71. Gregory Baum, "The Pilgrim State of the Christian Church," in Giuseppe Ruggieri and Miklós Tomka, eds., *The Church in Fragments: Towards What Kind of Unity? Concilium* 1997/3 (London, SCM, 1997) 118.

peace, even if these positions do not quite correspond to their deepest convictions."[72]

Here I suggest that the problem we have seen illustrated by our discussions in the earlier chapters of this volume is that the sense that there can be an "official" ecclesiology, a "definitive" interpretation of the documents of Vatican II, and "closure" on the part of the curial authorities on debates still raging throughout the church suggests that many in positions of ecclesial authority today are of the mistaken belief that such tensions *can* be resolved once and for all. Only true and honest dialogue can resolve such tensions in even a partial fashion. No longer can the church subscribe to Augustine's oft-paraphrased dictum, "Rome has spoken, the matter is closed." Rather, Rome can and must speak, but it also can and must listen—particularly to critical voices— and so, too, must it be attentive to the painful experiences of the faithful and those on the margins of both society and the church itself. Despite their intransigent and unforgiving attitudes toward some, one cannot help feeling that the exclusion of the Donatists was nonetheless a deep wound for the church in those times. Perhaps dialogue on all sides could have overcome the disagreements without the need for schism.

Baum himself reminds us that the church is also a place where the reality of sin is ever present,[73] and we have noted Curran's apposite reflections on this fact also. What Augustine apparently underemphasized at times was the fact that sin is present in its fullness also in church leaders, and even at times in the institution itself: Recall again Congar's dictum that "institutions also speak,"[74] and Baum's concept of "institutional illness." If institutions can suffer from other malaises, they can also suffer from institutionalized sin. John Paul's millennium apologies for the sins committed by those within the church almost conceded as much. But the nagging doubt that was created by the desire to somehow preserve the stainless character of the *institution* (as opposed to the sacramental mystery) of the church itself means that the apologies may have left necessary words unsaid.

All of this may be applied in an especially pertinent way to the contemporary challenges facing the Catholic Church. Recall that Baum declares that "mission is the faithful dialogue of the church with other religions and ideologies as a means of offering redemptive transformation

72. Ibid., 118–19.
73. Ibid., 119.
74. Yves Congar, "Towards a Catholic Synthesis," in Jürgen Moltmann and Hans Küng, eds., *Who Has the Say in the Church?*, *Concilium* 148/8 (1981) 72.

to all the participants, the church as well as the others."[75] This is a crucial point and must be emphasized. And here I want to update and commend a similar methodology for our postmodern times: we must first honestly and openly engage with the divisions and disagreements within the church, but then enter into genuine dialogue in charity so that the church may renew itself and its mission for today.

Again I would stress that all that is here said concerning dialogue with those *outside* the church can also, and first of all, be said of dialogue *within* the church. Intra-and inter-ecclesial dialogue is also the path whereby we can all discover "more deeply" what "God's will for" the church is. And if such true dialogue is entered into in light of the "signs of *our* times," it would once again appear that the neo-exclusivistic path is not one that we should discern as being more in tune with the gospel than alternative ecclesial pathways—quite the opposite. Baum followed a path from initial Christian ecumenism to dialogue with the Jewish faith, then broadened his considerations and methodology toward the entire human family. As Carolyn Sharp has said, "Gregory Baum is an outwardly directed theologian" who argues for "an outwardly directed church."[76] Thus Baum's ecumenical theology took on an increasingly political and social character. In this we see mirrored the direction of much theology and ecclesial engagement in the spirit of Vatican II. Like Baum, in our efforts to discern the signs of our times today we should learn to heed that call again and in a new way for this new age with its new challenges.

At the beginning of this part of our volume, following the spirit of *Gaudium et Spes* and Vatican II in general, we emphasized that *pastoral* needs should have priority in any ecclesiology. Baum concurs, and stresses that such an ecclesiology must be open to the sinful realities of the church as well as their effect on the lives of the faithful: "We are in need of a pastorally-sensitive ecclesiology that interprets for Christians their actual experience of the church: their faithful attachment to the gospel and the Christian tradition, their confusion over the disunity of the Christian church, and their anguish over many aspects of ecclesiastical life and teaching that appal them."[77]

---

75. Baum, *Faith and Doctrine,* 118. This is also discussed by McKenna, "The Transformative Mission of the Church," 630–34, (with the quotation at 631), which focuses on Baum's understanding of the transformative power of dialogue.

76. Carolyn Sharp, "The Contribution of Gregory Baum to Political Thought," paper given at the seminar "The Work of Gregory Baum: An Appreciation," Toronto, 2002.

77. Gregory Baum, "The Pilgrim State of the Christian Church," 116.

Baum thus provides the church with a loving yet self-critical account of its merits and faults. He highlights with total honesty where the ecclesiological fault lines lie and how we need a healthy dose of realism in our attempts to address their reality. As with Rahner, Gregory Baum also helps us draw together our earlier considerations from this chapter and to point toward fundamental ecclesiological themes to be discussed in the following chapters. Referring to *Dialogue and Mission*, a document released by the Vatican's Secretariat for Non-Christian Religions in 1984, he offers the following beautiful prose, evocative of some of the deepest truths and mysteries of the faith and yet, in light of our considerations thus far, obviously challenging to many in today's church in its ecclesiological implications:

> *Dialogue and Mission* presents the church as the living sign of God's love revealed in Christ, with a mission to love humanity as Christ has loved us, towards the full manifestation of God's reign which has begun in him. (#9) The church is called to dialogue because of its very faith: God is love, and in the trinitarian mystery Christian faith glimpses in God a life of communion and interchange. (#22) This was a theme dear to Pope Paul VI more fully explored in his encyclical *Ecclesiam suam* (1964), which proposes dialogue as norm and ideal for the church of Christ on every level. Recognizing that the Spirit also works outside the visible confines of the Mystical Body, *Dialogue and Mission* argues that the church is impelled to discern the signs of the Spirit's presence and to serve as its humble and discreet collaborator through a commitment to dialogue in its many forms. (#24).[78]

So dialogue, for Baum also, is a primary ecclesiological virtue. Let us further explore how the realities of fostering such transformative dialogue might become reality in the church of our times.

Ecumenical Investigations—
Toward a Wider Ecumenical Engagement for Our Time

It was at the fifth Faith and Order Conference of the World Council of Churches, held at Santiago, that the then WCC General Secretary, Konrad Raiser, challenged theologians to foster a constructive dialogue among cultures without dissolving difference into consensus. In other words, he was espousing the need for an "ecumenical intercultural hermeneutic." Such a challenge not only brings together divided Christians but draws

---

78. Baum, *Amazing Church*, 114.

human pilgrims of every background onto common ground. It might well be termed a call to *communion in mission.*[79]

Here I wish to suggest in particular that Catholics today should also take up this challenge posed by Raiser, i.e., to foster that constructive dialogue among cultures *without* dissolving difference into consensus, as well as his call for measures toward "opening space for a culture of dialogue and solidarity."[80] But first, in order for our efforts to bear fruit and in order to counter the anti-pluralistic polemic that has surfaced across many Christian denominations in these postmodern times, we need to channel our energies into further developing what liberation theologians call "total ecumenism" or "macro-ecumenism,"[81] defined as follows:

> This is not just an attitude of mind, but a spirit that inspires attitudes and derives from a spiritual experience, an experience of God in the world and history, and from a particular way of understanding the world and its processes. We could say that in our religious experience we have encountered "God's ecumenism." God is ecumenical. God is not racist, or linked to one racial group or culture. God does not belong exclusively

79. Echoing the ARCIC document *The Gift of Authority* (London: CTS, 1999). Also of relevance in developing ecclesial dialogue is the work of a large number of emerging projects and collaborative undertakings. To name but a few (some of which the author is obviously familiar with through personal involvement!): The Chichester Project, which began in the UK and fed into the Ecclesiological Investigations Research Network that gathers together a range of people from diverse ecclesial and denominational backgrounds; the Ecclesiological Investigations Program Unit of the American Academy of Religion and related international research network; the Durham University "Receptive Ecumenism" Project; and the work of a variety of research centers and networks such as Boston College's Church in the 21st Century, Liverpool Hope University's Church in Our Times: Centre for the Study of Contemporary Ecclesiology, the University of Leuven's Centre for Ecumenical Research, and the Center for the Study of Society and Religion, Colombo, Sri Lanka, along with organizations such as INSecT and MISSIO.

80. Cf. Konrad Raiser, "Opening Space for a Culture of Dialogue and Solidarity— The Missionary objectives of the WCC in an Age of Globalization and Religious Plurality," Lecture at the *SEDOS* Seminar, Ariccia, 19 May 1999 (this can be viewed at www.sedos.org./english/raiser_2.html). On these themes see also Mannion, "What's In a Name? Hermeneutical Questions on Globalisation, Catholicity and Ecumenism," *New Blackfriars* (May 2005). Again consider the many calls for dialogue by John Paul II and now Benedict XVI. The reality that in recent decades obstacles have again been placed in the way of genuine dialogue cannot be overlooked here.

81. See Pedro Casaldáliga and José María Vigil, *The Spirituality of Liberation* (London: Burns & Oates, 1993) 165–73. Here I fully agree with Tracy that although we cannot go down the route of embracing an "easy pluralism" there is nonetheless a need to defend "polycentrism." David Tracy, "On Naming the Present" in Claude Geffré and Jean-Pierre Jossua, eds., *The Debate on Modernity, Concilium* 1992/6 (London: SCM, 1992). See also his *The Analogical Imagination*, 454. Nonetheless, here I repeat that I retain the use of the term pluralism in a positive sense.

to anyone. The New Testament revelation breaks down the walls of the "Jewish" God and shows us the universal God, the God who wants all human beings "to be saved and to come to the knowledge of the truth" (1 Tim 2:4).[82]

Again this points our thinking toward the *theological* necessity of dialogue. In essence this concept of "macro-ecumenism" is identical to what Gregory Baum calls a "wider ecumenism" (which we discussed above), governing our relations with those within and outside the church, mirroring the openness to the world that much of the teaching of Vatican II sought to foster, for if anything exhibits a positive dimension to the postmodern age (and thus for our ideas of ministry and mission) it is that the world can be and often is a much more open place, for all the risks involved in its being so.[83]

Hence "wider" or "macro"-ecumenism is a task for church leaders as well. Through engaging in it wholeheartedly we may both transcend divisions and transform our own community and the perspectives within it, but in a manner that avoids extremes—whether the postmodern poles of unity or radical diversity or the extremes of globalization and uniformity on one hand or extreme and nihilistic relativism on the other: true dialogue and consensus can help the church steer clear of all such extremes. And we remind ourselves that such charity begins at home, as Herman Pottmeyer states—for from such intra-Catholic and intra-Christian charity comes forth that spirit of dialogue that helps fulfil the gospel: "However, in order for the church to show itself 'the sign of that brotherliness which allows honest dialogue' among all human beings, it will be necessary 'to foster within the church itself . . . dialogue with

82. Ibid., 165. Note that such a notion was also discussed in the debates at Vatican II, e.g., the speech by the Bishop of Cuernavaca, Mexico, Sergio Méndez Arceo, "The Church as an Open Community," in Yves Congar, Hans Küng, and Daniel O'Hanlon, eds., *Council Speeches of Vatican II* (London and New York: Sheed and Ward, 1964) 118–21, especially 119–20. Some years later David Tracy would speak of "a new kind of interreligious ecumenism as part of theological self-consciousness." David Tracy, "Beyond Foundationalism and Relativism," 133. Somewhat presciently Tracy spoke of the impact on Christian theology of the day when "the new Islamic reality" throughout Europe "becomes a central theological concern," ibid.

83. Hermann Pottmeyer admirably sums up the scope of this "wider ecumenism": "Although we have limited ourselves . . . to the discussion of dialogue within the church, we must not forget that Vatican II also used the term "dialogue" to refer to communication with separated Christians, with non-Christians and atheists, with the entire human family, and with the world. This aspect deserves our attention even more than the use of the dialogue model for exchanges within the church." Pottmeyer, "Dialogue as a Model for Communication in the Church," in Patrick Granfield, ed., *The Church and Communication* (Kansas City: Sheed and Ward, 1994) 97–103, at 103.

ever abounding fruitfulness' *(Gaudium et spes* 92). The important goal of global dialogue on which the future of humanity depends will not be served by a relapse into preconciliar one-way communication."[84]

And, as we noted earlier, historical consciousness is fundamental to a "critical" conception of catholicity and ecumenicity.[85] Sectarian mind-sets (including those we have here termed neo-exclusivism) work against the lived reality of Catholicity itself.[86] We might go theologically further still: In all such endeavors the very being of God is revealed. We gain an entrancing and transforming, yet forever partial, glimpse of the ecumenical "face of God." Casaldáliga and Vigil concur:

> After a period in which many versions of the image of God in the ambit of Western civilization had been too closely tied to one culture—or to a set of hegemonic cultures, Greek, Latin, Saxon—Christian thought and discernment in recent times have given us back a clearer view of the ecumenical face of God. For Catholics, the Second Vatican Council was a crucial moment in this process, especially in its decrees on the church, the modern world, ecumenism, mission and the lay apostolate. Today we see more clearly the presence of God's Spirit down through history, in all peoples and all cultures.[87]

In our age of increased and at times seemingly runaway globalization these priorities become ever more urgent. Thus Casaldáliga and Vigil help demonstrate the link between our previous discussion and our movement toward embracing the ecclesial, doctrinal, and moral necessity of dialogue in a variety of macro-ecumenical forms.[88] There must be both a *method* and a *meaning* to our dialogue, and the two are intertwined. Our concern is not simply with method for its own sake. Any methodology, by nature, should be facilitating, a means to an end:

84. Pottmeyer, "Dialogue as a Model for Communication in the Church." See also Karl Rahner, "Dialogue in the Church," 104: "even in questions of the absolute nature of the church's own assent of faith and her ultimately missionary purpose, the church can conduct an open dialogue with all men and groups of men because in such a dialogue, without prejudice to the divine truth, the church can and must be she who learns as well, she who is capable of being led into still deeper levels of her own truth and her understanding of that truth. In such a dialogue she can be purified from misunderstandings and distorted interpretations such as may have attached themselves to her understanding of her faith, and she can herself become more believing."

85. See also David Tracy, "Beyond Foundationalism and Relativism," 133–36.

86. Charles Curran, *The Church and Morality,* ch. 4.

87. Casaldáliga and Vigil, *Spirituality of Liberation,* 165–66.

88. Here see also a definitive collection of essays on various debates pertaining to "wider ecumenism," Peter Phan, ed., *Christianity and the Wider Ecumenism* (New York: Paragon House, 1990).

the prime concern is the end itself, that community enhancement to which the church is called. In shaping the conversational method, naturally, theologians, those theoretical experts and professional practitioners of God-talk, can and should help. That, after all, is their vocation, whether they all fully appreciate it or not. But again we must caution against any idealistic notions that dialogue and charity may easily and swiftly overcome divisions and disagreements. The church has always faced interior struggles, and its members from the earliest times have frequently found it difficult to display toward others within, just as to those outside, that very Christian love that is meant to characterize the Christian life. So our considerations are not only hope-filled. They are equally humbling and indicative of the long road that dialogue all too often represents. But if the journey is embarked upon resolutely, the communion we desire comes ever closer.

Now we must ask: What themes need to be examined in more detail to facilitate the shaping of this method? We explore these questions in what follows.

Chapter Seven

The Promise of Comparative Ecclesiology: Toward "An Ecumenical Intercultural Hermeneutic"

Re-envisioning the Open Church

In a passage that captures the situation of the Christian church in the contemporary world in a most vivid fashion, the Anglican theologian Christopher Duraisingh tells us that

> The gospel story is for all places and times, but it is never available to us apart from its embodiment in particular cultures. The story of God's love in Christ becomes the good news only as it is enfleshed in a particular culture; yet this gospel can never be identified with any one of its particular expressions, for it transcends them all. While all cultures are worthy expressions of the gospel story, no cultural expression of it, even the classical, can become the exclusive norm or exhaustive means for drawing out the richness of God's love in Christ. It is only as the multiplicity of traditions that mark the global church are recognised and brought into dialogue with each other that the church can discern and witness to the "multi-colored wisdom of God" that the author of the letter to the Ephesians speaks of.[1]

In this chapter I want to suggest that our ecclesiological undertakings today can flourish all the more if we take our lead from theologians like

---

1. Christopher Duraisingh, "Contextual and Catholic: Conditions for Cross-Cultural Hermeneutics," *Anglican Theological Review* 82 (Fall 2000) 687.

Gregory Baum and work toward contributing to such an "alternative consciousness" to that of reductive postmodernity, and of globalization in particular. Our efforts today will benefit if we remind ourselves that *ecumenical issues* always demand attention in any theological conversation, be it obviously so, as in historical and ecclesiological explorations, doctrinally so as in systematics, or morally so in ethical debates. Indeed, cannot the case be made that all true theology must be "ecumenical theology," because the formation and enhancement of communities is the teleological priority for humanity? Hence the ongoing task of "bridge-building," without which no true reconciliation can take place, finds its natural applied and theoretical home in the science of theology.

All of this is the nature and task of that *macro-ecumenism* discussed in our previous chapter, which is simply to say that we should not forget that ecumenism is not simply about the *church and the churches.* As we have noted, the church has increasingly understood its mission as involving dialogue and closer relations with people of all faiths and none. From John XXIII through Vatican II and even down to certain teachings of Pope John Paul II, a "wider agenda" for ecumenism is already there in the church also—a call to bring about the greater unity of the entire human family, a task that Christians were set as far back as when Jesus of Nazareth wandered around first-century Palestine preaching that radical and transformative gospel of love, justice, and *reconciliation.*

Thus if all such hope is allowed to develop further, our structures can change, our understanding of authority and governance may be transformed, and so too might our conception of what it is to be and live as church. Better relationships might flow, opportunities could be increased, and all of this could be achieved through dialogue at both a global and a local level. This quest for macro-ecumenism articulates our seeking to unite all beings so that all may live as fulfilled a life-in-community as possible. Consider the words of the Church of Scotland theologian Duncan Forrester, who has done much pioneering work not just in ecumenical theology but also in practical and public theology. He is commenting on Eph 2:13-15: "Notice that God's purpose is to create a single new humanity—the unity of the church is simply a sign and foretaste of the broader unity of humankind which is God's goal. . . . The New Testament teaches that the way the church is structured and operates is to be at the service of the gospel. *The Church points to, and already expresses in a partial way, the coming unity of humankind.*"[2]

2. Duncan B. Forrester, *Truthful Action: Explorations in Practical Theology* (Edinburgh: T & T Clark, 2000) 191 (italics supplied).

In fact, was not *Gaudium et Spes* unique in that it addressed not simply Catholics or even Christians, but rather "the whole of humanity" (§2)?[3] And did it not proclaim that "the People of God and the human race in whose midst it lives render service to each other? Thus the mission of the church will show its religious, and by that very fact, its supremely human character" (§11). Roger Haight outlines the reality of this call for the church in our postmodern times: "To be ecumenical, Christian theology must both attend and transcend the specific authorities and magisteria of particular churches. . . . [T]his Christian church co-exists with other religions in a new common human history. *This new context imposes what might be called a dialogical situation.* Christian theology in this situation will attend to the faiths of other peoples and, being influenced by them, reformulate its self-understanding accordingly."[4]

Here we see tentative methodological fundamentals laid down for the "comparative ecclesiology" Haight would go on to develop at much greater length, and which we consider below in more detail. We should acknowledge that our postmodern age is radically different from earlier times and hence the church needs to adopt a radically different approach to the formulation of mission priorities and the identification of the ecclesial ministries, structures, and modes of governance necessary for our times.

What form of dialogue is emerging here? It is one that begins within the Catholic Church, spreads throughout it and beyond, embracing the entire human family. That first step of trying to transcend divisions within the Catholic Church demands a return to the source of many such divisions, as outlined in parts I and II above, namely, differing understandings of and responses to postmodern reality and its challenges. As Roger Haight has said, "Looking back [over the course of church history] it becomes plain that positive constructive dialogue and comparison are a better way to forge communion than polemics or claims to juridical authority."[5] But how exactly might such polemics be transcended?

Once again, in many ways such polemics are really of a very postmodern character and the need to transcend them is often as much a methodological (even epistemological) and theological task as it is an ecclesiological one. Quite often the divisions in ecclesiology stem from

---

3. This vision is again further encapsulated by *Gaudium et Spes* §55; cf. also §§92–93.
4. Roger Haight, "The Church as Locus of Theology," in *Why Theology? Concilium* 1994/6, 22 (italics supplied).
5. Roger Haight, "Comparative Theology," in Gerard Mannion and Lewis Mudge, eds., *The Routledge Companion to the Christian Church* (London: Routledge, 2007).

divisions in one or more of these other areas. So there is a need, as David Tracy among many others suggests, to move beyond foundationalism on the one hand and relativism on the other.[6] Recalling our discussions in the previous chapter, and the idea of a "wider ecumenism" in general, note that Tracy relates the shift in epistemology to the "new" Europe where Christianity's superiority, understood in modern developmental terms ("schemata with a secretly evolutionary sense of time and a culturally colonist sense of space"),[7] is no longer an assumption taken for granted. Thus, recalling our discussions of the wider or macro-ecumenism, Tracy suggests that theologians from every continent

> now believe that all serious theology today will try to work out an adequate Christian theology only by trying to understand Christianity in culturally and politically non-Eurocentric ways. Perhaps only by trying to understand the meaning of the other great religions can a modern Christian achieve an appropriate Christian self-understanding in the late twentieth century. This latter "new ecumenism," moreover, needs to be worked out from the beginning of a theology and at every crucial moment in theology. The question of the "other religions" can no longer be left for an appendix to a theology.[8]

Tracy was writing at the beginning of the 1990s and perhaps his optimism was soon necessarily put on hold—for witness the emergence, and in some quarters the triumph, of neo-exclusivism in the years since. Back then, works such as John Milbank's *Theology and Social Theory*[9] were brand new, and radical orthodoxy had not been heard of. In short, much work remains to be done. Polemics have not disappeared in our times; they have rather been intensified. But Tracy *was* anticipating something of the great potential offered to all branches of theology, including, as we shall see, to ecclesiology, by the emerging discipline of comparative theology. And Tracy also offered the insightful warning that in the postmodern world we can no longer live within a tradition as we once did. The stark choices are to go the way of retrenchment (foundationalism) or to take flight (the path toward relativism), or else to progress via a third route:

6. David Tracy, "Beyond Foundationalism and Relativism: Hermeneutics and the New Ecumenism," ch. 12 of his *On Naming the Present: God, Hermeneutics, and Church* (Maryknoll, NY: Orbis, 1994); again, similar themes are discussed at greater length in his *Blessed Rage for Order: The New Pluralism in Theology* (New York: Crossroad, 1975), and *The Analogical Imagination: Christian Theology and the Culture of Pluralism* (New York: Crossroad, 1981).

7. Tracy, "Beyond Foundationalism and Relativism," 132.

8. Ibid.

9. John Milbank, *Theology and Social Theory* (Oxford: Blackwell, 1990).

. . . what Paul Ricoeur nicely named a "second naiveté" toward one's tradition (enter critical philosophy and revisionary theology) allied to a genuine openness to otherness and difference. Ulysses-like, theologians need to wander: through modern critical approaches; through an exposure to other ways—religious, non-religious, antireligious. . . . The only serious question becomes: is a second naiveté possible? If so how? Many of us may rediscover our traditions, i.e., experience a second naiveté toward its beauty and its truth, in and through discovering others, their difference, and their truth. But is it possible to honor the truth of one's own religious tradition while being genuinely open to other great ways as other? Clearly the answer must be yes or we are all lost in a Hobbesian state of the war of all against all.[10]

And yet is Tracy here not simply reappropriating much of the spirit of Vatican II? When one examines the many humble expressions there of appreciation, of generosity, of the debt the Catholic Church owes to other Christians and people of other faiths and indeed of no faith, we hear in Tracy's words an echo of their sentiments living on.[11]

And yet our polarized relations wound the very heart of the church itself. It seems that in our times it is becoming more difficult to accept and embrace even our own ecclesial sisters and brothers *as* others. Thomas P. Rausch offers a brief program for overcoming divisions that touches on many of the themes encountered in these three chapters. He particularly recommends that Catholics rediscover the enormous potential of the fundamental Catholic principles of catholic inclusivity, legitimate diversity, theological humility, faith seeking understanding, the complementarity of faith and reason, historical consciousness, and ecclesial theology itself, of an evangelical theology, an ecumenical theology, the conversation-facilitating concept of a hierarchy of truths and, finally, respect for the other.[12] We move closer, then, toward identifying key priorities.

Overcoming Polarization:
Lieven Boeve and Postmodernity's Ecclesiological "Interruption"

Of course, as we saw in our earlier chapters, the initial difficulty is overcoming divisions *within* the church. Such a challenge applies equally to theological method itself, for none of the above is possible if we remain

10. Tracy, "Beyond Foundationalism and Relativism," 138.
11. See Yves Congar, Hans Küng, and Daniel O'Hanlon, eds., *Council Speeches of Vatican II* (London: Sheed and Ward, 1964), especially those contained in Part III, "Reunion of All Christians," 95–191.
12. Thomas P. Rausch, *Reconciling Faith and Reason* (Collegeville: Liturgical Press, 1998), ch. 8, "Towards Common Ground in Theology," 115–26.

entrenched in theological and ecclesiological enclaves trapped between oscillations from pre-modern to modern to anti-modern thinking and the practice influenced by such thought. Here the recent work of Lieven Boeve proves particularly valuable and informative. Boeve's work is analogous to the aims of this book, for, in his own words, he aims to explore the *recontextualization* of theology in an age "which is characterized by irreducible plurality, radical particularity and contextuality, and an increased sensitivity towards irreducible alterity."[13] Boeve and his research group have explored possibilities for the "recontextualization of Christian theology in a postmodern context" and this, of course, has many ecclesiological implications. Boeve seeks to steer between naïve forms of correlation that simply reiterate their own theological presuppositions or totalize human experience and any theology of "rupture" that attempts to wash its hands of contextualization altogether and to articulate Christian identity today in a closed and defensive fashion.[14]

In one of his more explicitly ecclesiological writings Boeve asserts that theology in our postmodern age can move beyond the polarization between modern and anti-modern theological methods by drawing on the epistemological category of "interruption," for here "both continuity and discontinuity are held together in tension."[15] Boeve rejects the label of "postmodern theologian" assigned him by his critics. He asserts rather that he is not a pre-modern, modern, anti-modern, or postmodern theologian.[16] He is simply a theologian who works in a postmodern context. As Eamonn Conway has illustrated, Boeve's "Leuven Project" has sought to chart a middle way between radical orthodoxy and what conservative ecclesial mindsets have called "going native" and capitulating to the world in one's theological and ecclesiological thinking and practice.[17]

13. See Lieven Boeve, "Research Profile," www.kuleven.ac.be/cv/u0000317.htm.

14. Ibid. Boeve's most relevant work here is *Interrupting Tradition* (Leuven: Peeters, 2004). See also his earlier essay, "Bearing Witness to the Different: A Model for Theologizing in the Postmodern Context," *Louvain Studies* 20 (1995) 362–79.

15. "Beyond the Modern and Anti-modern Dilemma: Theological Method in a Postmodern European Context," in J. Verstraeten (ed.), *Scrutinizing the Signs of the Times and Interpreting Them in Light of the Gospel* (BETL), Leuven: Peeters Press, 2007 (forthcoming). (Page references are to a copy of the original conference paper.) Also published in German as 'Der schwierige Dialog zwischen Glaube und Kultur: Jenseits des modernen und anti-modernen Dilemmas', in C. Wessely (ed.), *Kunst des Glaubens—Glaube der Kunst. Der Blick auf das, unverfügbare Andere'* (FS. Gerhard Larcher), Regensburg: Verlag Friedrich Pustet, 2006, 11–26 (cf. III, VIII).

16. Here recall Tracy's categories in "On Naming the Present" (see ch. 1 above).

17. Eamonn Conway, "Speaking a Constant Word in a Changing World: Recognizing and Resolving Tensions and Tendencies in a Postmodern Context," *New Blackfriars* (March 2006) 110–20.

Thus Boeve quite rightly challenges then-Cardinal Ratzinger's rejection of the view that *Gaudium et Spes* offers a charter for "an unrestricted dialogue." As Boeve summarizes, the Cardinal had argued that "the Pastoral Constitution was not meant as a starting point for an unrestricted dialogue, but rather determined its limits; moreover, it is the Dogmatic Constitution on the Church that ought to direct a contemporary hermeneutics of the Pastoral Constitution and not the other way around."[18] These considerations return us to the themes of our reflections in chapters 3 and 4 of this book and that specter of neo-exclusivism that haunts contemporary Christianity. For, Boeve concludes, the result of such thinking is "radical critique, not only of the modern presumption of theology's dialogue with the late modern context, but of the principle of dialogue itself. For anti-modern theological epistemology, the identity, plausibility, and relevance of Christian faith are not reflected upon from the presumption of continuity but of *discontinuity* with the world. Theological rationality is at odds with the rationality of the world."[19]

For Boeve the problem is greater because, while such anti-modern theologies may concur with the critique of modernity presented by many postmodern thinkers, they attempt to combat the challenges of postmodernity "by introducing pre-modern theological thinking patterns."[20] Of course, I have also suggested that such "pre-modern" patterns have been used in a distinctively postmodern fashion; nonetheless, Boeve's methodological reflections certainly assist in taking our debates forward. His deliberations bring to mind Karl Rahner's own understanding of true dialogue: ". . . an open dialogue still has a certain meaning even in those cases in which it does not imply that kind of unity which consists in mutually holding the same opinion, but rather in accepting the other person in his uniqueness and otherness, the difference of 'viewpoint' being only a very secondary expression of this."[21]

18. Boeve, "Beyond the Modern and Anti-Modern Dilemma," 4. Cf. idem, "*Gaudium et Spes* and the Crisis of Modernity: the End of the Dialogue with the World?" in Mathijs Lemberigts and Leo Kenis, eds., *Vatican II and its Legacy* (Leuven: Peeters, 2002) 83–94. Boeve is referring in particular to Joseph Ratzinger, "Angesichts der Welt von heute. Überlegungen zur Konfrontation mit der Kirche im Schema XIII," in *Dogma und Verkündigung* (Munich and Freiburg: Wewel, 1973) 183–204, especially 199–200. (English: *Dogma and Preaching*, tr. Matthew J. O'Connell (Chicago: Franciscan Herald Press, 1985.)
19. Boeve, "Beyond the Modern and Anti-Modern Dilemma," 4.
20. Ibid.
21. Rahner, "Dialogue in the Church," *Theological Investigations* 10. *Writings of 1965–67 II* (London: Darton, Longman, and Todd, 1973) 104. On the hermeneutics of the other see, again, Gerard Mannion, "What's In a Name? Hermeneutical Questions

Thus we see that an openness to learn, to listen, and to engage must be paramount in encountering the other, for—as we have seen so many theologians here emphasize—such a "dialogical imperative" lies at the heart of the gospel message itself. The postmodern "interruption" of Christian tradition does not have to be met with a contemporary version of the siege mentality once so prevalent in Catholic reactions to the wider culture. Instead, it can be seen as opening space and opportunity for wider and more genuine (more truly catholic) dialogue to take place.

Thus, in contrast to the present "postmodern" understanding and exercise of the magisterium and the move away from the "open church" toward a neo-exclusivistic understanding of it, Boeve helps us appreciate that theology and the church can actually learn a great deal from currents of thought in the postmodern era.[22] Echoing Baum's appreciation of critical theory, Boeve commends how postmodern thought can help us appreciate the need today for a different "kind of sensitivity in the midst of our awareness of irreducible multiplicity."[23] This can lead us to an appreciation of the reality in which we live, and to acceptance of the "otherness" the postmodern era vividly brings before our cultural horizons. Hence, for Boeve, the "key to postmodern critical consciousness" involves such an appreciation.

> Indeed, this irreducible multiplicity implies otherness as such, irremovable otherness that cannot be reduced to a single narrative nor subsumed within a particular totalizing perspective. Whatever we do to encompass otherness within a single narrative, it will always place itself beyond our grasp. Sensitivity towards the other in his/her/its irreducible otherness lies at the basis of what we might refer to as postmodern critical consciousness, which consists of our reference to irreducible otherness and our ultimate witness to that otherness.[24]

Here, then Boeve helps add further weight to our argument that an official ecclesiological paradigm (or, again, as N. M. Healy terms it, a "blueprint ecclesiology"), particularly one imposed "from above," is especially ill-suited for furthering the mission of church in our times. Of course, this returns us to the "postmodern" understanding of the magisterium and the "official" interpretations of communion ecclesiology,

---

on 'Globalisation,' Catholicity and Ecumenism," *New Blackfriars* (May 2005) 204–15.

22. Note that I have argued in this volume that the present Catholic "antimoderns" are also "anti-" much of what comes after modernity.

23. Boeve, *Interrupting Tradition,* 90.

24. Ibid., 90–91. Along similar lines, cf. Mannion, "What's in a Name?"

which offer something very different from a "postmodern critical consciousness." So, reminding ourselves of our conclusions in chapter 4, let us recall that Boeve goes on to argue that "Every (closed, master) narrative that aims at the authoritarian reduction of multiplicity on the grounds of its own premises (thus stripping the other of his/her/its otherness) is open to criticism. From the postmodern perspective it would appear that only those narratives which admit to the specificity and limitedness of their own perspective and which witness to the impossibility of integrating the remainder are worthy of any claim to legitimacy."[25]

So our deliberations in this part of the volume have finally brought us to this fundamental question: What sort of ecclesiological methodology might be developed in light of such "postmodern critical consciousness," and how could an ecclesiology embrace and respect, indeed celebrate the other *as* other, while remaining comfortable in the celebration of fundamentals of its own tradition?

Toward a Comparative and Dialogical Ecclesiology

So we can now bring together the various themes of this section of our book. In doing so we seek to draw on the recent methodological insights of comparative theology, in particular Keith Ward's notion of "Pluralistic Christianity"[26] and Roger Haight's call for a "dialogical" mission to complement the church's mission of witness.[27] In underlining the need for (and inescapability of) the "new ecumenism," David Tracy also highlights the path that comparative theology itself might take in efforts to "find new ways to learn from the other traditions."[28] Such a path is the route between conservative retreats into foundationalism and utter relativism, and may allow us to further appreciate just why neo-exclusivism and the tone of texts such as *Dominus Iesus* cannot serve the church in our times well. One will begin close to home[29] and cherish what is of value there, but one will also venture out to learn

25. Boeve, *Interrupting Tradition*, 91.

26. See, for example, Keith Ward, *Religion and Community* (Oxford: Oxford University Press, 2000), and *A Vision to Pursue* (London: SCM, 1991). The writings of Francis X. Clooney provide a further example of pioneering work in this field.

27. Roger Haight, "The Church as Locus of Theology," in *Why Theology?* 13–22.

28. David Tracy, "Beyond Foundationalism and Relativism," 137.

29. "On the one hand, ecumenism agrees with the heart of all the classic religious journeys: the universal is to be found by embracing the particular. Indeed, those who break through to a universal religious message are always highly particular in both origin and expression. Surely this route through the particular is a wiser way to find truth than seeking that ever-elusive goal, a common denominator among the religions.

from what may enhance that homestead: "The new search is likely to become that of more and more religious persons: stay faithful to your own tradition; go deeper and deeper into its particularities; defend and clarify its identity. At the same time, wander, Ulysses-like, willingly, even eagerly, among other great traditions and ways; try to learn something of their beauty and truth; concentrate on their otherness and differences as the new route to communality."[30] Comparative ecclesiology is simply the ecclesiological *application* of such insights, and those of comparative theology, to the study of and discourse about and reflecting on the church.

Embracing a Comparative Ecclesiology

As with Gregory Baum and Lieven Boeve, we find Roger Haight addressing similar problems but for this new age. A true Jesuit, Haight has written extensively in the fields of systematic theology, liberation theology, christology, and, of course, ecclesiology. He excels in assessing where the churches and theology currently find themselves in the contemporary world and in suggesting ways forward for the future engagement of the churches with those across numerous other churches, other religions, and beyond the confines of either. It is thus that he champions the need for the church to embrace a *dialogical* mission. His most extensive work to date in ecclesiology is a monumental and pioneering two-volume study in *comparative* ecclesiology.[31] In brief, he defines this methodology thus: "Comparative ecclesiology consists in analyzing and portraying in an organized or systematic way two or more different ecclesiologies so that they can be compared."[32] It is characterized by, first, using social and historical science in the study of ecclesiologies; second, attention to representative and authoritative sources of particular ecclesiologies; third, organizing the different ecclesiologies under comparison according to a common pattern or template. It acknowledges that "it is no longer possible to think that a single church could carry the full

---

Some people can speak Esperanto. Most of us would rather learn Spanish or Chinese or Arabic or English." Ibid.

30. Ibid.

31. Cf. Roger Haight, *Christian Community in History.* 2 vols. (New York: Continuum, 2004). Vol 1: *Historical Ecclesiology.* Vol. 2: *Comparative Ecclesiology.* See also his "Comparative Ecclesiology," in *The Routledge Companion to the Christian Church,* 2007.

32. Haight, *Christian Community in History* 2:4.

flow of Christian life in a single organizational form."[33] Of particular relevance to this book, Haight develops his two-volume study toward the following conclusion: "just as the Catholic Church has begun to adjust to the modern world of Christian pluralism, the context is on the verge of changing again, just as radically, to a postmodern, globalized world of the multicultural with ecclesiologies across the Christian traditions and new ones reflecting this diversity. In sum, comparative ecclesiology does not undermine the basic thrust of historical ecclesiology but sharpens its tensions and makes it considerably more interesting."[34]

It is all the more disappointing, then, that a focus on Haight's inspiring and pioneering work in this area only serves to highlight further that "hermeneutical refusal" of the Vatican's Congregation for the Doctrine of the Faith in recent times (a refusal evident in neo-exclusivism in general). Haight's work in christology was publicly condemned, and in February 2005 he was prohibited from teaching Catholic theology and so forced to leave his post in the Weston Jesuit Theological Institute and to transfer to the longstanding "Hermeneutical-Pluralist" haven of Union Theological Seminary in New York City. Not least, the Vatican condemnation made it clear that the CDF took issue with Haight's affirmation of the need for Catholics to take the contemporary pluralist reality seriously. And, as with so many other theologians investigated by the CDF in recent decades, one must ask whether it is actually Haight's *ecclesiological* work that was the prime focus of CDF attention.

In a later writing Haight clarifies his definition of comparative ecclesiology further, stating that "Comparative ecclesiology studies the church in a way that takes into account the various levels of pluralism which mark its existence today. . . . The thematic that constitutes an ecclesiology as comparative is precisely the various ways ecclesiology explicitly interacts with pluralism."[35] He thus indicates all the more that comparative ecclesiology offers the best hope for meeting the challenges of dialogue and pluralism in the postmodern age that we have been discussing throughout this book.

In seeking to integrate aspects of these positive ecclesiological developments in our own contexts and churches, particularly in our efforts to provide the church with a renewed and continued relevance today,

33. Ibid., 2:7.
34. Ibid., 2:9.
35. Haight, "Comparative Theology," in *The Routledge Companion to the Christian Church*. A third volume exploring ecumenical ecclesiology of *Christian Community in History* is in progress.

to enable the gospel to be put into practice in our communities all the more, and to resist the rise of neo-exclusivism, we might especially gain from adapting and building on four theses "against sectarianism" offered by Haight in his 1994 article. These are formulated vis-à-vis certain radical transformations our age has witnessed in our understanding of the idea of *place,* the idea of *church,* the *idea* of theology, and, finally, the *focus* of theology.

Let us examine each of these in turn. They afford us insight into the nature and role of theology today in relation to the church, as Haight contends that the interrelationship between theology and church has been transformed by developments in knowledge, ecumenism, interreligious dialogue, and the movements for human liberation. In all Haight here offers, in effect, a systematic theology in brief and the embryonic outline of his later project. It thus merits our attention and citation at length, particularily so as to avoid any potential misunderstanding of his work and the intentions behind it.

"The idea of *place*" constitutes the first focal point of Haight's essay. By this he means that the complexification and explosion of knowledge has transformed our very understanding of what a "place" actually is. He argues, however, against any compartmentalization and localization of theology such as some have advocated in a reaction to the developments of postmodernity: "The localization and compartmentalization of theology is a temptation for many today. Some theologians have become seduced by the very systems of modernity and postmodernity which they attack. That is, they try to escape them by isolating the church from culture and conceiving of theology as a purely confessional and fideist discipline."[36] For Haight the significant point that needs to be grasped here is that theology *transcends* church and addresses *all* reality. The reality of human life is one, and so theology must embrace all human life and reach out into the wider world also.

Second, Haight turns to "the idea of *church.*" Echoing our earlier discussions, he addresses the rise of historical consciousness and of the ecumenical movement. The church cannot be restricted to one confessional movement, and any genuine ecumenical theology must transcend particular authorities and particular *magisteria.* The *entire* Christian church is theology's primary context.

> More and more today Christian theology is becoming an ecumenical discipline in fact without particular theologians surrendering their confes-

---

36. Haight, *The Church as Locus of Theology,* 15.

sional alliances and identities. But if these reflections on the ecumenical character of theology are accurate, then the role of the authority of any particular church relative to the theologian and his or her theology will have changed. And by extension, the role of the authority of individual churches shifts with respect to the discipline of theology itself. In an ecumenically conscious theology the witness and data of the magisterium of the particular theologian by definition ceases to be the sole point of reference for authoritative statements.[37]

In fastening on these questions of ecumenism, ecclesial identity, magisterium, and authority in general Haight thus also draws together many of those issues we have earlier identified as priorities for the church in our times and that therefore demonstrate and further accentuate the ecclesiological necessity of dialogue. He continues,

> Again, by extension to the discipline, ecumenical theology must consider a variety of authoritative witnesses from many churches. It must also employ various comparative and dialectical procedures to frame a more general statement of the issue than will be reflected in the particular view of only one church. Theology that is ecumenically conscious is led by a logic other than reliance on the magisterium of a single church and is forced to consult the authorities of all churches in a reverent and critical manner.[38]

Haight's analysis leads him to argue that we cannot confine theology to patently ecclesial matters alone, nor can one church alone authorize and dictate the shape and form of theology in our ecumenical age. "It should not be thought that the role or importance of the magisterium of any particular church is minimized by these considerations. Only exaggerated claims of the authority within any particular communion is affected. Particular structures of authority in different communions are essential for preserving the distinctive spirit of these traditions in a pluralistic church."

37. Ibid., 16.
38. Ibid., 16–17. He continues: "Theology in the Roman Catholic Church after Vatican II's endorsement of ecumenism is roughly analogous to theology during the Western Schism (1378–1417). Catholic theologians then existed within the sphere of one of the two popes or three popes. Theoretically they were bound by the magisterium and papal authority of their particular pope. Yet most of those theologians, especially those in the university centers, knew they had a higher loyalty to the *congregatio fidelium* which was one in Christ. Here theology rose above 'local' or 'sectarian' or 'confessional' authority, was critical of it and of the situation itself, and in this transcending role helped form the atmosphere or situational climate in which a resolution was effected." Ibid., 17.

But none of this is to dismiss the need for teaching authority, for magisterium altogether; far from it. Instead, Haight's analysis allows us to appreciate that in our contemporary world such a magisterium must be shaped by dialogue and ecumenical spirit as opposed to being driven by fear of dissent and of the other, and thus entrenched. As he suggests, "A magisterium is absolutely necessary to define the beliefs of a particular tradition, to establish boundaries of this or that communion, to organize and regulate and thus preserve the identity of it and the people in it. What the internalization of the ecumenical imperative by the churches has done, then, is to moderate the absolutistic or universalistic claims of certain structures of authority in particular churches."[39]

But this "internalization of the ecumenical imperative" is currently under threat from the forces of neo-exclusivism we encountered earlier. A new dogmatic and exclusivistic imperative would appear to be in the ascendancy, driven by the *fear* of postmodernity. But Haight's alternative vision embraces ecumenism, the world in which we find ourselves, and turns toward a truly pluralistic agenda that is neither fearful nor suspicious of the pluralistic reality of the world and the human family. So first, what does this mean *within* the Christian church? As Haight suggests, it is a call to acknowledge even the plurality of teaching authorities, of *magisteria* that are at work in the service of the gospel today, and thus to dialogue with and learn from each of them.

> Let me summarize this point in the form of a thesis. It is directed against another form of sectarianism. The church is the place for theology. But the church at the end of the twentieth century as a result of the ecumenical movement is recognized to be the whole or total church, despite its disunity and divisions. This means, negatively, that the church in the sense of a particular communion cannot by itself be a final or exclusive limit or constraint or criterion or norm for Christian theology today. Rather, positively, the many magisteria of various churches are witnesses to Christian truth and sources for data for Christian theology.[40]

The third consideration in Haight's analysis is of "the *idea* of theology" in light of the reality of pluralism. Here he addresses the encounter

39. Ibid., 17–18.
40. Ibid., 18. Cf. Richard Gaillardetz, *Teaching with Authority: A Theology of the Magisterium in the Church* (Collegeville: Liturgical Press, 1997) 276: "It is difficult to imagine a formalized unity among the churches that does not include some shared understanding of doctrinal teaching authority. Even so, Roman Catholics cannot afford the hubris of thinking that their structures and understandings of authority *in toto* and as presently constituted provide the only viable possibility."

of Christian theology and the church with world religions. Theology has much to learn and gain from its dialogue with other faiths, which establishes new horizons for its sources and norms. Again echoing our earlier discussion, he reminds us that we now live in a "dialogical situation" that calls for unending conversing *and* learning from such encounters. Haight's sentiments help provide further grounding for our suggestions concerning the need for ecclesiologies that are both dialogical and prophetic and the inseparability of such from the task of evangelization itself:

> The development entails a new posture of the church *vis á vis* other religions and consequently a new dimension for theological reflection within the church. In very broad terms one can define the new stance of the church in terms of the categories of witness and dialogue. The mission of the church in one respect remains the same: it is a mission of evangelization or giving witness to its faith in God mediated by Jesus Christ. Its intent is to be a sign of this faith and to establish and nurture a local church to continue the mission of Jesus. But at the same time the notion of dialogue has come to inform and qualify the method and immediate goals of the witness.[41]

Thus we return to our central theme of dialogue. Haight has a particularly developed and empowering understanding of the concept: "Dialogue means entering into a respectful and attentive exchange with people, their cultures and their religions. The metaphor of a dialogue or conversation supplies the rules for how the church should encounter the people of other religions at all levels. In other words, a phenomenology of an authentic dialogue reveals the characteristics that should qualify the unfolding of the church's mission."[41a] And one must conclude that such an understanding of dialogue has been shaped, nurtured, and brought to fruition in the creative and energizing waters of theological and cultural inquiry to which Vatican II helped give rise. Indeed, one might suggest that Haight has also only taken the spirit of Vatican II to its logical conclusion, ecclesiologically, theologically, and morally. Thus Haight speaks of such dialogue complementing the mission of church, with the sources and data for theology greatly expanded through this dialogical situation. He goes on to offer what could serve as a summary of our key concerns and aims in these chapters, echoing many of the insights outlined in the thought of Gregory Baum about the transformative nature of encounter and dialogue in these postmodern times and in our varying contexts:

41. Haight, *Church as Locus of Theology*, 9.
41a. Ibid.

Secondly, and correspondingly, in a situation that can be characterized as dialogical in nature, as opposed to being initially polemical, Christian theology is attentive to the voice of dialogue partners. Christian theology is open to learning. The experience of non-Christians becomes in some sense data for Christian theology. The consequences of this have been clearly described by theologians who have engaged in inter-religious dialogues: the understanding of their own faith has been changed. The dialogue, the passing over and entering into the world of the other religion, to whatever extent this is possible, and the return, transform Christian self-understanding.[42]

And we are drawn back to our earlier considerations once more, for in Haight's words we hear echoes of Paul VI's own call to dialogue in *Ecclesaim suam,* where a pluralistic reality is also viewed in positive terms for the church. Humanity is seen in terms of a series of concentric circles that incorporate the whole human family, all those of religious faith, all Christians, all Catholics with, finally, the church itself at the center. Note in particular that Paul speaks of the first "concentric circle" within which the church is located, along with all others to whom it must display love *(caritas)* and with whom it must engage in dialogue:

> The first of these circles is immense. Its limits stretch beyond our view into the distant horizon. It comprises the entire human race, the world. We are fully aware of the distance which separates us from the world, but we do not conceive of it as a stranger to us. All things human are our concern. We share with the whole of the human race a common nature, a common life, with all its gifts and all its problems. We are ready to play our part in this primary, universal society, to acknowledge the insistent demands of its fundamental needs, and to applaud the new and often sublime expressions of its genius. But there are moral values of the utmost importance which we have to offer it. These are of advantage to everyone. We root them firmly in the consciences of men. Wherever men are striving to understand themselves and the world, we are able to communicate with them. Wherever the councils of nations come together to establish the rights and duties of man, we are honored to be permitted to take our place among them. If there is in man a "soul that is naturally Christian," we wish to respect it, to cherish it, and to communicate with it.[43]

42. Ibid., 19–20.
43. *Ecclesiam suam* §97. Of course, the qualification of this spirit of dialogue in *Ecclesiam suam,* i.e., those passages that still border on the superior understanding of the church, are quite rightly counterbalanced and challenged by the "signs of the times" the church has since been called to discern—and Haight's own sentiments help to explain this in vivid and yet no less positive terms. Obviously one must take into

But we must be prepared to challenge those who believe the church is at the center of the world and God's priorities. Rather love, *caritas*, is at the center, for Christians believe in a God who is love in the depths of divine being. So the evidence again suggests that something of a "Copernican ecclesiological revolution" is indeed called for. But Paul VI himself is here not so much privileging the Catholic Church as showing the necessary *stages* of dialogue that need to proceed in order for the gospel mission to be fulfilled in his times. That is, charity must first begin at home: love those closest to us and we are given the vision and energy to go out and love those beyond. If we cannot even love those in the midst of whom we live, how much harder it will be to love those beyond our immediate confines.

The method for facilitating conversation, then, demands that true dialogue should be aimed at overcoming polarizations and factionalism: for example, striving to establish some common ground between "competing" ecclesiologies within Catholicism. Rahner, as so often, pre-empts our concerns here, warning that charity can often be all the more difficult to display the closer to home one encounters its need:

> . . . the world of intellectual pluralism is present within the church herself. And because of this a dialogue within the church is inevitable and necessary even if it makes things far more difficult and toilsome for us than formerly, especially since this dialogue is in many respects more difficult than a dialogue with the world outside the church. This is because however lovingly we may try to behave in a family dispute it still has a special sharpness and bitterness of its own. It is also because this dialogue within the church is conducted among complex and heterogeneous schools of thought within a single body governed by the same Christian faith and by the one social organization of the church. Thus these "limits" offer less possibility of avoiding the dispute than in the case of the dialogue carried on outside the church.[44]

Haight's painstaking work in developing this comparative method in ecclesiology is fully in step with such a vision, such a call to charity: to dialogue in love that encounters and embraces the other as other. But again we must be wary of any tendency to lapse into language that is laudable in intent but is not supported by actions. Recall that we are

---

account that the non-inclusive language employed in the encyclical sits uneasily with later readers.

44. Rahner, "Dialogue in the Church," 109. See also Bernard Lonergan, "Unity and Plurality: the Coherence of Christian Truth," in his *A Third Collection*, ed. Frederick E. Crowe (London: Geoffrey Chapman, 1985) 239–50.

making a case for the *necessity* of dialogue, ecclesially, theologically (indeed, doctrinally), and morally. In our ecclesiological investigations today we are called to such dialogue, for any reflection on the current life of the church leads one to such a conclusion. The most positive and enduring response to postmodernity must be dialogue. Our interpretive considerations lead us logically to this place. Thus Haight's thinking, as outlined above, supplements the franker analysis offered by Christof Theobald:

> The most serious issue is a hermeneutical one. We have in fact become aware of the diversity of cultures, their multiple interactions and the threat that an abstract and systematic globalization poses to all of them. The gospel cannot simply come to them from outside as a transcultural doctrine or a collection of practices and rites, thought to affect them all in their specific corporeality. It has to be received, in order to fall into the ground there before being recreated in some way by those who have already begun to live by it. This infinitely complex process is turning the church of the nations, which is still too structured by Latinism, into a vast laboratory.[45]

Theobald is not alone in adopting such a tone, for here, too, the further wise words of Rahner seem remarkably ahead of their time in their apparent foresight with regard to the challenges faced by the church in our times. In particular he addresses the church-world continuum of relations in the postmodern age in which the church finds itself:

> . . . if the church of today is to conduct a dialogue with the world, then it must not be overlooked that this "world" is not simply "outside," but is rather present in the church herself. This means that the first, and perhaps the decisive dialogue with the world is that which takes place precisely within the church. In fact the "world" which is to be the church's partner in the dialogue that is necessary today is, in the first instance, not only present where non-Christian groups have already emerged as social organizations with a firm ideological basis of their own. No such social organization needs to be achieved for the world to be constituted as a partner to a dialogue with the church.[46]

45. Christof Theobald, "The 'Definitive' Discourse of the Magisterium: Why be Afraid of a Creative Reception?" in Gerard Mannion, Richard Gaillardetz, Jan Kerkhofs, and Kenneth Wilson, eds., *Readings in Church Authority: Gifts and Challenges for Contemporary Catholicism*, (Aldershot, England, and Burlington, VT: Ashgate, 2003) 118.

46. Rahner, "Dialogue in the Church," 106. See also idem, "A Small Question Regarding the Contemporary Pluralism in the Intellectual Situation of Catholics and the Church" in vol. 6 of *Theological Investigations* (London: Darton, Longman, and

To summarize, this dialogue and embracing of pluralism is not only necessary on theological (doctrinal), ecclesiological, and moral grounds, but also on hermeneutical grounds: reading the signs of our times, ecclesial discernment. It is so also on intellectual and epistemological grounds. Who could not acknowledge, echoing our considerations in chapter 4, as well as Bernard Lonergan,[47] that the engagement between cultures across time *and* space, this ongoing series of what A. N. Whitehead called the "adventures of ideas," also points toward the life-giving properties of real pluralism. Here Rahner offers still further support:[48]

> Prior to the formation of any such ideological groups different from the church herself the necessity for a dialogue between the church and the "world" arises from the almost incalculable pluralism of ideas which constitutes the situation in which modern man lives, and which on the one hand is prior to the formation of the ideologies and their upholders, and on the other cannot fail to have a bearing upon the faith of the church. By the term "intellectual pluralism" as understood here we mean the sum total of the experiences, insights, impulses and human possibilities in all spheres of human living . . . .[49]

Pluralism is not an ideology; rather it is first of all a descriptive term for the way things are, for reality. At the same time it is also the name for the healthiest and most appropriate response to the way things are, as opposed to turning away from and attempting to deny that reality in various modes of self-delusion and community delusion. Pluralism is all around us and inescapable. But why would anyone seek to escape the riches of the diverse gifts God gives humanity to share?—unless, of course, they have allowed themselves to become fearful of the vast

---

Todd, 1965). For a discussion of Rahner on pluralism see Richard Lennan, "Faith and Ambiguity in a Pluralistic Age," ch. 6 of his *The Ecclesiology of Karl Rahner* (Oxford: Oxford University Press, 173–211).

47. Lonergan, "Unity and Plurality," 239, 250. See also "The Second Enlightenment," 63–64, part 6 of ch. 3 in the same volume, and idem, "The Transition from a Classicist to a Historicist Worldview" in his *A Second Collection* (London: Darton, Longman, and Todd, 1974), as well as his *Doctrinal Pluralism* (Milwaukee: Marquette University Press, 1971). For a discussion of Lonergan on pluralism see John J. Burkhard, *Apostolicity Then and Now: An Ecumenical Church in a Postmodern World* (Collegeville: Liturgical Press, 2004) 154–57.

48. Again he does so in a way that can be bracketed as neither anti-modern nor counter-modernity and neither postmodern nor halfway between modernity and postmodernity. The picture is far richer and more beautiful and awe-inspiring than such restrictive interpretations can do justice to. See Mannion, "Being True: Williams and Meynell on Reason and Virtue," *The Heythrop Journal*, forthcoming.

49. Rahner, "Dialogue in the Church," 106. Cf. Lonergan, "Unity and Plurality."

wonders of postmodern existence and to retreat from the world into the perceived "comfort zone" of "certainties" that ultimately prove to be quite the reverse on both counts.

Embracing pluralism[50] allows us to put the gospel into practice all the more effectively in our times, "just as you did it to one of the least of these who are members of my family, you did it to me."[51] The parable of the Last Judgment, of course, clearly indicates that the gospel itself, at its very heart, is both a call to embrace pluralism and to praxis—in short, to put one's celebration of pluralism into practice. Thus in our account of Haight's developmental "comparative ecclesiology," essentially a charter for pluralism and macro-ecumenism, we finally turn to "the *focus* of theology." Here Haight reflects on the population explosion and the attendant massive suffering the world has witnessed through this and other global developments: ". . . in common with other religions, human beings must address the elements of our common existence which are senseless, murderous and scandalous. God's revelation to human beings in this world is for human existence in this world. To be credible and relevant, theology must address the actual lives of human beings in this world by formulating its meaning in social-historical terms as well as interpersonal and transcendent terms."[52]

This is most appropriate for addressing the questions that confront the church *in our times.* The methodological lesson to be learned here is that theology must address *real* lives and must always bear in mind the fundamental social and public dimensions of human existence as well as the interpersonal and transcendent. In other words, theology should never be a purely individualistic discipline with regard to its chief areas of concern.

Essentially Haight is seeking to move theology, and especially ecclesiology, beyond all narrow sectarian, absolutist, and universalizing stances: "Theology transcends the church." There is a new reality for the church to take account of, and this naturally means a new reality for authority, structures, and theology itself throughout the Christian church. An acknowledgment of this points further toward and helps develop the particularly ecclesiological implications of such arguments.

50. Hence I believe the term can still be employed, despite the valid challenges put to certain uses of the term by Johann Baptist Metz, who prefers the term "polycentric."
51. Matthew 25:40.
52. Haight, "The Church as Locus of Theology," 22. See also Janet Crawford, "Women and Ecclesiology: Two Ecumenical Streams," *The Ecumenical Review* 53 (2002) 14–24.

For our contemporary times the church has *yet* to adequately harmonize its mission to humanity with its evangelical mission. Comparative theology and the sub-discipline of comparative ecclesiology—or comparative studies in and reflection on the various religious (and other) communities to be found in the world offer a better methodology for taking the church forward than any neo-exclusivistic outlook. If the latter becomes the new guiding methodological starting point and principle, churches risk performing a retreat to the debates of the 1930s and perhaps further back still.

Comparative ecclesiology, then, offers a most promising basis for the development of that necessary "ecumenical intercultural hermeneutic," and the comparisons can prove fruitful across a variety of synchronic and diachronic forms. They can be across history, across communion and denomination or even within denomination, or even between differing ecclesiological methodologies or between the visions of the ecclesial authorities and local church realities. Haight has shown us examples of so many varieties here as well as demonstrating the insights that can issue from a comparison of ecclesiology "from above" and "from below."

Space prevents a detailed reflection on what fruitful insights might be gleaned from engaging with the ecclesiological visions of those from differing contexts—be they viewed in geographical, cultural, social, interest-group, or gender terms or a combination of several such, but our final chapters will help support the contention that if we engage in specific "comparative ecclesiological explorations" toward such ends, they will be fruitful. In particular I wish to commend the promise of the ecclesiological thinking and practice being shaped in the creative waters of the various "emerging theologies" (particularly liberationist, contextual, and feminist theologies) that have seen their own development bracket much of the postmodern era.

Concluding Remarks:
The Promise of Comparative Ecclesial Hermeneutics[53]

Whether one wishes to acknowledge and celebrate the fact or not, theological and ecclesiological pluralism both are and have always been a lived reality in the church. But, as Rahner indicates, this is something positive for the church; it empowers the church in its missionary activity

---

53. As we have seen, the work of both Gregory Baum and Roger Haight takes such hermeneutical, ecclesiological, and ethical considerations further as they seek to offer positive suggestions for the relation between theology and the church today.

in the world: "Since Christians, in spite of their unity of faith, are pluralistic in theology, they must discuss their theologies at least in order to assure themselves sufficiently that in spite of the differences between their theologies the unity of their creed is maintained, a fact which today is far more difficult to establish than was formerly thought to be the case."[54] No more, then, the myth of timelessly self-evident absolute, fixed and defined truths and rigid uniformity, for such rears its ugly head only when the church has lost its way, and its present form in the church is a curiously postmodern take on a very modern tendency at that. Context-specific *interpretations* of truth can distort the value of such truth itself and even lead away from truth altogether.

What emerges from the foregoing is the need for a more durable, transferable, and flexible ecclesiology that is always pastorally/praxis-oriented. This requires more self-critical, sustained, and open ecclesiological reflection. Ecclesiology should and must be *empowering*: the key question in forming any vision of the church should be how to enable the enhancement of justice, freedom, and love within *and* outside the Christian community (as *Gaudium et Spes* made clear), but never one without the other. We must never be afraid to engage in conversation. Our dialogue must take place at *every* level of the church and beyond, to embrace all religious and communitarian "families" in our world, in our times.

54. Rahner, "Dialogue in the Church," 110.

PART IV

ANALOGIA ECCLESIAE:
THE VISION OF A VIRTUOUS COMMUNITY

Chapter Eight

Analogia Ecclesiae

In the previous section I made a contemporary case for the theological, moral, and ecclesiological *necessity* of dialogue within and outside the church. In this final section we consider the methodological and practical implications of this necessity. Here I will seek to underpin further those theological, moral, and ecclesiological grounds for dialogue and pluralism (or "polycentrism") in contradistinction to other prevailing contemporary ecclesiological methods and visions.

Along the way this book has sought to discern particular ecclesial "vices" and to identify potential ecclesial "virtues." This final section tentatively suggests ways forward for an ecclesiological response to the challenges of postmodernity and the questions facing the church in our times. I wish to suggest that we allow our ethical insights and means of moral discernment to inform our ecclesiological thinking as well as our ecclesial being and praxis.

So in the following chapter I briefly introduce and seek to apply the resources offered to contemporary ecclesiology by virtue ethics. In passing I will discuss one famous alternative example of the appropriation of virtue ethics, namely the work of Stanley Hauerwas, in order to indicate that what is being suggested here is something very different, even, in some respects, antithetical to that type of ecclesiological vision.

Instead, building on earlier chapters, I embrace the perception of Christian tradition as an "open narrative" as opposed to an inward-looking "closed narrative."[1] In keeping with the content of Part III of

1. Again Lieven Boeve's work and that of Lewis Mudge are relevant to the ecclesiological thinking here.

this volume and the themes discussed there in relation to contemporary challenges facing the church, pluralism or "polycentrism" is commended as an ecclesial and ecclesiological *virtue*. It should be embraced and allowed to permeate every aspect of ecclesial life. Dialogue with and understanding of the "other" are the natural means by which such a virtue is cultivated, developed, and exercised.[2]

But first, in this chapter, we engage with more fundamental aspects of any ecclesiological method for our time, still. Although much church teaching and theological discussion speak of the church in analogical terms,[3] here I will suggest that the full implications of such language, not least its practical implications, might be developed at greater length and offer considerable hope for ecclesiology in its efforts to discern the path for the church in our postmodern times. In particular we will seek to build on the promise of trinitararian ecclesiology in order to discern the theological and practical ecclesial implications of the *analogia ecclesiae,* the *analogy of church.*

"Uneasy Existential Alliances": An Analogical Path Toward Virtuous Being and Witness?

This book has sought to consider the problems generated by conflicting ecclesiological visions, models, and paradigms and conflicting views of the most urgent priorities and understandings of mission for the church today. It has looked at possible ways by which such divisions might be transcended, by which different ecclesial perspectives and ways of being church might mutually flourish and enhance each other. Dialogue has loomed large in this suggested route for the church to take in its various postmodern contexts and in its reaction to the challenges they present. But the reality and depth of the differences within the church have not been underplayed, nor has the immensity of the task of transcending such divisions, given the ascendancy of the neo-exclusivistic ecclesial mindset in recent decades in a "trans-denominational reformation." Such are the struggles in a church torn between various aspects of the pre-modern, modern, and postmodern cultural horizons. So we have been seeking to discern how a very tentative and (to borrow

2. On the theme of dialogue with other *as* other see again Gerard Mannion, "What's in a Name? Hermeneutical Reflections on Globalisation, Catholicity and Ecumenism," *New Blackfriars* (May 2007) 204–15.

3. E.g., *Catechism of the Catholic Church* §774: "The Church, then, both contains and communicates the invisible grace she signifies. It is in this analogical sense that the Church is called a 'sacrament.'"

David Tracy's now famous phrase) "uneasy" alliance may be conceived or, more accurately, *re*-conceived. The church has been here before. Tracy himself, in using the phrase, referred to an alliance between aspects of Catholic theological method, modernity, and postmodernity.[4]

Following Friedrich Von Hügel, Tracy made a very strong case for the need to harmonize (albeit through creative *tension* being acknowledged and permitted) the religious (or mystical, for Von Hügel), the intellectual (which I prefer to speak of here as prophetic, i.e., discerning and proclaiming the word of God), and the institutional elements of any religion (and so here, of course, applied to the church), if it is successfully to meet the challenges of the postmodern age. Only when all three elements of any religion are flourishing "may the religion itself be said to flourish."[5] For all three to be in harmony, for such flourishing to shape the life of faith as opposed to one or two elements taking priority to the detriment and neglect of the other(s), there must be a sense of equilibrium, of existential balance. We might here speak of this as a virtue—the latter being fundamentally understood as a disposition, a way of being, a mean between excesses that orients one toward a right goal, end, or state of being.

Tracy also suggests that a "great divide" has opened up in recent decades across the traditions,[6] between those who still believe there can be a correlation between theology and the cultural and intellectual ferments in the contemporary world and those who feel the correlationist project has failed and wish to preserve Christian tradition from the detrimental effects of such cultural forces. In many ways Tracy is describing a particular aspect of the "trans-denominational reformation" I described in chapter 3. His proposed solution for Christian systematic theology in our times—now famous though still too little engaged, and yet all too often contested—is captured in the following quotation:

> Indeed, the reality of self-exposure to the other is a condition for the possibility of authentic conversation in our day. The need for conversation—expressed in the differing strategies of confrontation, argument, conflict, persuasion and above all, concentration on the subject matter—should

4. David Tracy, "The Uneasy Alliance Reconceived: Catholic Theological Method, Modernity, and Postmodernity," *TS* 50/3 (1989) 548–70.

5. Ibid., 548. J. H. Newman, of course, addressed the need for such "creative tension," also.

6. Ibid., 556. "Harmony," of course, literally means "joining together" in a fitting or pleasant fashion. The "uneasy alliance" indicates conflict and tension will prove constant features of the relationship. Nonetheless, the end at which the aliance ends must be something harmonious or an ugly cacophony is the only alternative.

free the Christian theologian to the fuller contemporary possibility of an analogical imagination. Under the rubric of a comparative and critical hermeneutics, the real similarities and dissimilarities, the continuities and the discontinuities present in the contemporary pluralist situation should be allowed their necessary emergence. When the ability to listen is present, the fear of confrontation, conflict, argument are not shunned. Rather they are necessary dialectical moments in every analogical conversation.[7]

Our concerns from Part III of this volume are thus brought into sharper relief. Here I wish to build on Tracy's insightful work in two ways.[8] First, I will suggest that our proposed use of virtue ethics offers the best hope for successfully reconceiving such an "uneasy alliance." Indeed, I believe we can rightly see those three elements of Catholic, indeed Christian life—religious, prophetic, and institutional—as *analogous* to the three (God-given) theological virtues, *corresponding* respectively to faith, hope, and charity.[9] The last may raise some eyebrows! Few today think of the institutional church as the embodiment of charity. But this chapter (indeed, this whole book) points to some tentative steps toward forming a "virtue ecclesiology" whereby the church is primarily understood as a "virtuous community."[10] Thus the church's institutional facets should always aspire to be the embodiment of the love, the *caritas*

7. David Tracy, *The Analogical Imagination: Christian Theology and the Culture of Pluralism* (New York: Crossroad, 1981) 446–47.

8. Tracy's primary works on this subject, besides *The Analogical Imagination,* include *Blessed Rage for Order: The New Pluralism in Theology* (New York: Crossroad, 1975); *Dialogue with the Other: the Inter-Religious Dialogue* (Leuven: Peeters, 1990); *On Naming the Present. God, Hermeneutics, and Church* (Maryknoll, NY: Orbis, 1994). For assessments of Tracy's work see, again, Werner G. Jeanrond and Jennifer L. Rike, eds., *Radical Pluralism and Truth. David Tracy and the Hermeneutics of Religion* (New York: Crossroad, 1991), and Gareth Jones, "Tracy: Halting the Postmodernist Slide," ch. 5 of his *Critical Theology* (Cambridge: Polity, 1993) 113–34.

9. Such theological virtues are in themselves analogous of the triune being of God.

10. Not, then, in Stanley Hauerwas' words, "A Community of Character." The difference is subtle but vital: the church is not a community trumpeting its distinctiveness and (even if only implicitly) its superiority to other communities and to the world in general, but rather a community that seeks to live its values, its virtues: in other words, a community that embodies such virtues in its daily life, as does the virtuous person (not the "person of character"). The subtle difference lies in avoiding all tendencies toward existential and moral hubris. For, as has been repeated so often, even before Augustine's remonstrations with the Donatists, the church is a community of sinners and saints. The difference is that it aspires toward ever more holiness. Such holiness is here understood to be the aspiration toward being the community that embodies and lives out its virtues in practice, in statement, in mission. It is thus I have commended ecclesiology as an *aspirational* undertaking. Community is, of course, a loaded, some would say dangerous term but, given the theological connotations of communion that we have been working with throughout this volume, I will continue to employ

that Christians believe is expressive of the very being of God. The task for the institutional church is to bear witness *in its daily operations and fulfilment of its mission* to the God of love, the love of God.[11]

Tracy's work, along with the particular ecclesial perspective on it offered by T. Howland Sanks, comes into play here in a second sense. His monumental study, *The Analogical Imagination*, sought to discern the fundamental character of Christian theology as analogical and to show how this offered great hope for theology in a pluralistic context. Tracy first defined the "analogical imagination" in 1977: "In more familiar and traditional language, analogy articulates both the significant differences and similarities between human beings and the rest of life in the cosmos and, above all, between human beings and God as disclosed in Jesus Christ."[12] As T. Howland Sanks indicates, such language is not equivocal, nor univocal, nor dialectical.[13] Sanks applies this notion in examining differing forms of ecclesiality: "Put simply, my thesis is that the church is and always has been an analogical notion, that the various ways in which the church has taken on historical concreteness have been conditioned by historical particularities and therefore were partly alike and partly different—analogous rather than univocal."[14]

As witnessed in our earlier discussion of the promise of comparative ecclesiology (and the work of Roger Haight in particular), such a view

---

it in a positive and constructive sense while bearing in mind that all conceptions of "community" must be subject to the hermeneutics of suspicion.

11. Here one must of course be attentive to the danger of overlooking a situation somewhat analogous to the tension in sacramental theology between overt emphasis either on understanding the sacramental significance as *ex opere operato*, i.e., "through the performance of the work," or *ex opere operantis*, i.e., "through the work of the worker." The church does not have to be a perfect and stainless community in order to fulfill its mission. But at the same time, on a virtue-based understanding, the church cannot truly bear witness to the gospel and the God of love if the actions repeatedly done within it and on its behalf are contrary to the gospel and the God of love, for virtue comes from habit and through voluntary choice. Here I do mean to emphasize that the church is called to bear witness while at the same time recognizing and acknowledging that it also learns from the world outside itself.

12. David Tracy, "Presidential Address: The Catholic Analogical Imagination," *Proceedings of the Catholic Theological Society of America* 32 (1977) 234–44. Cited in T. Howland Sanks, "Forms of Ecclesiality: the Analogical Church," *TS* 49 (1988) 703; see David Tracy, "The Analogical Imagination in Catholic Theology," ch. 2 of John B. Cobb and David Tracy, eds., *Talking About God: Doing Theology in the Context of Modern Pluralism* (New York: Seabury, 1983).

13. Sanks, "Forms of Ecclesiality," 703.

14. Ibid., 696. Sanks cites the use of the term also in José Miguez Bonino, "Fundamental Questions in Ecclesiology," in Sergio Torres and John Eagleson, eds., *The Challenge of Basic Christian Communities* (Maryknoll, NY: Orbis, 1981) 148.

offers the contemporary church a very positive underlining ecclesiologi-cal principle that could prove fruitful in attempts to transcend "compet-ing" ecclesiologies. Sanks primarily employs the notion in order to highlight the fact that imposed uniformity in ecclesial structure, or in defining the parameters of what constitutes church, has never really been the Christian tradition. In particular he urges a reconsideration of any rigid understanding of parish, and analogously (in a twofold sense!) applies this analysis also to the magisterial authority of episcopal conferences (*contra* the disparaging and conceptually muddled assess-ment of their authority in the 1988 pre-synodal *instrumentum laboris,* "Theological and Juridical Status of Episcopal Conferences"). As he writes: ". . . we need to remember that the Catholic tradition is indeed characterized by the analogical imagination. 'Church' is and always has been an analogical notion, and the forms in which it has been embodied are historically conditioned but analogously related to one another. This means that there will be differences within similarities, but then that is precisely how the focal meaning of Catholic Christianity, the Incarnation, has enabled us to envision or imagine all of reality."[15]

But Sanks, at least here, seems to overlook the still greater ecclesio-logical potential of his analysis and of this very conclusion. For by simply focusing upon the Incarnation (and, in particular, "where two or three are gathered in my name, I am there among them"),[16] as the primary analogate, Sanks underplays the further significance of perceiving "church" in analogical terms, for the concept of *incarnation* is, as Athanasius so eloquently explained, itself only analogous to a primary analogate: the threefold being of God.[17]

Of course, a trinitarian focus in ecclesiology has been explored at various times in the development of Christian tradition,[18] most notably

15. Sanks, "Forms of Ecclesiality," 708.

16. Matt 18:20, also discussed by Sanks, "Forms of Ecclesiality," 703.

17. After all, one could argue that any alternative interpretation of the doctrine could not hold that Jesus of Nazareth was fully God *and* fully human. The paradoxical tension could not be maintained in univocal, equivocal, or dialectical language: no dichotomous mode of thinking could justify the Incarnation. I.e., the Chalcedonian fathers *left* the doctrine *as* paradoxical—it was affirmed as faith, as opposed to being explained in univocal, equivocal, or dialectical terms.

18. Recall *Communionis notio* §3, as quoted in ch. 3, and also David McLoughlin: "Like the Trinity, the church's reality lies in an essential orientation towards relationship. Our God is a being-in-communion. If we share *koinonia* with God in Christ then we will find ourselves in *koinonia* with each other" ("Authority in the Service of Communion," in Noel Timms and Kenneth Wilson, eds., *Governance and Authority in the Roman Catholic Church: Beginning a Conversation* [London: S.P.C.K., 2000] 129).

in the East, and has also had a significant impact on recent trinitarian and ecclesiological thinking in the West. Marie-Dominique Chenu has provided a wonderful sketch of how, thanks largely to influences from the east, the council fathers at Vatican II came to re-embrace the trinitarian implications of ecclesiology.[19]

It is a primary aim of this chapter to emphasize the *trinitarian* dimensions of the *analogia ecclesiae* and, in the following chapter, with the aid of insights from virtue ethics, to apply this in exploring a dispositional, transferable ecclesiology attentive to context and historicity, able to celebrate polycentrism and the other and to serve the church well in its efforts to be church amid the vagaries of postmodern times.[20] If "church" is in fact an analogical term, then any uniform ecclesiology imposed "from above," be it one of *communion* or not,[21] must be an

---

19. "The New Awareness of the Trinitarian Basis of the Church," in Giuseppe Alberigo and Gustavo Gutiérrez, eds., *Where Does the Church Stand? Concilium* 146 (New York: Seabury, 1981) 14–21. Chenu's insightful study helps further demonstrate that issues of church and world, historical consciousness and doctrinal attentiveness or forgetfulness, can all affect ecclesiology. Citing the 1968 speech of Ignatius IV Hazim, then Metropolitan of Lattakia (in Syria), to the General Assembly of the WCC at Uppsala on a more positive understanding of God's relation to the world and the implications of this for church renewal (thus somewhat pre-empting aspects of our discussions in this book of the phenomenon of "neo-exclusivist" ecclesiology), he writes: "We cannot fail to notice, behind this provocative condemnation of the deism of present-day spirituality, the expression of the Trinitarian theology of the eastern church, according to which the circumincession of the Father, Son and Holy Spirit takes place in the Unity of the Mystery, and this establishes the church in history" (ibid., 14).

20. Another recent author who particularly seeks to bridge the so-called "east-west" divide is Miroslav Volf: *After Our Likeness: The Church as the Image of the Trinity* (Grand Rapids: Eerdmanns, 1998). John D. Zizioulas' now famous work, *Being as Communion* (New York: St. Vladimir's Seminary Press, 1993), obviously enters into these considerations throughout its pages, although Zizioulas' thinking can be used to serve as justification for ecclesiological hierarchy—something this present volume seeks to challenge (and on trinitarian grounds). This is despite the *relational* interpretation of ministry and hierarchy Zizioulas offers. As Volf states, ". . . in Catholic and Orthodox thought earthly hierarchies tend to mirror the heavenly one. Given the conflictual nature of all social realities, the church not excepted, a hierarchical notion of the Trinity ends up underwriting an authoritarian practice in the church. In contrast I have tried to develop a non-hierarchical but truly communal ecclesiology based on a non-hierarchical doctrine of the Trinity" (*After Our Likeness*, 4). Roger Haight has illustrated how Zizioulas employs the "iconic imagination" in his trinitarian ecclesiology, *Christian Community in History* (New York: Continuum, 2004) vol. 2, *Comparative Ecclesiology*, especially 444–48. Haight also indicates how the trinity features in the ecclesiological thinking of Calvin (ibid., 141 n. 30), Luther (ibid., 141–42), the Orthodox churches in general (ibid., 435–37), and in the World Council of Churches (ibid., 381–82).

21. See chs. 1–4 and especially our earlier discussions of *Communionis notio* and *Dominus Iesus*.

ecclesiology ill-suited to our time or any other. Such might also be seemingly ignorant of much of the Christian ecclesiological tradition and especially of its quintessentially catholic aspects (recall chapter 6 and our discussion of the true meaning of "catholicity").[22] For Sanks himself, analogical thinking should be contrasted with "dichotomous" thinking, "which stresses that relationships are either/or: either completely alike or completely different. This mode of thinking does not see proportional relationships between different entities or structures but stresses only the differences. It can only replicate its focal meaning rather than allow that focal meaning to illuminate new experiences of structures."[23]

Thus a further key aim: we here refer to the *analogia ecclesiae* as an alternative to any ecclesiology based on either/or, right/wrong, that

22. Despite relative inattention in much Catholic scholarship (notwithstanding attention to trinitarian themes in the "official" *communion* ecclesiology and the ecclesiological thought of Joseph Ratzinger which, as we have seen, raise a number of problematic issues), Catholic scholars *are* now increasingly re-engaging with the trinitarian dimension of ecclesiology, not least through and thanks to ecumenical encounters. See, for example, two essays by Paul McPartlan in Bernard Hoose, ed., *Authority and the Roman Catholic Church* (Aldershot: Ashgate, 2002): ch. 8, "Trinity, Church and State," 117–28, and ch. 10, "The Same But Different: Living in Communion," 149–67. See also his two books, *The Eucharist Makes the Church: Henri De Lubac and John Zizioulas in Dialogue* (Edinburgh: T & T Clark, 1993), and *Sacrament of Salvation: An Introduction to Eucharistic Ecclesiology* (Edinburgh: T & T Clark, 1995). Much church teaching in recent decades has engaged the same. Nonetheless, this chapter suggests that the *practical* implications of such trinitarian thinking have yet to make as significant an impact on the life of the Catholic Church in its day-to-day operations and organization as it should. Hence some further *theological* and especially analogical thought is required. We must emphasize the promise of trinitarian work being undertaken in various "emerging ecclesiologies." Furthermore, this chapter and the next stress the *moral* implications of such trinitarian engagement in ecclesiology, thereby also building on and taking account of the critique of the approach by some liberation theologians, e.g., Leonardo Boff, "Trinity," in Jon Sobrino and Ignacio Ellacuría, eds., *Systematic Theology—Perspectives from Liberation Theology* (London: SCM, 1996) 75–89, and also his *Trinity and Society* (Tunbridge Wells: Burns and Oates, 1988), as well as theologians such as Jürgen Moltmann, *The Trinity and the Kingdom of God* (London: SCM, 1981), and his *History and the Triune God* (London: SCM, 1991). Of particular relevance to the themes under discussion in this chapter and volume in general are the works by Bradford Hinze, *Practices of Dialogue in the Roman Catholic Church: Aims and Obstacles, Lessons and Laments* (New York: Continuum, 2006); "Synodality and Ecumenicity: Marks of a Trinitarian Church," in Jaroslav Z. Skira and Michael Attridge, eds., *In God's Hands: Essays on the Church and Ecumenism in Honor of Michael A. Fahey, S.J.,* BETL, no. 199 (Leuven: Leuven University Press, 2006), and "Dialogical Traditions and a Trinitarian Hermeneutic," in Jacques Haers and P. De Mey, eds., *Theology and Conversation: Towards a Relational Theory.* BETL 172 (Leuven: Peeters, 2003) 311–22. Part I of the same collection contains a further twenty essays on the theme of "Reflecting on God and Creation: Conversation and Trinity."

23. Sanks, "Forms of Ecclesiality," 703.

seeks to impose uniformity and univocity, denies that difference should be encountered, engaged, and celebrated, and shuns genuine ecclesiological hermeneutics and thus denies the ecclesial necessity of dialogue.[24] As Keith Ward so convincingly demonstrated *contra* W. G. Maclagan's critique of the use of theology in ethics, all moral language is itself symbolic, figurative, and employs analogy and metaphor in the attempt to discern the good and our relations to it. It points toward truth, regardless of the vagaries of the fact/value debate. So even a "secular" moral philosopher like Iris Murdoch could pen a volume entitled *Metaphysics as a Guide to Morals*.[25] Such considerations have added weight to the cumulative case that religion and metaphysics do have a part to play in moral discernment.[26]

Here I want to take such notions as those offered by Tracy[27] and Sanks further still. The concept of a "virtue ecclesiology" is really the

24. The concept of virtue itself seeks out a mean, a midpoint between two extremes. Here also see the earlier Avery Dulles' use of Aquinas' understanding of the term "connaturality" with regard to our discernment of the *mystery* of the church, and his statement that "We cannot fully objectify the church because we are involved in it; we know it through a kind of intersubjectivity . . . . The mysterious character of the church has important implications for methodology. It rules out the possibility of proceeding through clear and univocal concepts, or from definitions in the usual sense of the word. The concepts abstracted from the realities we observe in the objective world about us are not applicable, at least directly, to the mystery of man's communion with God" ("The Use of Models in Ecclesiology," in Gerard Mannion, Richard Gaillardetz, Jan Kerkhofs, and Kenneth Wilson, eds., *Readings in Church Authority: Gifts and Challenges for Contemporary Catholicism*, (Aldershot, England, and Burlington, VT: Ashgate, 2003) 66, quoted from ch. 1 of Dulles' *Models of the Church* (2d ed. Dublin: Gill and Macmillan, 1988).

25. Iris Murdoch is herself a leading figure in the revival of interest in virtue ethics, and her work is of interest for our attempt to use that school of moral thought in this tentative analogical ecclesiology. She joins with other philosophers steeped in the classical tradition; hence their preference for virtue ethics. Thus the *virtue* of analogical thinking and of analogical discourse is further commended.

26. W. G. Maclagan, *The Theological Frontiers of Ethics*, London, George, Allen & Urwin, 1961; Keith Ward, *Ethics and Christianity*, London, George, Allen & Urwin, 1970. For a discussion of the Maclagan-Ward debate as well as the relationship between religion and morality in general see Gerard Mannion, *Schopenhauer, Religion and Morality* (Harmondsworth: Ashgate, 2003), especially ch. 5.

27. Obviously Tracy's later works do explore the doctrine of God and its implications for Christian theology and Christian living in a postmodern world much more fully than do *Blessed Rage for Order* and *The Analogical Imagination,* with their christological emphasis. The importance of mystery and a mystical approach in tandem with a hermeneutical and practical approach has been increasingly accentuated in these later works, developing from its earlier brief outline in writings such as "The Uneasy Alliance Reconceived." Lieven Boeve has used Tracy's work in his own account of Christian tradition in postmodern times, including his "Negative Theology: God's

practical and theoretical outworking of an *analogia ecclesiae*—an analogy of church. This means that in its actions and in its being, its daily life, the church—however imperfectly, provisionally, and tentatively—should always strive to bear witness to, to be the sign and the mediation of the very self-communication of God to the world, to be a sacrament of grace, of salvation, "for God so loved the world." Christianity believes in a God whose being is a community of love, of blissful *perichoresis*, of unity in diversity—celebrating the differing "modes of being," the "relational distinctions," the classical understanding of *persona* (role in the community), all of which represents our tentative steps toward grasping the nature of God's own self *and* that self in its salvific activity in the world (in other words, the respective immanent and economic articulation of our theologizing).

None of this is to strive for an idealistic unobtainable "perfect" church, but to ask fundamental questions about the "wherefore" of the "pilgrim church." Pedro Trigo summarizes the "realism" of our quest: "There is room, then, in our culture, to conceptualize ourselves, and to live, as images of God—but not without a profound transformation of many of the elements of that culture."[28] Here I simply narrow the focus somewhat: without profound transformations of our contemporary ecclesial culture and practices we can never aspire to see our church living as even an approximate, analogical image of God. So, too, might we apply Leonardo Boff's wider "social doctrine" to our ecclesiological thinking today: "Here are the Trinitarian roots of a Christian commitment to the transformation of society; we seek to change society because we see, in faith, that the supreme reality is the prototype of all other things, and that this supreme reality is the absolute communion of three distinct Realities, each of equal dignity, with equal love and full reciprocal communion of love and life. Furthermore, we wish our society, our visible reality, to be able to speak to us of the Trinity through our egalitarian and communitarian organization, and thus afford us an experience of the three divine persons."[29]

For "society" we here first insert "church," not that Boff is not alive to the ecclesiological implications of his statement—far from it, for he continues:

Interruption of Christian Master Narratives," ch. 8 of his *Interrupting Tradition*, 147–62.

28. Pedro Trigo, "What are the Traits of the Image of God?" ch. 13 of his *Creation and History* (Tunbridge Wells: Burns and Oates, 1991) 224.

29. Leonardo Boff, "Trinity," in Sobrino and Ellacuría, eds., *Systematic Theology*, 77–78.

The Roman Catholic Church, especially, tends to live a societal model rather than a communitarian one. Power is centralized in the clerical corps, and the faithful are guided in a manner that tends to be authoritarian with very little differentiated participation on the part of all. A monarchical conception of power was imposed on the church historically. Here it was not a trinitarian reflection, a mindset governed by the notion of communion, that prevailed; instead, the dominant view was pre-trinitarian, even a-trinitarian. If we accept, in faith, that the holy Trinity is the best community, and that it is by communion that the divine persons are joined together in one God, we can then postulate a model of church more adequate to its source, from which its life and oneness spring (cf. *Lumen Gentium*, no. 4).[30]

Of course, the "social doctrine of the trinity" has its numerous critics, but I feel that some of their number, at least, have missed something very significant about the essential intention behind such approaches to trinitarian theology in contemporary times. It may be that the *ecclesiological* implications of such may help bring these to the foreground. For, as we shall see, this is not so much to project human ideals[31] onto our understanding of God, but rather to enable the church to strive, however imperfectly, to be both the sign and mediator of that perfect community of love, the love that is poured out as gracious self-communication to all the world. Although one finds attention to trinitarian themes in many

30. Ibid., 85–86. For a critique of such approaches, often referred to collectively as the "social doctrine of the Trinity," see Brian Hebblethwaite, "Trinity" in his *Philosophical Theology and Christian Doctrine* (Oxford: Blackwell, 2005) 82–90 (examining arguments of those for *and* against the notion). Examples of more specifically critical accounts include Karen Kilby, "Perichoresis and Projection: Problems with Social Doctrines of the Trinity," *New Blackfriars* (October 2000) 432–45; Norman Metzler, "The Trinity in Contemporary Theology: Questioning the Social Doctrine of the Trinity," *Concordia Theological Quarterly* 67 (2003), 270–88; and Mark Chapman, "Theologies of Community and Theologies of Conflict," ch. 4 of his *Blair's Britain: A Christian Critique* (London: Darton Longman and Todd, 2005) 43–58. From a feminist perspective, Catherine Mowry LaCugna has reflected on trinitarian aspects of ecclesial life in her *God For Us: The Trinity and the Christian Life* (San Francisco: HarperSanFrancisco, 1991). Interpreting and building on her work, Natalie Watson explores LaCugna's thesis that the church is "the continuation of the incarnation of the Triune God in the concrete, embodied and sexual lives of women, men and children," and Letty Russell's contention that "The life of the church is the continuation of the liberating praxis of Jesus and of the life of God's Trinitarian activity." See Watson, "Feminist Ecclesiologies," in Gerard Mannion and Lewis Mudge, eds., *The Routledge Companion to the Christian Church* (London: Routledge, 2007), and her *Introducing Feminist Ecclesiology*, (Cleveland: Pilgrim Press, 2002) 118, 120, and Elisabeth Moltmann-Wendel, *A Land Flowing with Milk and Honey* (London: SCM, 1986) 181–202 (and 172-74), especially 181–85.

31. Or the best-known form of human relationships and community.

writings that influenced the "official" *communio* ecclesiology discussed in chapter 3, I want to suggest that an ecclesiological commitment to build on the trinitarian reflections from such emerging ecclesiologies and, in particular, a move toward greater emphasis on the church as bearing sacramental witness to the Triune God would better point the church's ecclesiological thinking and practice in the right direction for these postmodern times.

Hence, we are not speaking about projection but, again, approximation, tentative conclusions, natural theologizing on the one hand (or what Brian Hebblethwaite would call "*a priori* arguments for Trinitarian theology")[32] *and,* let us not forget, "revelation based arguments" on the other hand.[33] In other words, our attempt to make sense of God's own *self*-communication involves both reflection on human love and community and reasoning from this to what a God of love calls humans to do and be in their relations to one another, and so to further reason what all this might tell us of the being of such a God. But also, such attempts reflect on human experience of that self-communication itself, particularly the experiences of those whose lives, faith, and hopes are recorded in the biblical testimony. Did not Karl Barth call the doctrine of the trinity "church exegesis of biblical revelation"?[34]

Certainly there are several different versions of social trinitarianism and a number of them are flawed in many ways, some perhaps irredeemably so,[35] but here I suggest that ecclesiology can learn much from some versions of this approach, and in particular from the general principle.

32. See Brian Hebblethwaite, "Trinity," in his *Philosophical Theology and Christian Doctrine,* 78–80.

33. Again, for additional examples see ibid., 80–82.

34. Karl Barth, *Church Dogmatics* I:1 §§8, 9. Of course, Barth tells us that other *vestigia trinitatis* (traces of the trinity) should be shunned because they risk confusing *vestigia creaturae in trinitate* with *vestigia trinitatis in creatura.* That is, they risk confusing the traces of creation in the trinity with traces of the trinity in creation, i.e., they impose things on the trinity that are worldly and alien rather than looking to aspects of the trinity revealed in the world, the created order itself. For Barth, the danger is that we would end up with a different source for the doctrine of the trinity than God's own revelation, and this in turn would lead to a different concept of God and subsequently a different doctrine of revelation. Although Barth shunned what he understood by the term "natural theology," here I would argue that such exegesis inevitably entails allowing some form of what a broader understanding of natural theology would involve.

35. Again see Hebblethwaite's "Trinity" for a discussion of various types of social trinitarianism. Mark Chapman's essay does identify some forms of the doctrine that tend toward what is, at times, naïve projection; see "Theologies of Community and Theologies of Conflict."

I would reject any forms that are subordinationist as well as those tending toward tritheism. Whether that leaves one hovering close to modalism is open to debate, albeit with the caveat that all our trinitarian speculations (even on what are deemed revealed aspects of trinitarian divine reality) are only approximations, analogical attempts to say something about the being of the God of love.[36] I would also reject those forms[37] that see the need to emphasize the term "person" in a manner analogous to the contemporary meaning of the term.[38]

What is appealing about Boff's form is the particular emphasis on *perichoresis* and the social implications for human communities.[39] This term, I suggest, lends itself to ecclesial reality and aspirations alike. It can prove illuminating, inspiring, and prophetic—providing some sense of what God calls the church to be and *how* it should be in every generation. The doctrine is an analogy, then, and an aspirational one at that.[40] It is thus a key resource for our construction of social

36. Indeed, one could add the further caveat that the social doctrine is the best bulwark against *either* subordinationist or tritheistic heresies and therefore the most coherent form of the doctrine of the trinity itself.

37. Again see the discussion of a number of such versions of the social doctrine in Hebblethwaite, "Trinity," 80–90.

38. Hence stressing three distinct "centers of consciousness" in the divine being. As Hebblethwaite adds, "it is the opponents of social trinitarianism who are working with the model of persons as isolated individuals" ("Trinity," 89).

39. Boff, *Trinity and Society.*

40. As Hebblethwaite writes in relation to the social trinity, "The question at issue is whether sense can be made of the supposition that the one infinite is best thought of as internally differentiated and interrelated in three mutually loving and interpenetrating subjectivities" ("Trinity," 87). Drawing on David Brown's writings on the trinity, especially "Trinitarian Personhood and Individuality," in Ronald J. Feenstra and Cornelius Plantinga Jr., eds., *Trinity, Incarnation and Atonement: Philosophical and Theological Essays* (Notre Dame: University of Notre Dame Press, 1989) 48–78, Hebblethwaite goes on to state: "To focus attention too literally on the finite, human aspects of the social model—three separate, externally related, finite individuals, such as those portrayed in the Rublev icon—is to fail to do justice to the way in which separate, autonomous, self-conscious persons are already something of an abstraction, even in the human world, let alone where the infinite paradigm of personality and relationality is concerned. Even in the human world, it can be shown that communion is more basic than the individual, and that persons in relation, not least an intense loving and mystical communion, glimpse or achieve a unity that transcends separateness" (ibid., 87–88). Brown, as he notes, writes that the term "individuality," as opposed to individualism, can be properly applied to the trinity. I would suggest that the "minefield" of discourse about persons to which Karl Barth and Karl Rahner alike helped draw modern attention is still very active. I actually believe that we still can profit from further exploring the ancient, classical sense of *persona*, (i.e., building on its original meaning of a mask for actors) when the term was used to refer to one's role within the *polis* or community. Hence to speak of personhood aside from community

ontologies[41] (and ecclesial versions thereof in particular). Thus Boff goes on to speak of unity in diversity in relation to ministry and participation, thereby further helping to focus our concluding discussions: "To the extent that anyone creates communion, that person becomes a sacrament of the holy Trinity. In the church community a consideration of the trinitarian communion ought to prevent the concentration of power and open the way for a broad, egalitarian participation on the part of all. Not everyone can do everything. Each person performs his or her own task, but in communion with everyone else. In this fashion the whole church is transformed into a sign of the Trinity: after all, now it lives the essence of the holy Trinity itself, which is communion."[42]

Thus the being of the church, its daily life, forms, and manner of organization, its activities, its statements, its words and deeds, should seek to approximate the very act and being of the God whom Christians proclaim to be a community of love, between whose act and being, Christians believe, there is no distinction. Hence the church is called to do so not merely in "immanent terms," to be a "community of character," but at one and the same time to do so in "economic terms," for the one is ultimately identical to the other even if differing points of perception and focus can nonetheless serve the church in relation to its mission. Thus the call is for the church—at one and the same time— to be and to proclaim a "virtuous community."[43]

---

was literally nonsensical. This lends itself more to a justification of the social doctrine and therefore also to a preference for the doctrine for ecclesiological ends.

41. See the discussion of this term, as well as of "community," in Gerard Mannion, "Genetics and the Ethics of Community," *Heythrop Journal* 47 (2006), especially 230–31 and n. 17, and also n. 23 on the "ethics of community." In the same paper, n. 20, I discuss Jürgen Moltmann's words: "a *person* is not an *individual*. The distinction is simple, but seldom made. According to its Latin meaning, an *individuum* is something ultimately indivisible, like 'atom' in Greek. A person, in comparison is—as Martin Buber showed (following Hegel, Feuerbach, and Hölderlin)—the individual human being in the resonant field of his or her relationships, the relationships of I, Thou and We, I-Myself and I-It. In the network of relationships, the person becomes the human subject of taking and giving, listening and doing, experiencing and touching, hearing and responding. We approach humanism only when we pass from individualism to personalism" (Jürgen Moltmann, *God for a Secular Society—The Public Relevance of Theology* [London: SCM, 1999] 156).

42. Boff, "Trinity," 86.

43. I believe it was to a significant extent the reappropriation of trinitarian elements into ecclesiological thinking, as witnessed in various exchanges on the Council floor at Vatican II, that helped smooth the way for the conciliar embracing of the notion of the open church, of dialogue, of affirming the world, and of communion itself. These were just some of the major ecclesiological concepts and priorities to emerge from such a reawakening to trinitarian theology among some of those present. Chenu again has

Countering Ecclesiological Confusions and Doctrinal Quandaries

In addition to this general ecclesiological "malaise" brought about by the divisions evident in our contemporary ecclesial situation—which, as we shall see, resembles Alasdair MacIntyre's portrait of modern moral philosophy's fractured state[44]—I am concerned to address tendencies toward what we might term a belief in "ecclesial impassibility," whereby the church is viewed as an unchanging, timeless institution preserving equally timeless truths in uniform modes of expression down through the centuries. Second, following Karl Rahner, Michael Himes, and John Beal, among others, I believe there is a need to counter what has been referred to as "ecclesiological monophysitism." Himes succinctly unpacks this term with reference to Adam Möhler's foundational work in modern ecclesiology, where christology is seen as the basis for ecclesiology.[45] Himes agrees with such a principle, but warns that if the christology one is working with is skewed, then so, too, will be the ecclesiology it informs. Going further, he suggests that in the last five hundred years (in the liturgy, in popular writings, etc.), the christology of much of the Western church has been *monophysite,* i.e., in practice we have allowed the divine in Christ to subsume the human as if Jesus were "really divine, acting human." And so, Himes continues, our debates in contemporary ecclesiology mirror this situation—the Ratzinger/Kasper clashes in recent years being prime examples: all too often there is the presumption that the church is "really divine, acting human," whereas the truth lies in the discernment of the mystery of its two natures.[46]

Himes believes that a fear of history and the nineteenth-century ecclesial agenda in relation to this still dominate ecclesiological debates. To

suggested that the eastern prelates and other fathers at the Council helped bring about this reawakening. "It was by their original presentation of the mystery of God and its manifestations that the eastern prelates exercised a growing influence . . . . Trinitarian personalism subtly and effectively reduced the deism to which western thought (including even the concepts used in Vatican I) had more or less succumbed. Some traces of it remained in the texts produced by the preparatory commission of Vatican II, where the Trinitarian revelation had not succeeded in imparting its characteristic sense and tone to the various statements which had been prepared." ("The New Awareness of the Trinitarian Basis of the Church," 14.) I suggest that this trinitarian basis needs reasserting in official Catholic ecclesiology and that it be allowed, once more, to transform the church.

44. I will thus seek to draw parallels between MacIntyre's moral malaises and the contemporary ecclesiological "malaises."

45. Again see attempts in liberation ecclesiology and the work of Leonardo Boff, in particular, to supplement and balance *overtly* christological ecclesiologies.

46. Michael Himes was addressing the Yale Conference on "Governance, Accountability and the Future of the Catholic Church," March 2003.

his analysis I would add that the postmodern debates in relation to history, as well as to relativism, the championing of the local over the universal, etc., have renewed such fears still further. But Himes gives a timely reminder of Newman's point[47] that the church does not look very much like the Christian communities of New Testament times *today* because things develop.[48] For Himes, the startling point in Newman's day—as it still is—is not *how* things develop but simply *that* they do. This can lead to fear, because things may decline as well as develop in a positive direction (again I would add that the lessons of modernity and the transition into the postmodern world demonstrate this all too vividly). For Himes any disparagement of the Enlightenment *in toto* is mistaken. Much was wrong with the Enlightenment, but more was right with it.[49]

Sharing similar concerns, the prominent American canon lawyer John Beal, sees the debate centering on the following:

> Thus, the challenge for ecclesiology and the canon law that seeks to serve it is not to exacerbate the tension between the juridic and *communion* tendencies, but to find ways to hold these two dimensions together in a dynamic unity. Failure to achieve and maintain the appropriate balance of these tendencies results in ecclesiological distortions reminiscent of the ancient (and sometimes not so ancient) christological tendencies. Radicalizing the tension between the juridic and the *communion* dimensions of the church results in a sort of ecclesiological Nestorianism; collapsing the tension altogether leads, usually, to ecclesiological monophysitism.[50]

As Beal laments, although the principle of "sacramentality" has often been presumed to provide a resource to hold together these divine/

---

47. In his *Essay on the Development of Doctrine* (London: Toovery, 1845).

48. New Testament scholars would argue that it does not technically makes sense to speak of a New Testament "church" or of "gospel values" and "gospel mission," "the gospel," etc. Certainly I agree with them that the notion of "church" in relation to the gospels and perhaps other New Testament texts is an anachronism. But, although we of course have four gospels, the church has always sought to distill the commonality of the essential message of what constitutes the "good news" proclaimed by Jesus of Nazareth. Hence "the gospel" is a term that has been and can be used in a meaningful sense today.

49. Here recall our discussions on the legacy of the Enlightenment in ch. 1.

50. John Beal, "'It Shall Not Be So Among You!' Crisis in the Church, Crisis in Canon Law," in Francis Oakley and Bruce Russet, eds., *Governance, Accountability and the Future of the Church* (New York: Continuum, 2003) 96. Beal is here drawing on Karl Rahner's "Current Problems in Christology," *Theological Investigations* 1 (London: Darton Longman and Todd, 1965) 149–200. This again points to the need for a mean, a midpoint between two extremes.

human, visible/invisible, juridic/*communion* elements of the church, in reality it has proved immensely difficult, particularly in the realm of canon law. For canon law lapses all too easily into ecclesiological mono-physitism in the "chronic difficulty" it displays with "making provision for both the possibility and the reality of human sinfulness when it de-ploys, structures, and provides checks on the exercise of power in the church."[51] Notwithstanding statements from those such as John Paul II apologizing to those wronged by church actions in the past, it ap-pears canon law is "unable to provide for the governance of the church except by angels."[52]

So third, as a mean, a proportionate midpoint, I will also seek to commend a "virtue ecclesiology" and the *analogia ecclesiae* against tendencies toward *any* situation whereby trinitarian perspectives in ec-clesiology are overlooked at the expense of certain perceptions of chris-tological elements. In the words of Beal, "The overemphasis on the christological perspective, which has even been described as 'christo-monism,' leads to the unspoken assumption that the Holy Spirit oper-ates in the church primarily, if not exclusively, through the mediation of the hierarchical authorities who act in *persona Christi* to mold and rule the priestly people in virtue of their sacred power. This christologi-cal constriction of the flow of the Spirit in the church renders suspect charisms or purported manifestations of the Spirit outside hierarchical channels, unless they can be, sometimes begrudgingly, legitimated or coopted by the hierarchy."[53]

I would even wish to steer the Christian "analogical imagination" away from the tendency *only* to perceive Christ as the primary analogate whenever this causes trinitarian and ongoing experiences of the living God to be overlooked or perceived as inferior.[54]

---

51. Beal, "'It Shall Not Be So Among You!'" 96.
52. Ibid.
53. Ibid., 96–97.
54. Of course a trinitarian focus is inclusive of a major dependence on the Incarnation and christological aspects of encountering and understanding God. The dialogical implications of trinitarian theology are further borne out by Karl Barth, who elucidates his reader's understanding of the Trinity by exploring various threefold illustrative schemes, one of which is the following: "the speaker without whom there is no word or meaning: the word is the word of the speaker, and the meaning, which is the meaning of both the speaker and the word" (Karl Barth, *Church Dogmatics* [Edinburgh: T & T Clark, 1975–77] I. 1, 364.

Chapter Nine

From Virtue Ethics to a
"Virtue Ecclesiology" for Today

Ecclesiological Parallels with
Modern and Contemporary Moral Philosophy

To draw the foregoing discussion and analysis together, and in an attempt to provide suggested starting points for such systematic foundations for contemporary and future ecclesiology, we can here profit by drawing some ecclesiological parallels with modern moral philosophy, particularly in relation to what became known as the *After Virtue* debate and subsequent developments in virtue ethics.[1] I want to make the case that the ecclesiological dilemma of the church, local and universal, mirrors the dilemma in modern moral philosophy to which recent virtue ethicists refer.

In particular, the current ecclesiological situation mirrors the famous parable that Alasdair MacIntyre sets out at the beginning of *After Virtue*,[2] where he compares the current situation with regard to ethics and morality to some futuristic scenario in which scientists and science have been assailed and persecuted to extinction (having been blamed for a series of environmental catastrophes). When, many centuries later,

---

1. The arguments presented here have developed out of my earlier "A Virtuous Community: The Self-identity, Vision and Future of the Diocesan Church," in Noel Timms, ed., *Diocesan Dispositions and Parish Voices in the Roman Catholic Church* (Chelmsford: Matthew James, 2001) 79–130.
2. Alasdair MacIntyre, *After Virtue* (2nd ed. London: Duckworth, 1988) 1–5.

people try to reconstruct science from various fragments of textbooks and surviving artefacts, the task is impossible because no one is sure any longer of the context in which such things gained meaning and were useful. MacIntyre believes that morality today resembles such a situation: assailed by the Enlightenment and modernity, most forms of ethical theory no longer make sense, having been taken out of the original contexts and wider frameworks in which they made sense.[3]

Thus, as so much of MacIntyre's work has sought to demonstrate, ethics has a history and is not timeless, universal, absolute, and unchanging in nature. In *After Virtue* he offered a bleak picture of modern ethics, with too many competing and contradictory moral frameworks jostling for primacy. Many such frameworks had long since been rendered meaningless, having been divorced either historically, culturally, or intellectually from the contexts in which they arose and were applicable and relevant.

I suggest an analogous situation exists in relation to contemporary ecclesiology. It is a parallel that not a few may have been drawn to make.[4] But the positive benefit to be derived from making such parallels

3. While recalling what was quoted from Michael Himes, as well as the work of Bernard Lonergan, Gregory Baum, Hugo Meynell, and David Tracy, the various critical theorists, etc., I do not wish wholeheartedly to endorse the rejection of the "Enlightenment Project" espoused by the MacIntyre of that work (although MacIntyre's primary target is the "project's" attempts to provide a solely *rational* justification for morality). As argued in this book at various points, the Enlightenment *in toto* need not necessarily be perceived to have been a bad thing. Much can be rescued from the Enlightenment. Obviously this book suggests that the retreat of many contemporary Christian theologians and ecclesiologists in particular into the "safety" of pre-modern thought systems is something I do not believe will serve the church well in the postmodern era. Again, the "virtue theory" approach leads toward a (contextually sensitive, and hence relative and proportional) mean.

4. I am aware that the applications of MacIntyre's work by Christian ethicists, moral theologians, and even ecclesiologists are legion. Still, I think more explicitly ecclesiological appropriations are less common, and those *combined* with attention to wider debates about the interrelation between ethics and ecclesiology are still fewer. For example, see the series edited by Robin Gill, *New Studies in Christian Ethics*, published by Cambridge University Press from 1992 onward, in which many of the monographs were "deeply influenced by the agenda raised by" MacIntyre's 1981 study (Gill, *Churchgoing and Christian Ethics* [Cambridge: Cambridge University Press, 1999] 2). For a different approach see also, Nancy Murphy, "Using MacIntyre's Method in Christian Ethics," in eadem et al., eds., *Virtues and Practices in the Christian Tradition* (Harrisburg: Trinity Press International, 1997) 33–38. I would question aspects of the use of MacIntyre by certain "Christian" apologists, most notably in Hauerwas' work. As Arne Rasmusson notes, scholars like Hauerwas and Milbank use MacIntyre "in order to help them see how the church might be a place for moral formation and reflection" ("Ecclesiology and Ethics: the Difficulties of Ecclesial Moral Reflection,"

is that certain aspects of the *solutions* MacIntyre and like-minded figures offer to address the plight of morality are also relevant to our ecclesiological debates. MacIntyre's preferred solution, as is now well known, was to advocate a return to the more transferable disposition of virtue ethics, which is relative to context and hence more durable against the poundings of the ebb and flow of culture and history. We shall explore that solution in more detail below.

In chapter 2, I outlined Roger Haight's commendation of "historical ecclesiology" carried out "from below" and also introduced the concept of "comparative ecclesiology." In chapter 6, I further explored the importance of historical consciousness (and the shift toward a socially attentive form of it) for dialogue in the church, and I went on (in chapter 7) to unpack the "promise of comparative ecclesiology." Here we see further parallels with the revival of virtue ethics and the approach taken by MacIntyre. For MacIntyre, in his earlier work as well as in *After Virtue* and since, probes the long history of ethical thought and practice not simply "from above" (metaethics and ethical theory) but also "from below," drawing on practical examples from the classical world onward.

In this sense MacIntyre's "genealogy" of morals is more effective and one might even say more honest than that offered by his antagonist in *After Virtue,* Friedrich Nietzsche. In effect MacIntyre engages in a *comparative* study of ethics, which leads him to conclude that fixed and determined ethical theories "from above," in which normative methods of procedure or fixed moral absolutes are imposed "from above," are doomed to failure in our contemporary age. Indeed, they have ceased to be effective in building up human communities for some centuries now, as most of them are piecemeal and patchwork bricolage of the ethical theories of bygone ages.

MacIntyre embraces virtue theory anew because it is not fixed and determined, or wedded to any particular culture and age: it is transferable across time and geographical and cultural location and is therefore relative in the most positive of senses, namely, that it can be applied to differing scenarios and meet differing communitarian needs. Signifi-

---

The Ecumenical Review 52 [2000] 183), yet they take him to task for how he perceives the interrelation between theology and philosophy (ibid., 183 n.14). (Cf. John Milbank, *Theology and Social Theory* [Oxford: Blackwell, 1990] ch. 11). Yet without agreeing with MacIntyre on the latter, how might one consistently use his work on the former?

cantly, he sees such ethics joined to particular "traditions" relative to their contexts.

Toward a Genealogy of Ecclesiology?

The promise of historical ecclesiology, leading into comparative ecclesiology, should lead us in a similar direction.[5] Paul VI called for the church to engage in ongoing self-critical examination,[6] which must involve the constant discernment of the "signs of the times"—in other words, an engagement with the lessons of history and with the facts that cry out "from below." In the words of the distinguished church historian Roger Aubert, history *is* the "self-understanding of the church."[7] Long before the publication of *After Virtue,* Anton Weiler described an analogous situation in ecclesial self-understanding to that which MacIntyre outlines for ethics, although he acknowledges that the scenario he refers to poses still further questions: "That there are various phases in the historical self-understanding of the church is not to be doubted. Our whole style of living today is making inescapably obvious the social and psychological phenomenon of change in the self-consciousness of the Catholic community—change that is affecting large groups of people."[8]

One such further question concerns the "essential identity" of the church that runs through its "various historical manifestations."[9] And so an additional problem to be faced is the reality of schisms and factions even within particular communions that (as we have seen demonstrated all too vividly in parts of this book) disagree about what constitutes that "essential identity." As Weiler states, "Sectarian groups on the Left and on the Right have each given the self-understanding of the church their own particular emphasis."[10] In one sense, then, *Ecclesiology and Postmodernity* has been about the exploration of such problems, and especially about the attempt to "impose" one very particular understanding of the church across its various communities "from above." But it is about more than this. Although we have had to engage, necessarily, in con-

---

5. I.e., being attentive to context and to the social reality as well as to moral issues.

6. On self-critique see also Elisabeth Moltmann-Wendel, *A Land Flowing with Milk and Honey* (London: SCM, 1986) 163–64.

7. Roger Aubert, ed., *History: Self Understanding of the Church. Concilium* 67 (New York: Herder and Herder, 1971).

8. Anton Weiler, "Editorial" in Aubert, ed., *History,* 9.

9. Ibid.

10. Ibid.

flictual analysis in order to move forward toward dialogue, the majority of the work has been concerned with *constructive* ecclesiology for, as Weiler continues, a further question must be what actually *is*

> this church, whose self-understanding we keep talking about? Who or what is said to "understand itself"? Does there exist a church above and beyond the churches, ecclesial groups and individual believers? A church which is able to comprehend and express itself as a totality, so that all the members recognize themselves in that self-expression, are able to endorse it, and thus turn it into authentic self-understanding? If so, what or who is the organ that formulates this self-understanding, that self-expression? Is it the pope, a council, the congregation at prayer, theologians . . . ? To this question also, whether from the historical or the theological side, a variable answer can be given.[11]

For Weiler the historian can only go so far, exploring and recording the various manifestations of the church's self-understanding "in ecclesiology, in prayer and devotion, in the activity of the church at all levels of [human] life."[12] Such a *comparative* method of procedure allows one to discern what remains constant and consistent in the evolving church.[13] Yet, again, one errs if one believes that a fixed and definitive account can be forthcoming. In Aubert's own volume, an edited collection of explorations by a number of international scholars, what becomes evident "is the plurality, both diachronic and synchronic, of the self-understanding of the church, and also the diversity of levels at which this self-understanding occurs."[14] It is to an acknowledgment of this very point that our explorations of the interrelations between ecclesiology and the age of postmodernity, and of the impact on and challenges posed to ecclesiology by "our times," have thus led us.

But what form might an analogous solution to that offered by virtue ethics take? Just as, in that debate, dispositional virtues (as against, for example, an emphasis on rules and consequences) were recommended as the foundation for a flexible and more transferable moral framework, so we should seek to develop a virtue- (or even character-) oriented ecclesiology (i.e., our considerations of what the church is and what the church does must *always* go hand in hand).[15] Such an ecclesiology

11. Ibid., 9–10.
12. Ibid., 12.
13. Ibid.
14. Ibid., 13. This is further illustrated in Part 3 of the present volume.
15. Aristotle's *Nichomachean Ethics,* in particular Book 2, offers much scope for ecclesiological reflection here.

would better enable the church to confront the "culture of death" and the prevalence of destructive forms of relativism it perceives in our postmodern age. It would be able to do so because such an ecclesiology would be less fixed, less imposed, and less alien to certain cultures and contexts since it would be based on a fundamental orientation of the individual and community toward the good and hence God (and vice-versa). This contrasts fully with any ecclesiology based on rigid conformity, authoritarianism, and fixed absolutes in orthodoxy along with a restrictive understanding of theological enquiry. We are not, then, simply or primarily concerned with what ends the church should be trying to bring about or what norms and rules those belonging to it must live by, but rather with what sort of community it should be. How should we live as Christians *in* the world of today?

This would *not,* however, be akin to Stanley Hauerwas' attempts to appropriate virtue ethics in his ecclesiological thinking. Instead, I suggest that Hauerwas might well prove mistaken in his interpretation of the nature of virtue ethics. If he were not, his ecclesiology would not have developed into the neo-exclusivistic and insular "resident aliens" concept that characterizes his recent thinking. (Again, parallels with Catholicism can be illuminating here.) Of course, there already exists a rich vein of material bringing together the concerns of Christianity with the discipline of virtue ethics. My aim differs in its attempt to explore how one might seek to integrate certain contributions from virtue ethics into the particular debates concerning ecclesiological vision in the Catholic Church as it strives to meet the challenges of a postmodern age. The gospel of life is commended as being a radical and transferable ethic of virtue in itself. It is both dispositional and communitarian in outlook.

For those unfamiliar with the revival of debate concerning "virtue theory," I offer a very basic summary here. Those to whom this background is familiar may safely skip the next section.

Virtue Rekindled[16]

What, then, of the virtues? Why might the recent revival of debate on the virtues, particularly in moral philosophy, help inform the ecclesiology of the communities studied? How might the problems affecting

16. For a fuller introduction see Roger Crisp and Michael Slote, eds., *Virtue Ethics* (Oxford: Oxford University Press, 1997). The literature in the field is now quite enormous; only a representative sample of studies and discussions might include Jean Porter, *The Recovery of Virtue* (London: SPCK, 1990), and also her chapter on virtue ethics in Robin Gill, ed., *The Cambridge Companion to Christian Ethics* (Cambridge:

many Christian communities today be confronted in a way that will facilitate greater pastoral vision and hence community enhancement?

After Virtue and Beyond

As indicated, "virtue ethics" is the name given to a revival of interest in the virtues in the second half of the twentieth century that aimed at shaping a different style of moral philosophy. There are many complex divisions even *within* the field itself. Space prevents a full introduction, so, though generalizing somewhat, I here seek to illustrate the nature of virtue ethics with reference to its pre-eminent classical "forefather" and the work of one major theorist in its late-twentieth-century revival, the aforementioned Alasdair MacIntyre.[17]

We have observed that in *After Virtue,* his now classic work in the field, MacIntyre argues that the modern era, particularly after the revolution in human thought and culture known as the Enlightenment, turned its back on a much older method in ethics. That method, he

---

Cambridge University Press, 2001); Greg Pence, "Virtue Theory" in Peter Singer, ed., *A Companion to Ethics* (Oxford: Blackwell, 1986); James Keenan, "What is Virtue Ethics?" in *Priests and People* 13 (1999) 405, and also his *Moral Wisdom: Lessons and Texts from the Catholic Tradition* (London: Sheed and Ward, 2004). On MacIntyre and the *After Virtue* debate see MacIntyre, *After Virtue,* (2nd ed. 1985), and John Horton and Susan Mendus, eds., *After MacIntyre* (Oxford: Oxford University Press, 1994). Also of interest are Iris Murdoch, *The Sovereignty of Good and Other Essays* (London: Routledge, 1991) and her *Metaphysics as a Guide to Morals* (London: Penguin, 1993); Philippa Foot, *Virtues and Vices* (Oxford: Blackwell, 1978); Richard Taylor, *Good and Evil: A New Direction* (London: Macmillan, 1970); Maria Antonaccio and William Schweiker, eds., *Iris Murdoch and the Search for Human Goodness* (London: University of Chicago Press, 1996); Daniel Statman, *Virtue Ethics: A Critical Reader* (Edinburgh: Edinburgh University Press, 1997); Roger Crisp, ed., *How Should One Live? Essays on the Virtues* (Oxford: Oxford University Press, 1998); Kieran Flanagan and Peter Jupp, *Virtue Ethics, and Sociology: Issues of Modernity and Religion* (New York: St. Martin's, 2001).

17. I am using MacIntyre as a representative and perhaps even paradigmatic example rather than seeking to endorse every aspect of his analysis either then or in later works. Space does not permit a detailed account and critique of all his writings, but we should be attentive to the fact that critics have pointed to MacIntyre's various flaws, fluctuations, inconsistencies, and reversals in later works. His changing understanding of tradition, his admission of having learned from his critics, and his revisions to fundamental aspects of his thinking all demand an exhaustive account that would require considerably more discussion than is here possible. For our primarily ecclesiological purpose, then, we confine ourselves to fundamentals of the MacIntyre of the *After Virtue* period. I am employing MacIntyre not particularly in a privileged sense, i.e., as *the* thinker whose theories may help foster ecclesial virtue, conversation, and communion better than others, but because his grappling with various issues provides useful parallels for our purposes here.

said, can be traced back to the Greek philosopher Aristotle. According to MacIntyre's thesis, until the modern era Aristotle's was among the more influential schools of moral theory. Again, for those unfamiliar, I shall elaborate a little on what all this entails.

The Virtues

Aristotle saw ethics as a branch of social or political science, the branch of science that studies what is good for human beings both individually and socially. His ethics can be called *teleological* because it is concerned with overall ends or goals for humanity (*telos* is Greek for end or goal). Aristotle believed that nature never produces anything without a purpose and he argued further that the purpose of each existing thing is to be itself in the fullest sense.

Aristotle thought that, in order to live a "good life," we should always focus on excellence—*on fulfilling one's task or purpose as well as possible.* The Greek word for excellence is *arête,* in Latin *virtus.* Hence virtue means an excellence, a fulfillment of some particular thing or person. Aristotle believed that the final goal of the human being was happiness, but not in a hedonistic or otherwise utilitarian sense. He saw happiness as a life of activity in accordance with reason. By this he meant that we would make what we did with our lives fit in with intellectual and deliberative virtues: theoretical ("scientific") and moral (practical) excellence in harmony together. For Aristotle the highest virtue, the best excellence of all, was pure, theoretical wisdom. But he also espoused a theory about other moral virtues, which he said were the rational controlling of our desires. Moral virtues were never forced upon one; they had to be voluntarily chosen. In Aristotle's opinion human beings initially learned virtues through education, that is, through instruction and command, but the more they practiced these virtues the more they would come to see them as the right things to do and so the virtues would become habitual.

So Aristotle could say that virtues were a mean, a midpoint between excessive and deficient desire, between desiring too much and desiring too little. So, for example, meanness is a deficient desire, while extravagance is an excessive desire. The virtue that is the midpoint between these two is generosity; the generous person is not too free with giving everything away so as to bankrupt himself or herself, but is not so tight-fisted as to be self-centered. These midpoints could never be fixed in any universal, absolute sense. They are always related to the individual (or to a given community). Hence what might be generosity for John Paul Getty Jr. is not the same as the generosity of a homeless person on the streets of Liverpool who shares a meal with another homeless person. Other prime virtues for Aristotle included temperance, liberality, magnificence, good temper, and even pride. Perhaps a key definition for Aristotle was the following:

> Virtue, then, is a state of character concerned with choice, lying in a mean, i.e., the mean relative to us, this being determined by a rational principle, and by that principle by which the man of practical wisdom would determine it. Now it is a mean between two vices, that which depends on excess and that which depends on defect; and again it is a mean because the vices respectively fall short or exceed what is right in both passions and actions, while virtue finds and chooses that which is intermediate. Hence in respect of its substance and the definition which states its essence virtue is a mean, with regard to what is best and right an extreme.[18]

None of this is to say that there is universal agreement on the virtues, or even which virtues are most desirable. Aristotle's teacher, Plato, spoke of four cardinal virtues (namely, temperance, courage, prudence, justice). Thomas Aquinas, who integrated much of Aristotle's key teaching into Christian theology, articulated a detailed interpretation of the three theological (God-given) virtues: faith, hope, and charity/love *(caritas)* and also spoke of humility as something of a master virtue.[19]

Aristotle fleshed out his theories in the *Nicomachean Ethics* (named after his son, Nichomachus). In that work Aristotle articulates his famous claim that the human is a social being.[20] Consequently he could assert that friendship is a prime necessity of life. And, in accordance with the theory of virtue as a mean between excess and deficit, he said that friendship is important because it reconciles the love of self with the love of the other and so involves seeing others as one might see one's self and treating them accordingly.[21] So Aristotle's ideal life was one of contemplation with an aspiration toward immortality. He felt that pure contemplation took one beyond the normal human state. His notion of the human as the political or social being was built on his

18. Aristotle, *Nicomachean Ethics* II:6, W. D. Ross translation (Oxford: Clarendon Press) 1908.

19. We have encountered these four virtues and their ecclesiological relevance at various stages of the present volume.

20. Book VIII. More famously articulated in his *Politics,* bk I, 2.

21. This again reinforces the case that dialogue toward communion is a necessity.

belief that our language made us bound to try to come together in a community, a *polis*. The *polis* was a community seeking the good life for all its members.

Of course, as we have noted, a wide variety of Christian theologians, perhaps most notably and quintessentially Aquinas, have used Aristotle's ethical thought in their works and seen in it a useful tool in helping to discern and explain the Christian's path toward God, both individual and communal. And just as virtue ethics has been the subject of much debate among secular moral philosophers in recent decades, it has also grasped the imagination of late modern and contemporary Christian ethicists and moral theologians.[22] Perhaps one of the best known Christian specialists in ethics who has recently attempted to use virtue ethics is the Southern Methodist Stanley Hauerwas. As indicated here from the outset, I do not share the direction in which Hauerwas' appropriation of virtue theory has developed. I now want to explore why Hauerwas and those who share his position might be considered misguided in their attempts to use virtue theory in an ecclesiological context.

The "Misappropriation" of Virtue Ethics in the Service of Neo-Exclusivistic Ecclesiology

Here in a brief excursus we first summarize the ecclesial vision *of,* and then the appropriation of virtue ethics *by* one of the leading exponents of the value of virtue ethics for Christian moral and ecclesial discussion, Stanley Hauerwas.[23] There is much that he has said in his many, many publications that few Christians would disagree with. This is the case even with regard to Christian ethics in general and virtue ethics in particular. So, for example, given the arguments outlined in this present volume, I can only agree with Hauerwas when he writes that "the claims [Christians] make about the way things are involve convictions about the way *we* are or should be if we are *able* to see truthfully the way things are."[24] I would express such thoughts more

22. Perhaps ironically, MacIntyre himself, makes a number of connections between the Christian moral tradition and virtue ethics, but this did not prevent the publication of several works by Christian scholars with titles such as "The *Christian* Case for Virtue Ethics."

23. Although we very briefly touched upon the ecclesiological vision of Hauerwas in ch. 3 in relation to the advent of a trans-denominational neo-exclusivism, this book has focused most of its attention on contemporary Catholic debates. Thus our encounter with Hauerwas' moral thought will be illustrative rather than exhaustive..

24. Stanley Hauerwas, *A Community of Character: Toward a Constructive Christian Social Ethic* (London: University of Notre Dame Press, 1981) 90. The idea is borrowed,

tentatively, however: we strive to discern the truth of "how things are" just as we try, however imperfectly, to discern the truth of "how things should be." Arne Rasmusson describes this vision: "This is not just a theoretical question. Our descriptions are closely related to the sort of life we live. The basic questions then, are 'what sort of community should we be?' The answers to that question determine 'What should we do?'"[25]

But Hauerwas, *theologically, ecclesiologically,* and thus *ethically* wanders far from such sentiments when he goes on to develop his thoughts on the "narrative" character of the Christian community to the extent that he concludes: "The truthfulness of Christian convictions can only be tested by recognizing that they involve the claim that the character of the world is such that it requires the formation of a people who are *clearly differentiated from the world.*"[26]

---

as Hauerwas would no doubt admit, from Iris Murdoch, who herself may have absorbed it from G. E. M. Anscombe, who in turn appropriated it from Wittgenstein, who— the only one of the group *not* to acknowledge his source—somewhat "lifted" it from Schopenhauer, who in turn came to this insight from an engagement with the moral traditions of the various world religions as well as the thought of Aristotle. See his *On the Basis of Morality* (Oxford: Bern, 1995). It would appear that Schopenhauer was less familiar with the works of that great Christian "virtue ethicist," Aquinas although Hauerwas, given his doctoral dissertation focus, is not.

25. Rasmusson, "Ecclesiology and Ethics," 185. Note that in this chapter the case is also made that the reverse can apply equally, and, today should be allowed to apply primarily; see ch. 7.

26. Hauerwas, *Community of Character,* 91 (italics supplied). Other representative works (a list that is by no means exhaustive!) include his groundbreaking *Character and the Christian Life: A Study in Theological Ethics* (2nd ed. San Antonio: Trinity Press International, 1985 [first publication 1975]), and his first book, *Vision and Virtue: Essays in Christian Ethical Reflection* (Notre Dame: University of Notre Dame Press, 1981 [first publication 1974]); *The Peaceable Kingdom: A Primer in Christian Ethics* (Notre Dame: University of Notre Dame Press, 1983); *Christian Existence Today: Essays on Church, World and Living In-Between* (Durham, NC: Labyrinth, 1988); Hauerwas with William H. Willimon, *Resident Aliens: An Assessment of Culture and Ministry* (Nashville: Abingdon, 1989); *After Christendom: How the Church is to Behave if Freedom, Justice and a Christian Nation are Bad Ideas* (Nashville: Abingdon, 1991); *In Good Company: The Church as Polis* (Notre Dame: University of Notre Dame Press, 1995); Hauerwas with William H. Willimon, *Where Resident Aliens Live: Exercises for Christian Practice* (Nashville: Abingdon, 1996); Hauerwas with Charles Pinches, *Christians among the Virtues: Conversations with Ancient and Modern Ethics* (Notre Dame: University of Notre Dame Press, 1997); *Sanctify Them in the Truth: Holiness Exemplified* (Nashville: Abingdon, 1998); *A Better Hope: Resources for a Church Confronting Capitalism, Democracy and Postmodernity* (Grand Rapids: Brazos, 2000); *With the Grain of the Universe: The Church's Witness to Natural Theology* (Grand Rapids: Brazos, 2001).

At times, and Hauerwas is far from being the only theologian guilty of this, his arguments suggest rather premature certitude. And yet, that the character of the world demands the formation of a people (i.e., a community)—does not necessarily demand that they "are clearly differentiated from" that world. Indeed, it would appear that Hauerwas can also appear to offer positions that sit uneasily with one another. Thus he can follow a statement that is seemingly contra-exclusivism, namely "It is not the task of the church to deny the reality of the multiplicity of stories in the world or to force the many stories into an artificial harmony"[27] with one that is clearly exclusivistic and more representative of his own ecclesial thinking: "Rather, the task of the church is to be faithful to the story of God that makes intelligible the divided nature of the world."[28] My concern is with what such sentiments entail for understanding the doctrine of creation in operation here, let alone the nature-grace continuum that is seemingly more misunderstood and misrepresented in Christian theology today[29] than it is faithfully articulated and lived.[30]

Continuing from that passage, Hauerwas becomes still more exclusivistic in his ecclesiological thinking, somewhat at variance with the more open tone of his first statement above: "The existence of the

27. Hauerwas, *Community of Character,* 91.
28. Ibid.
29. See the earlier discussion, in chapters 2 and 3.
30. For the debates on Hauerwas' work see Robert Jenson, "The Hauerwas Project," *Modern Theology* 8 (1992) 285–95; Stanley Hauerwas and William H. Willimon, "Why Resident Aliens Struck a Chord," *Missiology* 19 (1991) 419–29; Arne Rasmusson, *The Church as Polis: From Political Theology to Theological Ethics as Exemplified by Jürgen Moltmann and Stanley Hauerwas* (Notre Dame: University of Notre Dame Press, 1995); idem, "Ecclesiology and Ethics," 180–94, Samuel Wells, *Transforming Fate Into Destiny: The Theological Ethics of Stanley Hauerwas* (Carlisle: Paternoster Press, 1998); Emman Katongole, *Beyond Universal Reason: The Relation Between Religion and Ethics in the Work of Stanley Hauerwas* (Notre Dame: University of Notre Dame Press, 2000); Jeffrey Stout, "Virtue and the Way of the World: Reflections on Hauerwas," in Ulrik Nissen, Svend Andersen, and Lars Reuter, eds., *The Sources of Public Morality* (Münster: LIT Verlag, 2003); Frank Kirkpatrick, *The Ethics of Community* (Oxford: Blackwell, 2001), especially 106–12; Stephen H. Webb, "The Very American Stanley Hauerwas," *First Things* 124 (2002) 12–14, Michael J. Quirk, "Stanley Hauerwas: an Interview," *Cross Currents* 52:1, (Spring 2002) 4ff.; Rusty Reno, "Stanley Hauerwas," ch. 21 of Peter Scott and William Cavanaugh, eds., *The Blackwell Companion to Political Theology* (Oxford: Blackwell, 2003) 302–16; J. B. Thompson, *The Ecclesiology of Stanley Hauerwas* (Aldershot: Ashgate, 2003). The very particular and idiosyncratic take on how Christians should engage in moral discourse (given that Hauerwas shuns the term "Christian ethics") is embodied in the structure of Stanley Hauerwas and Samuel Wells, eds., *The Blackwell Companion to Christian Ethics* (Oxford: Blackwell, 2004).

church, therefore, is not an accidental or contingent fact that can be ignored in considerations of the truth of Christian convictions. The church and the social ethic implied by its separate existence is an essential aspect of why Christians think their convictions are true."[31]

Even though Hauerwas acknowledges that the world is God's creation, he undermines the significance of such an acknowledgment by going on to argue that the church, despite its own faults, is nonetheless the "earnest of God's kingdom" and has the task of helping Christians to understand and live their corrective and separatist lives in the sinful world.[32] He insists he is not a tribalist and does not want Christians to retreat into a "religious ghetto,"[33] but the logic of what he prescribes might well leave room for little else, particularly as he weds it to the more stringent anti-world outlook of certain proponents of Radical Orthodoxy in recent years.

Hauerwas asserts, without the smallest hint of irony, that the world "knows not God."[34] But might not sectarian and divisive separatist ecclesial thinking and practice really cloud Christians' understanding of God and tear them away from living the true communion that bears testimony to the essential nature of the God of love?

Hauerwas is at pains to champion the church's role against the "worldly" powers, but his idealistic ecclesiology is not only an example of ecclesiological monophysitism, but equally overlooks the fact that, whatever his conceptual and linguistic maneuverings with the term "Constantinianism," the church remains *a* worldly power and continues to fall prey to the temptations *of* worldly powers. For all his dismissal of general hermeneutical theories (as opposed to his preferred emphasis on narrative),[35] I would here rather emphasize that it is the church's task to *be* a hermeneutical community, to discern the signs of the times:

---

31. Hauerwas, *Community of Character,* 91–92. If we are to speak of "essences," then separatism can have no part in the aspirations of the Christian church and its members. The real "alienation" today is from communion with God. Hence the problem is not the world as such, but our forms of being in it, and especially our failings as Christians. The Christian "story" states that we continually fail to live in ways that draw us closer to God, hence the need for the Incarnation.

32. Ibid., 92.

33. Ibid. See also his introduction and first chapter in *After Christendom,* 1–22, and chs. 1 and 2 of Hauerwas and Willimon, *Where Resident Aliens Live: Exercises for Christian Practice.*

34. Ibid., 93.

35. *Christian Existence Today,* 55.

hermeneutics is the church's calling and perhaps never more so than in our present age.[36]

But why is a volume primarily (though far from exclusively) concerned with debates within Roman Catholicism devoting this amount of space to someone who is not a Catholic? First, as indicated in earlier chapters, it is because Hauerwas is closer in thinking to some contemporary Catholic ecclesiological and moral perspectives than many alternative Catholic viewpoints and ecclesial ways of being.[37] Second, Hauerwas is one of the foremost scholars of recent decades to attempt to use insights from virtue ethics in both his moral and ecclesiological thinking. I wish there to be no room for misunderstanding here. In championing the utility of virtue ethics for ecclesiology today I do not therefore endorse the exclusivistic aspects of either ecclesiological or the ethical outlook of Stanley Hauerwas. Quite the reverse, I hope, will be seen to be the case from the preceding chapters and what remains of this one.

But if we have raised concerns about aspects of Hauerwas' ecclesiological vision, what of his appropriation of "virtue ethics," more specifically in relation to this critique and our wider aim to shape considerations toward a contemporary "virtue ecclesiology"? While we cannot go into a detailed and exhaustive account of every aspect of the history, merits, and faults of virtue ethics here, a short passage from Robin Gill adequately captures its importance for ecclesiological thinking and practice and so for our debates:

36. I join with those such as David Tracy, Lewis Mudge, Werner Jeanrond, and Simone Sinn, each of whose work is discussed in Mannion, "Hermeneutical Investigations: Discerning Contemporary Christian Community" (forthcoming).

37. Some may feel, of course, that this picture of so much "common ground" between representatives of the official Catholic Church and the likes of Hauerwas, Milbank, and the proponents of Radical Orthodoxy is a little far-fetched. They should not. Hauerwas himself provided ample evidence when he recently claimed a most unlikely ally in Francis Cardinal George, Archbishop of Chicago. Hauerwas was particularly taken by a speech George gave in a Library of Congress series, entitled "Catholic Christianity and the Millennium." They are less strange bedfellows than one might think. It appears Hauerwas believes that because George offers as insular and inward-looking a neo-exclusivist vision as his own, this somehow defends him from the charge of being a "sectarian fideistic tribalist," cf. *A Better Hope,* 10. Hauerwas states that his own book is but a "footnote" to George's speech, but it seems neither can see the irony that their arguments serve only to create and sustain the impression that there actually *is* a definite divide between nature and grace.

. . . the specific insight of virtue ethics, which is especially relevant to a study of churchgoing and Christian ethics, is that the moral life is shaped by particular communities despite their actual frailties and ambiguities. Whereas there has been a tendency for moral philosophy to focus upon ethical decision-making as if individuals could act solely on the basis of autonomous reasoning, virtue ethics is more distinctly sociological in character. . . . [i.e.,] Moral notions are socially generated and—even when this is not realized by the participants themselves—rely upon specific communities for their support.[38]

Bear in mind this last sentence in particular, where we could easily replace "moral notions" with "ecclesial notions." It is thus that I would sum up the great value of virtue ethics: it is a type of ethical theory that teaches us both that ethics has a history and that ethics is fundamentally bound up with communities that likewise have their own "histories," i.e., their narratives and stories and past, present, and future concerns and anxieties. Virtue ethics focuses on what sort of persons we should seek to be and what sort of communities we should work to build[39] (not, of course, that other ethical theories are irrelevant to or are not employed in the church).[40]

But virtue ethics needs to be applied carefully and consistently, as does any ethical "method." As no ethical theory or method is ever truly neutral and context free, it is always sensible to "read between the lines" and look for any possible specific agendas when we see various ethical theories being applied; this is particularly true of virtue ethics in recent decades. In his various works Gill, both a sociologist and a theologian, has recently criticized Christians, most notably theologians and moral philosophers, whose response to postmodernity is to focus on an *idealized* as opposed to actual Christian community. He deems the work of those like Hauerwas

---

38. Gill, *Churchgoing and Christian Ethics,* 26.

39. Just as virtue ethics has proved its importance for sociology, hence for understanding and directing communities and their enhancement, so we can re-emphasize its importance for ecclesiology: furthermore, ecclesial visions that shun or at best remain aloof from the social sciences today in a separatist ecclesial outlook are likely to be ill-suited to the appropriation of virtue ethics in ecclesial thinking, for contemporary virtue ethics owes much to an engagement with the social sciences. It is perhaps often overlooked by some that, early in his career, Alasdair MacIntyre was employed as a lecturer in sociology. Cf. also Kieran Flanagan and Peter Jupp, *Virtue Ethics, and Sociology.* Flanagan is also a specialist in the sociology of religion.

40. A variety of such theories can be found in the Catholic moral tradition, often side by side (even when they are *conflicting* methodologies).

particularly representative of such attitudes.[41] Gill's main objection concerns the attempt of some people to appropriate *a* form of "virtue ethics" to support their moral and ecclesiological reasoning.

So we might suggest that part of the problem with Stanley Hauerwas and those who share his particular approach is that they are offering too inadequate and overtly insular an ecclesiology to sufficiently meet the challenges of a postmodern age, because it is one based on an *idealized* understanding of the church. As Gill writes: " . . . idealized communities ill fit a virtue ethic whether Christian or secular."[42] Indeed, as Gill's study seeks to demonstrate, neither the method nor the conclusions that follow from such an approach stand up when compared with the sociological evidence. He detects a distinct "bias" at work here: " . . . one side of the bias is to take the concept of Christian communities seriously, but the other side is to be deeply distrustful of actual Christian communities. . . . [T]he frailties and inadequacies of churchgoers themselves are regarded as all too obvious. As a result, amongst a number of recent theologians a high doctrine of *worship* is often combined with a low estimate of worshipp*ers*."[43]

Again, there are striking parallels with our issues of discussion vis-à-vis the Catholic community: for example, Gill's last sentence could even be describing aspects of *Christifideles laici,* the 1997 *Instruction on Certain Questions Regarding the Collaboration of the Non-Ordained Faithful in the Sacred Ministry of the Priest,* or the tone of numerous other official church pronouncements. Gill's analysis can be particularly illuminating when applied to the current Catholic Church, especially with regard to many of the attitudes adopted and ventures initiated by the church in recent times. Gill's warning against "idealized accounts" is most pertinent for the Catholic Church today. Thus the notion of "blueprint ecclesiologies" imposed "from above" is further found wanting.

41. Rusty Reno offers a succinct account of the earlier Hauerwas on virtue: Hauerwas "wants us to use character, rather than command, as the 'central metaphor' . . . . Character is the basis for the 'continuity' and 'integrity' of a person subject to a power that effects real and lasting change. Virtue denotes the qualities of character that establish continuity and integrity in lives changing for the better. Vice denotes those qualities in lives changing for the worse (and therefore disintegrating). . . . He wants to understand the particular ways the lives of Christians take on weight and solidity. He is eager to explain how this brick-like quality both collides with and resists the worldly powers that dominate our lives, and just this collision and resistance defines the political reality of Christian character" ("Stanley Hauerwas," 305–306).

42. Gill, *Churchgoing and Christian Ethics,* 13.

43. Ibid., 31 (italics supplied).

Hauerwas is also criticized by Frank Kirkpatrick for such insularity and its detrimental effect on the building of a true community, particularly in relation to his dependence on an "idealized" (and so *nonexistent*) church. Kirkpatrick argues that "anyone who has belonged to a real church, as opposed to the ideal one that Hauerwas projects, knows that this description is often far off the mark."[44] What Hauerwas offers, I would add, appears to be "mere" ideals, as opposed to any real ecclesiology of substance.

Yes, let us embrace the value of virtue ethics in our ecclesiological and ethical thinking, but *not* in the way in which Stanley Hauerwas attempts to appropriate virtue ethics in his own ecclesiological thinking, for the evidence suggests that Hauerwas might even be challenged on his interpretation of the nature of virtue ethics.[45] If he were not, his ecclesiology would not have developed into the neo-exclusivistic and insular notion of Christians relating to the wider society according to that concept of "resident aliens" that particularly characterizes his recent thinking.[46]

Hauerwas' misappropriation of virtue ethics has not only *ecclesiological,* but also, *metaethical* implications. As Jeffrey Stout,[47] Gill, and many others suggest, Hauerwas' idiosyncratic version of virtue ethics, together with an equally idiosyncratic (and occasionally even incompatible) appropriation of the theories of others such as MacIntyre, Yoder, and Milbank, looks very different from the form of virtue ethics found in the main classical, medieval, modern, and now postmodern proponents of such an ethical theory. Obviously there are and should be differing varieties of virtue ethics, but the model offered by Hauerwas may prove self-defeating, as it runs counter to what virtue theory really entails and seeks to foster.

To draw together the ecclesial and ethical aspects of our analysis, an additional dimension to such critique of Hauerwas, Milbank, those who share their approach (and so of their Catholic equivalents) is provided by Lewis Mudge, particularly in terms of their specifically *ecclesiological* thinking. Mudge worries at the direction in which such attempts to pull the church back from being slaves to the cultural and political

44. Kirkpatrick, *The Ethics of Community,* 109–10.
45. The concept of virtue does not appear to be a mean between deficiency and excess as Hauerwas uses it. His writings, like those of representatives of other varieties of neo-exclusivism, often contain a worrying degree of ecclesial hubris and other-worldliness, indeed even anti-world sentiment.
46. Again I believe that parallels with Catholicism can here be illuminating.
47. Jeffrey Stout, "Virtue and the Way of the World: Reflections on Hauerwas."

as well as cultural "pretensions of our times"[48] are developing. For if the church is supposed to stand outside the moral and social ways of the contemporary world, Mudge wants to ask: "how is this supposed to work?"[49]

His assessment of such ecclesiological-ethical thinking challenges its lack of sociological realism, when "Stanley Hauerwas and his school" speak as if "the congregation were a total cultural environment, as if it were *possible* to transform the world's story entirely within the Christian story."[50] They seem to suggest that the historical welfare of the world is somehow dependent on a "cultural Christianization of the world."[51] Mudge acknowledges that "'cultural Christianization' is not a Hauerwasian or Milbankian category. But does it not come to this? What else could it mean to rest our hopes exclusively on communities of Christian moral practice?"[52]

In his comparative study Arne Rasmusson summarizes Mudge's response to the Hauerwasian position, which entails that ". . . a true politics will be intelligible only in the framework of a full theological language that excludes secular people and people in other religions."[53] But Mudge also insists that Hauerwasian presumptions about congregational life, particularly that the church itself constitutes a "*total* cultural environment," are built on thin air, for such total cultural environments "scarcely exist" in a postmodern world. "A devout member of the Knights of Columbus may *also* be an avid baseball fan *and* a member of the Teamsters' Union! Readers from other cultures can readily supply their own examples."[54] Indeed they can, and here the insights of a number of feminist and womanist scholars demonstrate the multiplicity of "cultural worlds" and identities each of us today

---

48. *The Church as Moral Community: Ecclesiology and Ethics in Ecumenical Debate* (Geneva: WCC Publications, 1998) 77.

49. Ibid.

50. Ibid.

51. Ibid., 151, also discussed in Rasmusson, "Ecclesiology and Ethics," 189.

52. Ibid., 151–52. For analysis of Mudge's work see Mannion, "Hermeneutical Investigations," (forthcoming) and "What's in a Name?" Recall our discussion of Jean-François Lyotard in relation to the contemporary understanding and exercise of magisterium in ch. 4: "What their 'arrogance' means is that they identify themselves with the social system conceived as a totality in quest of its most performative unity possible" (Lyotard, *The Postmodern Condition: A Report on Knowledge* (Manchester: University of Manchester Press, 1984) 79.

53. Rasmusson, "Ethics and Ecclesiology," 189.

54. Mudge, *Church as Moral Community,* 77.

simultaneously occupies. Rasmusson's comparative study summarizes Mudge's alternative argument better than I could hope to:

> Christians themselves are much more part of the secular world than this language allows for. Most of us today "exist in a multiplicity of cultural environments, and engage in several different occupational and familial practices, each with its own symbolism, logic, customs, and the like. Pluralism enters our personhood."[55] Living in several different cultures, with permeable boundaries, we become "multiple selves." Thus we need guidance on how to live with this complexity, trusting that God is at work not only in the church, but in everyday life. ""Ecclesiology" maps only part of the setting for the faithful life."[56] Theologically, Mudge speaks of "a sacramental transfiguration of everyday life" which "engenders a capacity to discern how and where the Holy Spirit is at work as [Christians] know it."[57] It is precisely in this process that the community is formed . . . .[58]

Like Mudge, I would equally endorse an understanding of Christianity that is open to the world and more world-*affirming* than denouncing.[59] So, too, I would adhere to the understanding of the Christian's multi-dimensioned and simultaneous membership of a diverse variety of communities, as opposed to a Hauerwasian "resident aliens" conceptualization of the Christian life and those entailed by its parallel varieties in Radical Orthodoxy and Catholicism. Here one might see striking similarities between such odd bedfellows as John Milbank and Joseph Ratzinger.[60]

Here the issue of pluralism or polycentrism returns to the forefront in light of the challenges to the neo-exclusivists by those who hold that the reality of our pluralistic existence should be embraced. Again one finds similar sentiments in Frank Kirkpatrick, who writes:

> The difficulty I have with Hauerwas' sectarian understanding of church as community is that it fundamentally underestimates the scope of God's

55. Ibid.

56. Ibid.

57. Ibid., 81.

58. Rasmusson, "Ethics and Ecclesiology," 189. Recall our discussion of Francis Sullivan on the means of grace and the actualization of it, with the possession of the former not equivalent to possession of the fullness of grace, in relation to his critique of *Dominus Iesus* in ch. 3 (Sullivan, "Introduction and Ecclesiological Issues," in Stephen J. Pope and Charles Hefling, eds., *Sic et Non: Encountering Dominus Iesus* [Maryknoll, NY: Orbis, 2002] 56).

59. Cf. Mannion, "What's in a Name?" which utilizes and discusses Mudge's work further.

60. Recall Joseph Ratzinger's sense of the church being in a period of "Babylonian captivity."

involvement with the world beyond the church. Hauerwas too narrowly limits the scope of God's actions in history to the church and only to the church (wherever and however he finds and defines it). He has a sense of the universality of God's intention for the world, he understands the world as that which God loves and that which the church serves, but *he cannot bring himself to acknowledge that the world just may, in its own various ways, be doing more things to realize God's intentions than the church itself has done or has been able to appreciate.*[61]

We shall return to these differences of opinion about God's presence and activity in the world in drawing this book to a close. But here we must also consider that many critics of the neo-exclusivists find serious difficulties not simply with *what* is being said, although that is primarily the problem, but, also, because it compounds this very serious problem, with the *way* in which they say it.[62]

Thus ultimately, Hauerwas' appropriation of virtue ethics, like similar ecclesiological visions, does not engage the analogical mode of imagination but is rather dichotomous in character and even, at times, relies on assumptions grounded on little other than binary oppositional thinking. As Gill shows, Christians display a wide variety of values and virtues even within the same congregations, despite some differences between Christians and the surrounding population on many issues. Hence "The distinctiveness of churchgoers is real but relative. This is exactly the picture that Alasdair MacIntyre paints in *After Virtue*. Unlike the dichotomy . . . between church and society increasingly present in the writings of Stanley Hauerwas and others, MacIntyre avoids idealized depictions of churches."[63] The Neo-exclusivistic perception is much more than acclaiming "the" tradition; it is a distinctly postmodern privileging of *an* interpretation of *one* particular tradition. And yet a virtue, by definition, cannot be understood in binary either/or terms, only in mediatory ones. Whatever Hauerwas offers his readers, it is not, therefore, the most constructive appropriation and ecclesiological application of virtue ethics. And I suggest we have seen in our discussions throughout this book that elements of contemporary "official" thinking in the Catholic Church will fare little better.[64]

61. Kirkpatrick, *The Ethics of Community*, 110 (italics supplied).
62. Hauerwas frequently pleads that his critics have "got him all wrong" and he is no sectarian tribal fideist, but his defenses ring somewhat hollow, given the implications of his argument.
63. Gill, *Churchgoing and Christian Ethics*, 197–98.
64. Hence the need to learn the lesson that ecclesial concepts such as laity and ministry have a history no less than moral concepts—a lesson inspired, of course, by

Note that I am not simply using Hauerwas as a straw man but am quite deliberately drawing parallels with what has taken place and with the arguments put forth in parts of the Catholic communion in recent decades. As in our earlier chapter 3, I am discussing the ecclesiological thinking of those such as Hauerwas because it gives cause for concern in its own right. But another fundamental reason for doing so is that a number of Catholics may already agree with such analysis or be persuaded by it. If that is so, they must also persuade themselves that the very same difficulties and ecclesiological reductivism exists within the Catholic community and has been in the ascendancy for some decades now.

Alasdair MacIntyre's Own "Solutions" to Modernity's Ills

What of Alasdair MacIntyre's own suggestions concerning the way forward for ethics and for communities today? In *After Virtue* he argued that modernity had collectively given rise to what he called the "*Enlightenment project.*" I will provide only a brief outline of his now very influential and yet oft-contested arguments.[65] He believed that because the Enlightenment championed reason, the self, and autonomy (detached from historical and social context) it had detrimental effects on communities everywhere and hence on morality. As indicated, the result of all this is that we no longer have an effective sense of morality, but instead there are competing moral frameworks long since ineffective because they are divorced from the original contexts in which they had arisen. We now have the choice, he tells us, of following the Enlightenment project to its completion and ending, like Nietzsche, with a problem because we then no longer believe there is such a thing as objective

---

metaethical debates generated by the re-emergence of discourse concerning "virtue ethics." So, too, they are developed out of and thus contextually related to *specific* communities. We need to recognize the *true* lessons of virtue ethics and not simply manipulate its rhetoric. Sadly, working to their own differing agendas, various ecclesiological appropriators of virtue ethics in recent years, both Catholic and non-Catholic, can appear to "hijack" the rhetoric of "virtue" without paying due heed to the pluralistic reality many theorists behind the modern revival in virtue ethics sought to depict.

65. On the "Enlightenment project" see especially *After Virtue*, chs. 4–6, and cf. Horton and Mendus, *After MacIntyre* (1994) for a treatment of the debates surrounding MacIntyre's work. See also Kieran Flanagan and Peter Jupp eds., *Virtue, Ethics, and Sociology*.

morality, so we no longer can discern effectively how we are to live.[66] Alternatively, MacIntyre argues, we can reject the Enlightenment project of justifying morality altogether. He believes there is no third alternative.[67]

However, MacIntyre believes that modernity has tried to dodge this decision. He sees that modern humanity has refused to directly ask the question "What *sort* of person should I become?" Yet this is the very question that inquires what the end, the *telos* for human beings should be. It is *the* teleological question and is fundamental for human communities because on its answer depends our capacity for building and maintaining community. Instead, modernity (and now *post-modernity*) asks questions about the ends of human life only indirectly, from the standpoint of the individual. Too often in the past we have had rules and "oughts" as the topics of conversation in moral philosophy. Any talk about the qualities of character in people only becomes relevant if such qualities enable us to follow certain rules and principles. But that is doing ethics the wrong way around, claimed MacIntyre. Thus in an epitomizing and famous passage he writes:

> A crucial turning point in [our] earlier history occurred when men and women of good will turned aside from the task of shoring up the Roman *imperium* and ceased to identify the continuation of civility and moral community with the maintenance of that *imperium*. What they set themselves to achieve instead—often not recognizing fully what they were doing—was the construction of new forms of community within which the moral life could be sustained so that both morality and civility might survive the coming ages of barbarism and darkness. If my account of our moral condition is correct, we ought also to conclude that for some time now we too have reached that turning point. What matters at this stage is the construction of local forms of community within which civility and the intellectual and moral life can be sustained through the new dark ages which are already upon us. And if the tradition of the virtues was able to survive the horrors of the last dark ages, we are not entirely without grounds for hope. This time however, the barbarians are not waiting beyond the frontiers; they have already been governing for quite some time. And it is our lack of consciousness of this that constitutes

66. Here also we seek to apply a similar critique to any ecclesiology that is divorced from and inattentive to context.

67. Again note that I would maintain that the notion of a "new" or "second" Enlightenment offers much positive scope for our debates vis-à-vis postmodernity, as opposed to an outright rejection of the Enlightenment in general.

> part of our predicament. We are waiting not for a Godot, but for an-
> other—doubtless very different—St. Benedict.[68]

MacIntyre argued that we need to go back and look at the virtues *first of all* in order to understand the whole notion of how rules work and what authority they have. It is not "do this" because it is what you ought to do, but rather, "if you want to be a good and just and kind person, this is the sort of thing you should do." So MacIntyre goes back to Aristotle's virtue theory and looks at different types of moral character, different types of the self, and different types of society and community. MacIntyre stresses the teleological aspects of *arête* as *overall* excellence and goodness rather than particular forms of excellence and particular goods. This is a crucial point for the formation of a virtue ecclesiology that will overcome divisions and avoid imposing alien structures of community on parts of the church where they are clearly detrimental to that very community. MacIntyre suggested that we should rekindle the sense of a virtue as a mean between two extremes.

The *After Virtue* debate was and continues to be about putting the self in a new (communal) setting and having some notion of an overall end and purpose in life, rather than about rules and principles and consequences and individual happiness. We must also realize that there is a broader picture to be looked at than simply the self or one's im-mediate problems and needs. We need to rekindle the teleological aspect of ethics. So, in MacIntyre's view, moral philosophy in these times needed to reinvent itself and re-explain itself. It needed to change the questions it was asking as well as the language in which it asked those questions. MacIntyre asserted the need to "place" ourselves and our communities again, to embrace the notions of narrative, practice, and tradition in direct correspondence to our understanding of the self, society, and history. We each have a story, a collective story, and we can learn from and build on the past. So his vision entails that we shun in-dividualism, move away from moral visions that are predominantly fix-ated on rules and abstract concepts, and try to relate to our here and now in a way that brings us closer to fulfilling what our true end and *telos* should be.

This book has been describing an ecclesiological turning point just as MacIntyre was describing a moral and cultural one. But the church need not be as pessimistic as MacIntyre: after all, it teaches that hope is a *God-given* virtue. Neither do I mean to suggest that contemporary

68. MacIntyre, *After Virtue*, 263.

church leaders are barbarians. But some of MacIntyre's contentions can indeed be informative for the church. In theological terms one might paraphrase the above arguments thus: For Christians this is the building of open community and following the collective and individual path toward peace and union with God, a path set for us by Jesus of Nazareth, on which we are guided by the Spirit. *This* should be the meaning and purpose of ecclesial authority today, I suggest: empowerment, bringing forth the best of people, working toward a true community.[69]

Virtue theorists urge us to consider not only what sort of person one should be but also what sort of community one should help to build. Perhaps the virtues on their own are not enough to build a new morality, but many believe that without due attention to these issues Nietzsche's dethronement of morality and enthronement of the individual is the only alternative.[70]

A Virtue Ecclesiology

Aside from MacIntyre, we should also note how many other recent contributions from moral philosophy outside and apart from theology

---

69. Again, note my earlier attempts to explore the meaning of authority, working toward this communitarian emphasis in "What Do We Mean by Authority?" in Bernard Hoose, ed., *Authority in the Roman Catholic Church: Theory and Practice* (Aldershot, England; Burlington, VT: Ashgate Press, 2002). Note that in place of MacIntyre's "narrative" we have spoken of "historical consciousness," the microcosmic and macrocosmic in tandem.

70. Cf. Mannion, "Being True: Williams and Meynell on Reason and Virtue," *The Heythrop Journal* (forthcoming). Here again I am open to the idea that there may be many more consistent and indeed constructive thinkers and theories in addition to MacIntyre to discuss in relation to encouraging conversation and the building up of a virtuous community. Foremost among them is Jürgen Habermas and his theory of communicative action. The moral and even ecclesiological implications of Habermas' work are much discussed in German literature and increasingly in English. (Although the moral aspects have been receiving detailed treatment in English for some time now, the ecclesiological treatments are somewhat more recent.) Space simply does not permit an adequate discussion of Habermas' most ecclesiologically relevant works here. I am also mindful that much literature on community, in both critical theory and broader social theory, offers further rich resources and a necessary hermeneutic of suspicion of the concept itself in relation to its various forms and manifestations. An extremely useful discussion in relation to these areas of further debate is by Jacqui Stewart, "Theology, Conversation and Community: Bauman's Critique of Community," in Jacques Haers and P. De Mey, eds., *Theology and Conversation: Towards a Relational Theory.* BETL 172 (Leuven: Peeters, 2003) 519–30. I am also indebted to Jacqui for further very helpful suggestions concerning not only Habermas but the themes and thinkers under discussion in this chapter in general.

have much to offer Christian reflections on the virtues, despite the wealth of Christian tradition here. The list could go on and on, and Charles Taylor's name would feature prominently on it, but to highlight just two additional promising examples that might initially seem less obvious in their "ecclesiological implications," the recent works of Onora O'Neill and Allen Wood (both from a Kantian background) offer Catholic thought a further way of seeing that deontological and natural law insights in ethical thinking need not be incompatible with and indeed can be complementary to attention to virtue theory and the virtues in general.[71] Communitarian factors loom large in the works of both.[72]

But even in recent years it is not that the virtues, virtue ethics, and some of the issues outlined above have been ignored by theologians in relation to *ecclesiology:* far from it. Although Richard B. Hays has noted how the ecclesial setting of Pauline ethics has often been overlooked, many ecclesiologists have seen the importance of both ethics in general and the virtues in particular to the building up of church communities. So, to touch on only a few examples, the World Council of Churches between 1992 and 1996 coordinated a studies program on the interrelationship of ecclesiology and ethics, and their November 1994 document, *Costly Commitment,* is of particular relevance to the possibility of a "virtue ecclesiology."[73] The work of the late systematic theologian Colin Gunton has sought to interpret the church "as a school of virtue,"

71. The church also faces the challenge of harmonizing the various, sometimes conflicting moral traditions within its own midst and even in its official teaching.

72. See, for example, Onora O'Neill, *Constructions of Reason. Explorations in Kant's Practical Philosophy* (Cambridge: Cambridge University Press, 1989); eadem, "Vindicating Reason," in Paul Guyer, ed., *The Cambridge Companion to Kant* (Cambridge: Cambridge University Press, 1992); eadem, "Kantian Ethics," in Peter Singer, ed., *A Companion to Ethics* (Oxford: Blackwell, 1993); eadem, "Duties and Virtues," in Mary Warnock, ed., *Women Philosophers* (London: Everyman, 1996); eadem, *Towards Justice and Virtue* (Cambridge: Cambridge University Press, 1996); eadem, "Consistency in Action," in James Rachels, ed. *Ethical Theory* (Oxford: Oxford University Press, 1998). For Allen W. Wood see his *Kant's Moral Religion* (Ithaca: Cornell University Press, 1970); "Rational Theology, Moral Faith and Religion," in Paul Guyer, ed., *The Cambridge Companion to Kant* (Cambridge: Cambridge University Press, 1992); *Kant's Ethical Thought* (Cambridge: Cambridge University Press, 1999); and "The Final Form of Kant's Practical Philosophy," in Mark Timmons, ed., *Essays on Kant's Moral Philosophy* (New York: Cambridge University Press, 2000). Aspects of these works are discussed in Mannion, *Schopenhauer, Religion and Morality: The Humble Path to Ethics* (Aldershot, England, and Burlington, VT: Ashgate, 2003) chs. 4 and 5.

73. Thomas Best and Martin Robra, *Ecclesiology and Ethics: Costly Commitment* (Geneva: WCC, 1995).

relating trinitarian theology to the task of human formation. The pastoral-practical theology journal *Priests and People* devoted an entire issue to exploring the virtues and virtue ethics in an effort to see how virtue can be, as James Keenan puts it, a "bridge between church life and moral theology." Keenan's work in virtue ethics in general, particularly in elucidating aspects of the Catholic tradition in this field,[74] and the application of his invaluable work in this area to ecclesiological questions offers much hope and many resources for the development of any "virtue ecclesiology."[75] So, too, does Jean Porter's work loom large here for similar reasons, and numerous contributions from feminist theology and feminist ecclesiology have proved both groundbreaking and constructive in relation to virtue ethics also. This is because so many feminist ecclesiologists and other feminist theorists, along with various forms of "emerging ecclesiologies"[76] from around the globe, are essentially commending attention to virtues in their discourse about new and reformed practices in communities—hence, in effect, offering "virtue ecclesiologies."[77] In stark contrast, it might often appear as if

74. James Keenan, *Goodness and Rightness in Thomas Aquinas' Summa Theologiae* (Washington, D.C.: Georgetown University Press, 1992); idem, *Virtues for Ordinary Christians* (London: Sheed and Ward, 1996); idem, "Virtue Ethics," ch. 5 of Bernard Hoose, ed., *Christian Ethics: an Introduction* (London: Continuum, 1998); idem, "What is Virtue Ethics?" in *Priests and People* 13/11 (1999) 401ff.; idem, *Commandments of Compassion* (London: Sheed and Ward, 1999); idem, ed., with Joseph J. Kotva, Jr., *Practice What You Preach: Virtues, Ethics and Power in the Lives of Pastoral Ministers and Their Congregations* (London: Sheed and Ward, 1999); idem, with Daniel Harrington, *Jesus and Virtue Ethics: Building Bridges Between New Testament Studies and Moral Theology* (London: Sheed and Ward, 2002); and his *Moral Wisdom: Lessons and Texts from the Catholic Tradition* (London: Sheed and Ward, 2004).

75. Keenan, "What is Virtue Ethics?" (1999) 405. See also Richard B. Hays, "Ecclesiology and Ethics in 1 Corinthians," *Ex Auditu* 10 (1994); Colin Gunton, "The Church as a School of Virtue," paper presented to the Heidelberg Ecumenical Forum on The Trinity, the Church and the Christian Ethos, May 2000, published in his *Intellect and Action: Elucidations on Christian Theology and the Life of Faith* (Edinburgh: T & T Clark, 2000). Further representative samples of recent Christian approaches include Joseph J. Kotva, *The Christian Case for Virtue Ethics* (Washington, D.C.: Georgetown University Press, 1996); Romano Guardini, *Learning the Virtues* (Manchester, NH: Sophia Institute Press, 1998); Esther D. Reed, ed., *Virtue Ethics* (Edinburgh: T & T Clark, 1999); for a more specifically theological account see Romanus Cessario, *The Virtues, or the Examined Life* (London: Continuum, 2002).

76. As commended in the previous chapter. Note I do *not* mean the Emergent Church *movement* but rather those ecclesiologies informed by liberationist and contextual approaches, particularly those ecclesiologies from beyond the European and North American contexts.

77. See, for example, "Communities That Embody the Story of God: Towards a Feminist Narrative Ecclesiology," ch. 8 of Natalie Watson, *Introducing Feminist Ecclesiology* (London: Continuum, 2002). See also her "Feminist Ecclesiologies" in

the neo-exclusivistic approach seeks only to make conformity and obedience into "cardinal" virtues.

Nonetheless, there *are* many church documents that relate the virtues to ecclesiological issues and even to discussions of particular offices and ministries within the church (all too rarely, however, in a systematic fashion). The theological virtues of faith, hope, and charity were prominent features in the church's planning for the Jubilee celebrations. The rich monastic tradition through the Christian centuries has, of course, contributed much concerning how the virtues and the church's self-understanding go hand in hand. Thus the interrelationship between ecclesiology and the virtues is neither a controversial nor a completely new phenomenon. It is, then, all the better a focal point for transcending ecclesiological divisions by turning back toward such a valued part of the church's rich tradition.

Our present discussion differs, however, in its specific concern with how one might seek to integrate valuable contributions from virtue ethics into the debates over a contemporary ecclesiological vision in the Catholic Church. Obviously many of the problems identified in this volume and elsewhere are symptomatic of the "postmodern condition."[78]

Although MacIntyre might not explicitly say so in *After Virtue* itself, his thesis was a contribution to confronting the dilemmas of postmodern society. And just as the postmodern era has presented many challenges to the church and to each of those individuals who see themselves as part of that church, we have here been suggesting that the ecclesiological dilemmas of the contemporary church, local and universal alike, also mirror the dilemmas in modern moral philosophy to which virtue ethicists refer.

Hence many contemporary models, paradigms, and visions of the church have lost their true meaning, divorced from their original contexts. Furthermore, competing ecclesiologies make true community difficult to achieve. Just as modern moral philosophy slid into a polarization between deontological ethics (based on obligations) and consequentialistic ethics (based on outcomes) and various mix-and-match ethical frameworks in between, so the church has become polarized

---

Gerard Mannion and Lewis Mudge, eds., *The Routledge Companion to the Christian Church* (London: Routledge, 2007). See also Peter C. Hodgson, *Revisioning the Church: Ecclesial Freedom in the New Paradigm* (Philadelphia: Fortress Press, 1988).

78. James Keenan's work epitomizes many aspects of the ecclesiological appropriation of virtue ethics being suggested here.

between rival ecclesiological starting points as well as models and paradigms made up of various elements of both.[79]

How then, might we react? For some, as we have outlined in preceding chapters, the present curial governance of the Catholic Church is deemed to be a reactionary form of "conservative postmodernism" that asserts, at times even in a manner close to fundamentalism, the continued significance of rigidly fixed and determined, not to mention rigidly interpreted, "absolute truths" in the face of the slide toward relativism that characterized modernity and now is symptomatic of postmodernity.[80] Hauerwas' separatist agenda and those of similar ecclesial persuasion mirror this development. Relativism can, indeed, be a serious threat to religion, morality, and, above all, community. But is the correct reaction to the ills of our age to transform the community of the gospel of Jesus of Nazareth into an authoritarian or enclosed institution that tolerates little dissent for fear the cherished traditions of that church will be lost? Is this not rather the other extreme, the polar opposite of that good news? (Recall that virtue is a "midpoint," a mean between excess and deficiency).

I suggest the neo-exclusivistic, world-renouncing approach is *not* the most ecclesially virtuous approach to take. Nor is the correct response a flight into Nietzschean perspectivalism and/or emotivism and consumerist individualism (where one pretends that every significant factor in life is a matter of personal preference and choice). This leads to the loss of community and the absence of any agreed vision at all. But it is also not about an idealistic *via media,* if by such is meant a woolly compromise. Rather the analogical approach, attention to genuine hermeneutical engagement, and, finally, a "virtuous approach" can steer away from extremes without settling into crass and thus ineffective "middle ways."[81] Instead, a virtuous approach steers a middle course between two extremes in the manner appropriate to orientation toward the end that is good rather than the end that is least problematic, or that is convenient or diplomatic.

79. Once again with the qualification that we are dealing with paradigmatic theories and ideal types in engaging certain metaethical debates.

80. See David Ray Griffin, William A. Beardslee, and Joe Holland, eds., *Varieties of Postmodern Theology* (New York: SUNY Press, 1989).

81. See here chs. 9–11 of David Tracy, *The Analogical Imagination: Christian Theology and the Culture of Pluralism* (New York: Crossroad, 1981), and also his "Between Foundationalism and Relativism," in idem, *On Naming the Present, God, Hermeneutics, and Church* (Maryknoll, NY: Orbis, 1994). See also Lieven Boeve, *Interrupting Tradition* (Leuven: Peeters, 2004), Parts 2 and 3.

MacIntyre said that one of the grounds for hope was the fact that the virtues outlasted the previous age of barbarism, while other moral frameworks fared less well. This might encourage us to look for an adaptable ecclesiology that is less wedded to an era, paradigm, or failing grand narrative. So I suggest, instead, that we embrace an ecclesiology for postmodern times based not simply on aspects of MacIntyre's virtue ethics and those others who have recently embraced such a form of moral theory. We should also reinvigorate Catholicism's deep tradition of turning to the virtues in order to gain vision and energy to transform self, society, and world. Augustine, Bernard of Clairvaux, Aquinas, to name but a few, have each illustrated how the power of virtues and above all the priority of love permeates the treasures of Christian tradition. We should draw afresh from such a well, in dialogue with our age, when seeking to shape the vision that will inform our mechanisms of authority and governance, of empowerment and community enhancement for the church local and universal today.[82]

What is required is not a rigid plan and model, or a paradigm to be imposed, but a vision to replace the mix and match, make do and mend, rhetoric above reality, fire-fighting problem solving and cautious ecclesiological paradigm that today appears to dominate ecclesial life. The fixation on short-term ends is often ecclesially debilitating. In short, we need to focus on our true goals, to form a vision that is teleological rather than governed by rules and conditions or unduly influenced by church politics or financial considerations or any fixation on "intellectual," soteriological, and social "territory" (the paths toward exclusivism). We need a *dispositional* ecclesiology and one that is based on the virtues, which, of course, MacIntyre has described thus: "[The virtues are] those dispositions which will not only sustain practices and enable us to achieve the goals internal to practices, but which will also sustain us in the relevant kind of quest for the good, by enabling us to overcome the harms, dangers, temptations and distractions which we encounter, and which will furnish us with increasing self-knowledge and increasing knowledge of the good."[83]

82. Pope Benedict XVI's new encyclical *Deus caritas est* helps remind the church of the central importance of this virtue, for love provides a hermeneutic of the divine being itself.

83. MacIntyre, *After Virtue,* 219.

Recall Tracy's articulation of the need to harmonize the religious/ mystical, the intellectual, and the practical.[84] To hold such together in creative tension. As virtue ethics focuses *primarily* on character rather than on duties, commands, or consequences, there is a parallel lesson here both for the church as a community in general and for those who hold positions of ministry (service) and authority within the church in particular. But we have no ideal community in mind here. Rather the church itself—every Christian community—and every person who plays a role at whatever level within the church should be judged in terms of the motives behind their actions when those can be discerned and by their *deeds* where not. But the latter is not judgment simply in terms of consequences; rather it is a little natural moral theologizing at work: working backward from the effects to determine what the character who could do these things might or, in many cases, must be like.[85] No one in the church should seek to command respect because of any perceived *de facto* authority (hence power) connected with their position. Does the gospel not tell us as much itself? Aristotle said that people are "good in but one way but bad in many."[86] So also there are many ways of being church badly. But so is there only one way to ensure that we follow the right path toward being a good ecclesial community at both the local and universal level. It is the path of virtue, between ecclesial excesses and deficiencies alike.

So, too, a virtue-based model of ecclesial authority and governance should resemble such dispositions: it is not the title of bishop and due power invested in an individual that should command loyalty, cooperation, and respect; rather, it is how good a shepherd that bishop is and what virtues inform his vision and planning for the diocese. The same is true of any priest, lay minister, finance director, etc. We have noted how the deferential model of authority is in terminal decline in most areas of society and this, too, is a sign of our "postmodern times." The problem is that often this flight from authority is replaced, on the one hand, by indifference, apathy, and relativism; all authority is shunned. On the other hand the ugly head of authoritarianism rears itself anew. It would be no bad thing if the authoritarian and restrictive models currently in vogue in the church (and in society) were replaced with a

---

84. See the conclusions in Tracy, "The Uneasy Alliance Reconceived: Catholic Theological Method, Modernity, and Postmodernity," *TS* 50/3 (1989) 548–70, at 569–70.

85. The same is true of the communitarian equivalence of such reasoning.

86. Aristotle, *Nicomachean Ethics*, Bk II: 6, W. D. Ross translation.

virtue model of authority. The church might undertake to foster and encourage such an outlook as a matter of some urgency. In doing so it could once again be literally exemplary to those secular "powers" in the midst of which the church must and indeed should live.[87] Thus our task is to build a community where character truly matters, in both an individual and social sense.

---

87. Here recall that passage from *Gaudium et Spes* §92 we encountered in chapter 5.

Being Concerned with Love: Beginnings of a "Virtue Ecclesiology," Theological and Practical

A virtue ecclesiology would embrace the need to break free from the tensions between unity and diversity in the church and, as St. Paul urged, truly embrace unity *in* diversity.[1] In shaping this vision we simply must always pay heed to the *priority of love*.[2] We do need a vision of the church that can be adapted to take into account the context of the local church *wherever* groups of Christians find themselves struggling to be fully human and striving to adhere to the gospel vision itself, in *whatever* context. Virtue ethics, as an "ethics of being," a transferable and dispositional mode of moral reasoning and reflection, offers the best hope as a guiding (as opposed to exclusive) methodological framework.[3] We

1. See 1 Corinthians.
2. Recall our earlier discussion of *caritas*. But I do not mean this in the sense employed by Joseph Fletcher, *Situation Ethics* (Philadelphia: Westminster, 1966). Fletcher's ethics is more overtly consequentialistic, whereas virtue ethics seeks to move away from the narrower forms of consequentialistic concerns (which is not to imply that Fletcher's arguments can be dismissed so briefly, but space does not permit a full debate on situation ethics here). Some will rightly point out that some consequentialistic or teleological method might be needed to discern what counts as a virtue, to see what effect a certain "habit" might have, particularly on others. (I am most grateful to Professor Kurt Remele for raising this particular objection.)
3. Thus I am not seeking to rule out, in any absolute or crude sense, all forms of consequentialistic thinking (or, for that matter, deontological thinking). Rather, I believe that ethics cannot and should not be bracketed within the confines of

Christians do hold to fundamental truths, and among those truths are the power of love and the orientation of the human being and all creation toward the good, in itself some analogous yet imperfect attempt by which we seek to understand God. We believe, in a fuller sense even than Aristotle, that we are destined for community, that we exist with a fundamental purpose in mind: life is not meaningless, and we have a goal, a *telos* to aspire toward that involves the transcendence of this current state of affairs. Such things we assert in our attempts to discern what "truth" might be, for this, too, brings us closer to God, and Christ has taught us as much.

Above all, however, we do not seek to impose an interpretation of the truth, as if truth were something one might bottle and save up for a thirsty day. We believe that we must struggle to *live* the truth, and fundamental to doing so is to undertake this task together, united by Christ, as a *community,* a church. The church is called to be attentive to *being* true in every aspect of its daily existence.

We should avoid looking for our vision of the church in the wrong places, being overly concerned with finance or efficiency or public relations, with making the best of limited resources, with "waiting for Rome," even with simply praying and hoping our difficulties and divisions will go away. We should avoid being concerned with "guarding" our "territory," "defending" "our" "faith," with keeping "our" tradition "pure." Aquinas himself asserted the priority of *caritas* (love) in our path toward God, both personal and communal.[4] He saw love as the "form" of *all* the virtues, which depend upon it.[5] As Jean Porter has aptly illustrated, in Aquinas we see that by making *caritas* our guiding principle in all our actions we become closer to God, because all we do and desire becomes oriented toward God: *caritas* allows us to participate in the very mind and will of God. That, surely, must be the ultimate vision. The priority of love transforms our whole person, and yet it does much more: ". . . charity does not just secure the inner

only one exclusive methodology. As stated in the previous chapter, Catholic moral theology and moral teaching alike use several differing schools of ethical thought and moral traditions. The trick is to harmonize these and to avoid contradiction and the application of incompatible or conflicting reasoning processes.

4. Attention was given to this theme of *caritas* in chapter 5 of the present volume just as it was in so prominent a theme in Paul VI's *Ecclesiam suam*. See also David Tracy, "Caritas in the Catholic Tradition," in his *On Naming the Present* (Maryknoll, NY: Orbis, 1994).

5. For example, see Thomas Aquinas, *Summa Theologiae,* vol. 23 (1a 2ae. 55-67) (London: Eyre & Spottiswoode, 1969) 65.

unity that is the essence of peace. It is also the only sure foundation for that concord among individuals which is the basis for peace within the community."[6]

In chapter 7 we commended the fruits given to our church by the emerging ecclesiologies in other parts of the world and within our own. We also commended the promise of comparative theology and its ecclesiological counterpart. We delved into the promise of wider or macro-ecumenism, the new ecumenism of which David Tracy spoke as the path that could lead the church in our times beyond both the very postmodern poles of foundationalism and relativism. For Tracy such a journey demands that one "must try to hold together three virtues that would normally be kept apart: the virtue of self-respect and self-dignity maintained by all those who never leave their tradition; the virtue of a radical openness to other and different traditions; the virtue of ethical universality with a sense of justice by all who insist upon the communality of the human."[7] Such a journey may not, at times, be easy, but has the church in our times any real alternative if it is truly to be church and live out the gospel mission, to proclaim the good news to these times? Have we not suggested that here the "emerging ecclesiologies" elsewhere have much to teach the church in Europe and North America?

Here, then, I have commended living with difference, with plurality—even celebrating it. I do not commend a "woolly" pluralism, but rather the courage to live with tensions, even with conflict and disagreements: this must be possible just as dissent from or "creative fidelity" to official positions must be possible, in order for a communion to flourish. None of this is to suggest that inclusivity and acceptance of the other is necessarily limitless, for there are things that should not be accepted and those with whom conversation needs to be more critical. As Aristotle says, "not every action or every passion admits of a mean; for some have names that already imply badness." And such things "imply by their names that they are themselves bad, and not the excesses or deficiencies of them. It is not possible, then, ever to be right with regard to them; one must always be wrong."[8]

6. Jean Porter, *The Recovery of Virtue*, (Louisville: Westminster John Knox, 1990) 205. This again might raise the question why *Deus caritas est* does not explore the full *ecclesial* implications of the fact that *God is love*.

7. David Tracy, "Beyond Foundationalism and Relativism: Hermeneutics and the New Ecumenism," ch. 12 of *On Naming the Present*, 138.

8. Aristotle, *Nicomachean Ethics*, II: 6 (W. D. Ross translation). The examples he gives are spite, shamelessness, and envy for passions, and adultery, theft, and murder for

But that is why the path to a virtue ecclesiology will help illuminate what should and should not be accepted in the community as well as helping to determine the proportionate ecclesial "passions" (e.g., pluralism, openness, even community itself) and "actions" (e.g., conversation, consultation, active charity), *relative* to the context and to social needs and priorities. The level of dialogue that should be fostered, for example with those from another local Christian communion such as the Anglican Church, would be very different from the level, form, and character of dialogue with, say, South African Christians who sought to defend the apartheid regime. The form and level of charity to a priest who has a drinking problem would, one would think, necessarily be somewhat different in character to that provided to a cleric who is a serial child abuser. Some actions are just always wrong: for instance, the moving around of a serial abuser by his bishop, unbeknownst to those among whom the abuser will live and to whom he will minister in his new setting primarily for the purpose of avoiding scandal. The charity shown by the official church to theologians who dissent from official teaching, as well as the form of conversation entered into with them, should be truly governed by love in all things and proportionate to the nature and authority of the teaching concerned. Remember again John XXIII's words, which found their way into *Gaudium et Spes:* "Hence, *let there be unity in what is necessary; freedom in what is unsettled, and charity in any case."*[9] Such is a call to a virtuous community.

The various churches today can overcome their crisis of identity, their divisions and competing ecclesiologies, the lack of vision and misplaced plans and priorities by diverting some of their energies and attention away from structures and offices and rigid policies, from trying to conform to the will of an institutional church in Rome or their diocesan office or the mind of their parish priest or that of intransigent parishioners.

The churches can and must live with a great deal of disagreement; the church always has done so, and imposed unity is a contradiction in terms. Debate can be healthy as long as Pope John's maxim is followed: *in all things charity.* Nor should it be the case that Christians should always be in total agreement on *moral* issues; they never have been and perhaps never should be. Again virtue ethics offers the best way forward: search for the mean that is duly proportionate and relative to the context.

---

actions. Of course, proportionalism would urge us to qualify any such list. Certainly, as in one famous example, a hungry and destitute person who "steals" bread can be judged very differently. But is such truly "theft"?

9. *Gaudium et Spes* §92 (italics supplied).

Virtue is neither idealistic (in an everyday sense of the term) nor *anti-* organization and institutions. But a virtue ecclesiology would look carefully at the *motives* behind planning, strategy, and structural organization, with a view to emphasizing the priority of love. A virtue ecclesiology might enable Christians to explore in a comparative fashion what sort of communities their churches are in reality and what they aspire to be, in accordance with the gospel and the rich traditions of Christianity. Individual reflection will feed into community reflection and vice-versa. Christians might test their answers against what their ideals for themselves and their community should really be when reflected on in the light of making love the guiding principle in their personal and collective lives. The virtuous life is to be preferred over the predominence of the "institutional" (using the term here in a negative sense). When the institution becomes the end in itself, the *telos,* and is not driven by *caritas,* by embracing and bearing witness to the love of God, then it has gone seriously astray. This should not and cannot be a controversial point. Virtuous authority brings true freedom and a fuller enhancement of the community. Organizational norms and agreed priorities will follow. The shape/structure of their communities will take on a truly communitarian character the more the virtues become their own dispositional guides.

Thus will emerge a deeper sense of communion, in a truly lived sense, one greater than that perceived in terms of institutional "membership." The virtuous life, because it is dispositional by nature, calls the church to *continuous* renewal and reform: for example, not a diocesan assembly to once and for all solve the community's dilemmas, but regular gatherings to take soundings about the concerns of the members of that community and to discern if the diocese is heading in the right direction. A virtue ecclesiology embraces the notions of the church as mystery, sacrament, and community, for these notions of church all blend in with our very reason for trying to live by the virtues. The Christian understanding of God affirms the incomprehensible mystery of the ground of our being, and yet our faith attests also to the gracious and revelatory disclosure of that very being. The path to greater community with each other and hence with God: that is the sacramental nature of human existence—to grasp the offer of God's self-communication and transform oneself and unite with one's fellow travelers toward the ultimate union with the ground of all being: in Rahner's words, that infinite horizon where *all* other horizons meet.[10]

10. See Karl Rahner, *Foundations of Christian Faith* (New York: Crossroad, 1984).

A church guided by a virtue ecclesiology can do no other than constantly engage in dialogue and always view itself as servant.[11] A virtuous vision of the church brings to the fore a radical openness and faithfulness to the gospel. The aim and goal of a "virtuous community" should be to make all dispositions in the local church, from those operative in the prayer group, the catechesis class, the justice and peace society, the base community, the parish, the diocese, bishops' conference, curia, and beyond, *virtuous* dispositions. We have seen that over time other models, paradigms, and visions of the church lose favor and effectiveness, and cause divisions. A house divided cannot stand any more today than yesterday. The church in our times does not need a *rigid* paradigm for all peoples of all times in all places, but a *way,* a dispositional existential orientation: *the way of Jesus Christ.* The church in our times needs to rekindle the gospel ethic in our ecclesiological visions and structures alike in order that they may endure beyond the new postmodern age of the "barbarians." What will ensure this? The enduring nature of the virtues, but especially those Paul commends to ecclesial communities: "And now faith, hope, and love abide, these three; and the greatest of these is love. Pursue love . . . ."[12]

Comparative Ecclesiology:
As Path Toward Ecclesial Virtue and as Virtue Ecclesiology

We earlier explored and commended the promise of comparative ecclesiology, perceiving that it offers the church in a postmodern world the hope and resources necessary to meet the challenges of this new historical context and to transcend the competing ecclesiologies that have blighted inter- and intra-ecclesial relations in recent decades. Instead, comparative ecclesiology would allow genuine merits to be shared, differences to be openly acknowledged, and less profitable ecclesial approaches to be discerned.[13]

11. A dialogical vision might also facilitate aspects of the compatibilist model of a top-down with a bottom-up vision for the future of the church proposed by the organizational expert Louise Fitzgerald. See Noel Timms, ed., *Diocesan Dispositions and Parish Voices in the Roman Catholic Church* (Chelmsford: Matthew James, 2001), ch. 8.

12. 1 Cor 13:13–14:1.

13. Here we may further draw parallels between Roger Haight's work in ecclesiology and the broader systematic focus of Tracy, in particular his expression of the need, as an "appropriate response" to the present situation, for reflection "upon the pluralism *within* the Christian tradition in order to reflect upon the pluralism *among* the religious traditions or the pluralisms *among* the analyses of the situation. . . . The recognition

This book has been attempting to sketch a form of ecclesiology that brings ethics closer to ecclesiology and ecclesial life in general, embraces and celebrates the pluralistic realities in which the church will always find itself, celebrates the world as God's creation and the scene of God's self-communication and, finally, weds ecclesial vision (and so ecclesiological theory and rhetoric) to ecclesial praxis. Such reflections lead to the conclusion that comparative ecclesiology *is* a virtuous ecclesiology. One might even say that Trinitarian theology itself is a comparative attempt to understand the differing aspects of the being and salvific (economic) activity of God.

In this we are mindful to accord with all five "premises" of a comparative ecclesiology, as set down by Roger Haight,[14] namely, to immerse our explorations in historical consciousness, thereby inculcating the disposition of humility—both in methodological terms and, when one realizes how far short we fall of some of our ecclesial forebears, in terms of ecclesial life and practice as well. Second, as indicated, there is need for a positive appreciation of pluralism. Third is a whole/part conception of church, neither placing universal over and above local nor vice-versa. Fourth, we embrace the gifts and human challenges of religious pluralism. And the fifth premise is "Retaining a confessional or particular ecclesial identity."[15] This book has been addressed primarily to issues within the Catholic communion and is imperfectly composed by one who is grateful for and rejoices in being a part of that extended family, no matter what "family difficulties and disagreements" occur from time to time. As Haight himself writes,

> . . . comparative ecclesiology consists not in overcoming denominational Christianity or Christianity itself, but in transcending the limits of individual churches by expanding the sources brought to bear on the task of understanding the Christian faith, in this case the church. What is

---

that no classic tradition should abandon its particular genius in its entry into conversation with the others is a central key for enhancing a genuinely ecumenical theology" (David Tracy, *The Analogical Imagination* [New York: Crossroad, 1981] 447–48).

14. There is much scope to develop further aspects that are perhaps still tentative and suggestive in Haight's work to date because those works naturally had to focus on the historical and initial methodological outworking of a systematization of this form of ecclesiological inquiry. I believe that several such aspects of this method offer more promise than the methods and tone of the approaches more familiarly adopted in, for example, the writings of Hauerwas and much Roman curial documentation, and even in aspects of official teachings in recent decades.

15. The five are succinctly outlined in, Haight, "Comparative Theology," in Gerard Mannion and Lewis Mudge, eds., *The Routledge Companion to the Christian Church* (London: Routledge, 2007).

learned from these sources is brought back as further light on the particularities of any given church. The concern for the truth contained in
one's own community guarantees that the discipline remains Christian
theology.[16]

We are not, then "resident aliens," but citizens of God's creation,
despite our manifest and ongoing mistreatment of the gifts bestowed
on us and our all-too-often shoddy custodianship of the world. Pluralism itself (or again, if one prefers, "polycentrism") is commended
throughout this book and explicitly in this chapter as a further ecclesiological virtue, and sectarianism and insularity are denounced as ecclesiological vices.[17]

The point of this discussion thus comes into sharper focus: given
the exemplary, virtue- and character-based values attested by New Testament communities and throughout the long moral tradition of Christianity, we should not follow Caiaphas and ever believe that *expediency*
is a good enough justification for the actions for which we are respon-
sible. For Christians the ends *do not* justify the means. Let us put this
in more direct terms: if what we do actually *contradicts* the gospel of
love, then no amount of reasoning or appeal to higher authorities and
long-term ends can make right what is, according to gospel values,
wrong. One *cannot* bear witness to the gospel and further the gospel
mission by *betraying* any elements of the gospel itself. Our comparative
explorations of differing ways of being church and of understanding
the church can better help us proceed toward and then along the path
of ecclesial virtue.

One would be naïve to expect radical transformation overnight, but
perhaps a more modest expectation might be for due attention to be
paid to *one* virtue in particular. This could prove profitable as the initial
step forward. If we perhaps sought to live out this virtue in our ecclesial
being and allowed it to inform our ecclesiological thinking and discus-

16. Ibid. See Tracy, *The Analogical Imagination,* 448.

17. As Roger Haight concludes, "Comparative ecclesiology is an analogous notion
that includes a variety of subdisciplines that address the various levels of pluralism that
characterize Christian social existence in our time with distinct methods and goals.
Comparative ecclesiology in all its forms explicitly addresses the tension between
particularism, in the sense of a withdrawal into denominationalism, and universalism,
in the sense of a concern for religious community as such. All ecclesiology need not
be explicitly comparative in nature. There will always be a demand for denominational
studies. But, given globalization and the new sense of connection between religious
communities at all levels, one may expect that various forms of comparative ecclesiology
will assume a more important role for the self-understanding of the Christian churches"
(Haight, "Comparative Theology").

sions, then so much more would follow. However, it is not an easy virtue to master, or even to name.

"Plea for a Nameless Virtue"

Toward the end of his long and dedicated service to the church and the theological community, Karl Rahner wrote a short address, published in the final volume of his *Theological Investigations,* that is an impassioned plea "for a nameless virtue." Alluding to an analogous assessment of the state of moral thought and practice as sketched by MacIntyre in *After Virtue,* Rahner wrote that it was quite possible there could exist a virtue, though widely known because of its practice, that has nonetheless received less definitive treatment in moral theology and moral philosophy and so has yet remained "nameless."

> It is, however, possible that the theoretical reflection on the whole of morality has not grasped each and every individual element with equal clarity and explicitness with the result that one or other moral mode of behavior does remain nameless and is mostly lost sight of in a universal and abstract concept. The simple fact that the catalogues of virtues, ethical systems, and terminologies belonging to individual eras, civilizations, and styles of life were and are quite different and can hardly be brought into conformity with one another shows that something like this is quite conceivable. The lifestyle in one period of history unintentionally and unavoidably neglects this or that virtue which another lifestyle explicitly recognizes and cultivates. This cannot be explained solely by the fact that the extramoral and premoral conditions of human life vary and for this reason also require morally different ways of acting.[18]

Rahner, of course, had a definite example in mind and one that, as the above analysis suggests, might offer great hope in our dealings with the vagaries and challenges of the postmodern world. As with all proper "virtues" in the literal sense of the term, Rahner believed there could be a "middle way" between the two extremes of "skeptical relativism which thinks that it can dispense itself from making a decision and ideological fanaticism which wants to derive the absoluteness of the free decision from an absoluteness of the rational consideration, an absoluteness which does not really exist. . . . [Such] are the two false consequences that can very easily result from the insuperable difference

18. Karl Rahner, "Plea for a Nameless Virtue," ch. 3 of *Theological Investigations* 23 (London: Darton Longman and Todd, 1992) 34.

between the problematic nature of reflection and the absoluteness of decision, between theory and practice."[19]

Rahner here captures the essence of the postmodern dilemma exhibited in our contemporary intellectual and ethical pursuits, of which the ecclesiological problems we have focused on in this book are simply one prominent example. Rahner suggests that the middle way between these two extremes, this nameless virtue,

> takes seriously the antecedent reflection on the justification of a decision and . . . nonetheless does not demand more of the reflection than it can provide, . . . honestly admits its problematic nature and despite this does not stand in the way of the courage for a serene and brave decision; [it] is the hallmark of the proper self-understanding of a person who is neither the god of an absolute and universal certainty and clarity nor the creature of a sterile arbitrariness which views everything as equally right and equally wrong, a person who has human qualities that command respect even if these qualities do not have the effulgence of the divine or the transparence of the obvious.[20]

Rahner goes on to acknowledge that such a nameless virtue is difficult to practice, or even to discern. But in light of the questions for the church in our times that we have considered in this book, and particularly in light of the advent and rise of ecclesial and ecclesiological neo-exclusivism, the postmodern age cries out for this nameless virtue to be rediscovered and cultivated anew throughout the life and structures of the church. Rahner offers some hints that might aid such a quest:

> It belongs to that area of life wisdom which intellectual acumen cannot alone provide. Ultimately it does not matter whether one along with Saint Thomas Aquinas calls this virtue an intellectual virtue or whether one calls it a moral virtue. It is the virtue that takes theoretical rationality seriously and yet does not turn practice into a merely secondary derivation of theory, but rather acknowledges an ultimate independence and underivability of freedom and of practice. It is the virtue of active respect for the mutual relationship of theory and practice, of knowledge and freedom, and at the same time for their disconsonance. It is the virtue of the unity and diversity of the two realities without which one would be sacrificed in favor of the other.[21]

19. Ibid., 36.
20. Ibid., 36–37.
21. Ibid., 37.

I suggest that the discernment and commendation of the ecclesiological equivalent or rather the ecclesial practice of such a virtue is the purpose and fruit of the *analogia ecclesiae*,[22] and thus the focal point toward which this work has moved.[23] The problem with naming this virtue, of course, relates to the enduring problem of understanding the relationship between theory and practice. Rahner resists attempts to subsume it under the rubric of either wisdom or prudence, for it is a very specific virtue and would be lost in the generalities of either field. Instead, he ends his talk by saying: "Whether or not this virtue's name is known is in the end not so important. But this virtue ought to be practiced. Today, especially, when one could get the impression that the majority of humankind is divided into weary relativists and obstinate fanatics."[24]

Thus Rahner's "Plea for a Nameless Virtue" can be interpreted as concerning the joining of moral theory and practice, and this task in an ecclesial setting can itself be perceived as the business of ecclesiology.[25] One would not be so presumptuous as to attempt to give this

22. We might recall Aristotle's assertion that our final good and happiness lie in bringing about harmony between our intellectual and deliberative virtues; the excellence sought in both compounds our fulfilment (again see his *Nicomachean Ethics* and also Aquinas's discussion of the same task in *Summa Theologiae*, vol. 23 [1a 2ae. 55–67]). This approximates not only to Rahner's "nameless" virtue but also to Tracy's plea to construct that "uneasy alliance" anew: uniting the religious/mystical, the intellectual (what I have also termed prophetic and what could simply be called "hope,") and the institutional/practical/moral elements (love in action) of our faith. Recall also Kant's famous "three questions": "What can I know?" "What must I do?" and "What may I hope?"—which can all be reduced to the further question of "*What is the Human Being?*"Thus the questions come together to unite epistemological, moral, and soteriological concerns. The passage in Kant where these questions are raised is *Critique of Pure Reason*, B 832–33. Kant added the fourth in outlining these questions on other occasions (*Werke* 11:414; *Werke* 11:25).

23. See Tracy on "strategies" in the contemporary era, ch. 9 of *The Analogical Imagination,* and in particular his examination of the work of Johann Baptist Metz, to further assist in the discernment of the verities of recent ecclesial struggles toward what approximates to this virtue.

24. Karl Rahner, "Plea for a Nameless Virtue," 37.

25. Again the middle way between Rahner's two extremes is further illustrated and the constituents of that "uneasy alliance" envisioned by Tracy again widened still further by Tracy's own work: "Whether a thinker employs explicitly analogical language is not the real issue. What ultimately counts is the emergence of an analogical imagination for all those thinkers, secular and religious alike, who cannot accept either the brittleness of self-righteous ideologies masking some univocal monism or the privatized sloth of an all too easy pluralism masking either a decorous defeatism or some equivocal rootlessness. For all such persons, in fidelity to the concreteness of their own particularity, on behalf of the futural concreteness of all—of the concrete whole—there emerge, in both secular and religious form, the reality and the demands

virtue a name but, in its ecclesiological form and practice at least, the *analogia ecclesiae* and a virtue ecclesiology must commend its discernment and practice. The outcome must be what might (however clumsily) be termed a "Preferential Option for Social Ontology." Analogical ecclesiology approximates to the being of God and yet we learn that it is through attention to virtue that it embraces each of the fundamental aspects of Catholic ecclesiology: mystery, sacrament, and community. All this, and even that nameless virtue that offers ecclesial life so much, is captured well by those two contemporary servants of the church who embody it: David Tracy and David McLoughlin. "The Christian focus on the event of Jesus Christ discloses the always-already, not-yet reality of grace. That grace, when reflected upon, unfolds its fuller meaning into the ordered relationships of the God who is love, the world that is beloved and a self gifted and commanded to become loving. With the self-respect of that self-identity, the Christian should be released to the self-transcendence of genuine other-regard by a willing self-exposure to and in the contemporary situation."[26] "The Trinity will not be the luminous centre of Christian life till the life of the church reflects the mystery of divine life, at the heart of which is a unity without uniformity, distinction without separation."[27]

Postscript

The church begins the twenty-first century in a similar situation to that in which it found itself at the start of the twentieth century and, sadly, there are those who in many ways would have it set out on this journey into the future by displaying a similar attitude toward the world and adopting a similar position toward dissent within its own ranks—the

---

of a contemporary analogical imagination" (*The Analogical Imagination*, 454). Tracy could thus here be addressing the "heirs of Aristotle"

26. Ibid., 446.

27. David McLoughlin, "Authority in the Service of Communion," in Noel Timms and Kenneth Wilson, eds., *Governance and Authority in the Roman Catholic Church: Beginning a Conversation* (London: S.P.C.K., 2000) 135. See also Richard Gaillardetz's emphasis on the *relational* character of Vatican II's ecclesiology of communion, for which reason he commends the principles of conciliarity, collegiality, ecclesial reception, and the *sensus fidelium*, which go toward forming the constituent elements of such an ecclesiology (*Teaching With Authority* [Collegeville: Liturgical Press, 1997] 293). And see his "Reception of Doctrine: New Perspectives" in Bernard Hoose, ed., *Authority in the Roman Catholic Church: Theory and Practice* (Aldershot, England; Burlington, VT: Ashgate Press, 2002) 95–116, and Hoose's "Authority in the Church," *TS* 63 (2002) 108ff.

attitude that proved so stifling, mistaken, and ultimately counterproductive for the church of and immediately after Pius X. Certainly there is a very postmodern flavor and twist to the ecclesiological machinations of recent times. Nonetheless, those of such a mindset and given to such ecclesial visions should be wary of what they wish for, since their actions, and even their dispositions may stifle any chance for that nameless virtue to take root in the daily life of the church, both local and universal. As Hermann Häring reminds us, "Fear of decline and hope of renewal cohabit closely and are seen as being opposed; and the social *stigma of nonconformism* and opposition is experienced and suffered here more consciously than in other Christian communities—and sometimes it is provoked for the sake of a premature unity. Such a marked desire for unity also tends, however, to the fear of diversity and the obstruction of essential experimentation. Thus prophetic inspiration is suppressed by the concern for continuity."[28]

Our final chapters and conclusion have proposed that the church, now as in other times, should live as an analogical representation of the loving being of God. Does Christianity not claim to bear testimony to a God who is not uniform but community, a plurality of modes of divinity that are coequal, co-divine, and coeternal? How could the concepts of *perichoresis* (mutual indwelling/interpenetration) and *Seinsweise* (modes of being), which lie at the heart of so much recent trinitarian theology, as of so much early trinitarian theology, ever lend themselves to a sectarian, inner-looking, neo-exclusivist, world-renouncing ecclesiology? The question all churches in these times should ask is: how often do our ecclesiologies *actually* bear true witness to the love of the triune God?

In all this we discern something of what many Christian communities understand to be the sacramental nature and task of the church: that it should be both a sign and a mediation of the gracious and loving divine self-communication *to the world*. If such self-communication, such loving grace were limited to the confines of the church, ecclesiology would be nothing more than soteriological tautology, and in that

---

28. Hermann Häring, "The Rights and Limits of Dissent," in Hans Küng and Jürgen Moltmann, eds., *The Right to Dissent. Concilium* 158 (1982) 95. Two papers examining the contemporary situation in the Anglican communion offer similar suggestions. See Mark Chapman, "'By Schisms Rent Asunder, By Heresies Distressed'": Anglicanism and the Windsor Report," and George Pattison, "Church: Law, Community and Witness," both in Gerard Mannion, *Church and Religious Other*, Continuum/T. & T. Clark (forthcoming, 2008). Again we are reminded of Lyotard's warning against imposed unity and uniformity (see chs. 1–3 above).

case, fundamentals of our theology would collapse at crucial junctures. As Gustavo Gutiérrez famously said: "By preaching the Gospel message, by its sacraments, and by the charity of its members, the church proclaims and shelters the gift of the Kingdom of God in the heart of human history."[29]

Vatican II emphasized the pilgrim nature of the Christian church—and by this the Council sought to indicate that the church should be understood to be on a journey. This book has suggested that such a journey might best be seen as a journey of virtuous life and celebration with, no doubt, periods of decline and fall along the way, toward the *telos* that is the fullness of that kingdom.

Like many, the esteemed Dominican theologian Fergus Kerr has noted the ironies in our new pope's choice of name, not least how his vision of a new Christian Europe brings to mind the stark, depressing ending of Alasdair MacIntyre's *After Virtue,* quoted in the previous chapter.[30] Doubtless such postmodern times for the church do call for "a very different Benedict." Do they call for this particular Benedict? Our considerations might suggest that this papacy will raise still further questions for the church in our times.

29. Gustavo Gutiérrez, *A Theology of Liberation* (London: SCM, 1974) 11.
30. Fergus Kerr, "What's in a Name?" *New Blackfriars* (July 2005) 357–60.

Index